ll and
Locke

C000178572

Buying a property

TURKEY

CADOGANguides

Contents

About the authors, contributors and updaters

John Howell established John Howell & Co in Sheffield in 1979 and by 1997 it had become one of the largest and most respected law firms in the north of England, employing over 100 lawyers. On moving to London in 1995, John Howell has gone on to specialise in providing legal advice to clients buying property in France, Spain, Italy and Portugal and more recently Turkey and Croatia.

Tim Locke has never shaken off the travel bug, accumulating a fund of knowledge about places both in his native UK and across the globe. He has spent the past 19 years writing and editing guidebooks for AA Publishing, Which? Books, Reader's Digest, Cadogan Guides, Fodor's, Ebury Press and Thomas Cook, as well as exploring on foot, by cycle, by train and on cross-country skis. He is a qualified teacher of English to speakers of other languages and has worked for a year teaching in a language school in Japan. His other enthusiasms include archaeology, playing the piano and attempting to play tennis.

The publisher would like to thank specialist contributor to the first edition **Dr Bulent Bilmez**, plus the hardworking and knoweldgeable updaters of this edition: **Christian Williams**, author of Cadogan Guides' *Working and Living: USA*, and **Burcu Orhan**, attorney-at-law with London Legal International.

Cadogan Guides is an imprint of
New Holland Publishers (UK) Ltd
London • Cape Town • Sydney • Auckland

New Holland Publishers (UK) Ltd
Garfield House,
86–88 Edgware Road
London W2 2EA

80 McKenzie Street
Cape Town 8001
South Africa

Unit 1, 66 Gibbes Street
Chatswood, NSW 2067
Australia

218 Lake Road
Northcote
Auckland
New Zealand

Cadogan@nhpub.co.uk
www.cadoganguides.com
t 44 (0)20 7724 7773

Distributed in the United States by Globe Pequot, Connecticut

Cover photographs: front © Ilhan Balta – Fotolia.com; back © John A. Rizzo
Photo essay photographs © Tim Mitchell, © William McKelvie – Fotolia.com
Maps © Cadogan Guides, drawn by Maidenhead Cartographic Services Ltd
Cover design: Sarah Rianhard-Gardner
Editing: Linda McQueen
Proofreading: Dominique Shead
Indexing: Isobel McLean

Produced by **Navigator Guides**
www.navigatorguides.com

Printed in Finland by WS Bookwell
A catalogue record for this book is available from the British Library

ISBN: 978-186011-373-4

Please help us to keep this guide up to date. We have done our best to ensure that the information in this guide is correct at the time of going to press. But laws and regulations are constantly changing, and standards and prices fluctuate. We would be delighted to receive any comments. Authors of the best letters will receive a copy of the Cadogan Guide of their choice.

Introduction

01

Buying a property in Turkey can be as safe as buying a property in the UK. On reading a book such as this – which must explain the potential pitfalls if it is to serve any useful purpose – it can seem a frightening or dangerous experience. But if you go about the purchase the right way it should be neither, and only barely riskier than buying a house in the UK. If you are in any doubt, look briefly at a text book on British conveyancing and see all the horrible things that have happened to people in the UK! You do not worry about those dangers because you are familiar with them and, more importantly, because you are shielded against contact with most of them by your solicitor. The same should be true when buying in Turkey. Read this book to understand the background and why some of the problems exist. Ask your lawyer to advise about any issues that worry you and help you make sure you avoid the landmines!

This does not mean that buying property in Turkey is the same as buying a property in the UK. Only a few thousand British people currently own a home in Turkey, and away from the most popular areas you could be the first foreign buyer that an official has ever dealt with. The legal and administrative systems are less developed and less sophisticated than those in Western Europe. The estate agents are largely unregulated, though they have their own chamber now – there are a handful of established estate agency firms, but many have opened in the last few years to capitalise on the explosion in sales. Business practices and culture are very different from those in Western Europe; and comparatively few Turks outside Istanbul and Ankara speak fluent English. Thus the process of buying in Turkey cannot, at present, be as straightforward as the process of buying in France or Spain or some other European Union countries.

In many respects, dealing with Turkey today is comparable to dealing with Spain 20 years ago, and this is a huge attraction for many people. There is still a true local culture, the countryside remains unspoilt, and you can buy property near the coast at very reasonable prices. On the downside, many buyers will encounter non-compliance with the law, non-compliance with planning regulations, and a cavalier attitude to contracts and black market money – all of which were problems in Spain all those years ago.

This should not put you off buying property in Turkey. It is a wonderful, cultured and spectacularly beautiful country. It has huge potential for a growth in property values in the same way that property prices in Spain have exploded over the last 20 years. The cost of living is very cheap. So, whether you're looking to buy property for holiday use, for retirement or as an investment, Turkey is worth a very careful look.

About Turkey

02

There has been an explosion of interest in property in Turkey since 2003, particularly by British buyers. The roots of this can be traced back several years. During the boom years of the 1990s there was a specialist interest, especially among sailors and adventurers, but Turkey really came to the attention of the buyer of property overseas in 1999 when it became likely that the country might at last be considered for membership of the European Union. This prospect made people feel that Turkey had 'arrived'. Interest in buying property in Turkey was slow to start and then accelerated gradually.

Accurate numbers are hard to come by, because a large number of British buyers have bought property via Turkish company structures and are not separately recorded as British buyers. Our best guess is that in 2000 there were only a couple of hundred British people who had bought a house in Turkey. Recent figures are more readily available, and by 2007 17,000 Britons were registered as owning properties in Turkey. But this only forms a small part of the $2 billion investment by foreigners – largely northern Europeans – in Turkish real estate in 2006, a figure that is projected to double in 2007.

Why Turkey?

Why has there been this vast increase in demand?

• **Turkey has been 'discovered' by the British.** Tourism from the UK has increased from a very low level in the 1980s and 1990s to almost two million visitors a year. This is only a very small part of Turkey's overall tourism, which amounts to about 19 million visitors a year – a figure projected by the Turkish government to rise to 30 million by 2010. Most of this tourism, both from Britain and other countries, is concentrated on the southwest coast of Turkey, in the area from Alanya in the east to İzmir in the west. This is also the area where the majority of British people are buying.

• **Turkey is outstandingly beautiful.** The southwest coast of Turkey rivals anything in the Mediterranean, with great beaches and over 300 sunny days a year.

• **Turkey is not frightening!** Some people are initially concerned about buying property in a country where the majority of the population is Muslim, but they have quickly discovered that these worries are without foundation. Although the population of Turkey is overwhelmingly Muslim, the constitution of the country provides for a secular state. In many places, such as the big cities and in the tourist parts of the country, religion is less obvious and operates in the background: some local people drink; boys and girls walk hand-in-hand; women dress in Western fashion; many women – in particular younger women – work in conventional employment.

• **Turkey is exotic.** An engaging local culture is still intact here, not all but destroyed as along Spain's southern coast, where bland international ghettos have all too often taken over. Most people who buy property abroad value this cultural diversity – but want, at the same time, to enjoy Western levels of service and security and the home comforts and facilities they have come to expect at home. Turkey offers this balance.

• **Turkey is an inexpensive place to live.** A bilingual secretary might earn £6,000 a year, and a government clerk £3,000 a year. Depending on where you live, the cost of living will be between 30 and 50 per cent lower than in Britain. A British pensioner, even with only his or her state pension, can live well.

• **Turkey is also an inexpensive place to buy property.** It is less inexpensive than it was five years ago, as good property has risen in value at anything up to 50 per cent a year, but it remains much cheaper than other Mediterranean places. These days it is hard to find property in coastal Spain for less than about £80,000 and virtually impossible to find anything less than £55,000. A two-bedroom apartment on the Costa del Sol will cost £160,000. In Turkey, large two-bedroom apartments are currently available in less fashionable locations for about £35,000 and in fashionable beachfront locations for £80,000.

• **Turkey has low crime rates.**

• **Many people believe that they will make money by investing in Turkey.** They remember what happened to property prices in Spain, when tourism and property ownership exploded there. Houses bought for £5,000 sold a few years later for £50,000. Properties grew in value at up to 25 per cent a year – for many years. Many people believe they are still quite near to the beginning of this kind of curve in Turkey and that prices are likely to grow rapidly over the next 10 to 20 years. Certainly, many people who invested over the last year or two have made substantial sums of money; annual price rises of 10–15 per cent are anticipated for the next few years.

• **Turkey is increasingly stable politically.** Despite interventions by the military in recent history and large-scale demonstrations against Turkey's ruling AKP party, there is every sign that Turkey is emerging as an increasingly stable and mature democracy, as its EU membership discussions show. The success and behaviour of the AKP has also allayed fears that its roots in the Islamic movement will foster an anti-Western backlash. Its support and close alliance with fellow NATO member the USA has extinguished fears of it becoming embroiled in the troubles of neighbouring Iraq.

• **Turkey is increasingly stable economically.** Turkey went through a bad time in 2001, with huge inflation and a currency in freefall against other currencies; but the economy has since stabilised, then produced good growth, which has attracted large amounts of foreign investment to many economic sectors. Investment in large projects such as the golf courses around Belek, near Antalya, and the marinas in Marmaris, Göcek and Fethiye, is of particular relevance, creating conditions for economic growth in resort areas specifically.

• **Turkey has a novelty factor.** A few years ago, if you told friends in the pub that you had a villa in Spain or France their reaction was 'Wow!'; now it is more likely to be a yawn! Telling your friends that you have a house in Bodrum or Fethiye still has the desired effect.

Reality Check

Turkey is Turkey. The law says one thing and another happens. That is why you like it. But be careful – it may not always be thus. For example:

• **There are drink-drive laws.**

Despite popular imagery and the fact that the large majority of the population is Muslim, drinking and driving happens here too, although not to the same extent as in the West.

• **A foreigner from the EU needs a residence card or permit to stay in Turkey for more than 90 days.**

But thousands of citizens, mainly from Middle Eastern countries and the Balkans, have been there for many years with little or no paperwork at all.

• **A person who stays for more than six months is liable to pay tax in Turkey. Even non-residents must pay tax on income earned from letting their property in Turkey.**

Thousands have never paid a penny.

• **A developer needs planning permission before he can commence construction of a project. He can only put up buildings of the category authorised on that land. Just as in England, you cannot build a house in the middle of an industrial estate or a block of apartments on land used as a school playing field.**

Many developers in Turkey ignore these rules.

Things are changing, however. The number of people caught in the tax net is increasing. The police and other authorities are cracking down on foreigners' unlawful activity. Even planning consent is being enforced. And the pace of this change will increase. Turkey wishes to become a member of the European Union, but cannot do so until its systems comply more closely with the European norms. An important message of this book is that a prudent person should not proceed on the assumption that the current lax attitude to compliance with the law and taxation will continue in the years to come.

Turkish History

Turkey's unique position at the intersection of Europe and Asia has always made it fascinating to foreigners. This fascination goes back thousands of years. It is, perhaps, fortunate for modern Turkey that it led to successive invasions, takeovers, civilisations and evictions: Neolithic settlers, Bronze Age settlers, the

Dorians in the 7th century BC, the Megaron colonists, the Persians (513 BC), the Greeks, the Galatians, the Romans (AD 196), the Byzantine empire, the Crusaders and the Ottomans. Some of the influences were transient. Others lasted for hundreds of years.

The most obvious lasting influences have been the Roman (and, particularly, the later Byzantine) and the Ottoman. The combination of the characteristics of these two vast empires explains much about modern Turkey. By the beginning of the 20th century Turkey was a mixed society, dominated in the central areas by ethnic Turks but with thousands of Greek inhabitants controlling much of the coastal area that is today so popular with tourists.

Then, in 1923, the new Turkish state was formed by **Mustafa Kemal Atatürk**. The focus changed. The capital moved from Istanbul to Ankara. Sweeping social, cultural, educational and political reforms ensued. The Arabic script was abandoned in favour of the current Turkish script. Women were given the right to vote, released from the obligation to 'cover up' and generally emancipated. Atatürk is still a hugely important figurehead in Turkish society and stands for the values of freedom and equality, secularisation and education that he introduced. His picture (in a thousand different poses) is seen everywhere in Turkey.

Since 1923 the road has sometimes been rocky. There have been coups and counter-coups. The military have taken power. There have been good times and bad times. But the principles of secularisation and equality have held.

In 2002, a new government was elected with a huge majority of the popular vote. This was the government of Recep Tayyip Erdoğan. He leads an Islamic party, the AKP (the Justice and Development Party), but it is a party committed to change, to Westernisation, to entry into Europe and to the general modernisation of Turkish society and the Turkish economy. He is hugely popular, as his 2007 re-election by a massively increased margin attests: he won 47 per cent of the vote. In August 2007, foreign affairs minister Abdullah Gul was elected by parliament as the new president of the Republic (*see* 'Turkish Politics', p.9).

Translations: A Warning

Most English people do not speak Turkish. In this book, English terms are used, accompanied by the Turkish term within brackets and in italics, for example: 'You will need to sign the deed of sale (*tapu*) in front of the land registrar (*tapu müdürü*).'

At the back of the book is a list of the English and Turkish equivalents of a variety of legal and financial terms. Be careful. Words, when used in differing contexts, can mean radically different things. (My brother has an *interest* in a house in Turkey. Mr Smith is *interested* in buying it from him. He is concerned about future *interest* rates.) There is often no true translation of legal and financial terms because they can relate to institutions, systems or procedures that do not have an equivalent in the other country. In these circumstances, translations can give a false sense of familiarity and security.

Turkish Culture

At first glance, Turkey is unmistakably 'Eastern'. The minarets, the music, the smells and the chaos paint an instant and vivid picture for the new arrival in Istanbul. And Turkey *is* Eastern: although it straddles Europe and Asia, only one per cent of its landmass is within Europe.

Turkey is exotic. The very names of Constantinople and Istanbul fire the imagination and have done so through the centuries. A wander through the bazaars of the Sultanahmet region of Istanbul, selling gold and spices, cloth, saucepans, mousetraps and transistor radios, is a delight. The great covered bazaar, larger than the largest hypermarket, contains 5,000 independent shops in 200,000 square metres of land and bustles with noisy businesses, some of which date back centuries.

The huge majority of the population is Muslim and the minorities are, generally, diminishing in both size and influence. This is not a surprise, but it is not the whole picture, as Turkey is also a secular state. Since 1923 the constitution has prohibited the overt religious control of society.

So Turkey is, more than anything else, a country of cultural contrasts: a modern and efficient society with contemporary hospitals, schools and universities, and airports and airport security that are second to none. The culture varies significantly depending on where you are. The southwestern coastal part of Turkey (where most foreigners go on holiday and buy their properties) still bears signs of the Greek influence that endured there for 2,000 years. The European part of Istanbul is a great business and trading city set against the backdrop of its exotic Eastern pedigree. In the east of Turkey the life and culture is relatively conservative.

Turkish Politics

Turkey is a republican parliamentary democracy. Its current constitution was adopted on 7 November 7 1982, during a period of military rule that started in 1980. The 550-seat **Grand National Assembly of Turkey** (Türkiye Büyük Millet Meclisi), which represents 81 provinces, has the only legislative power. According to the Election Law, any party drawing less than 10 per cent of the national vote is excluded from parliament and their votes discarded, regardless of the result in individual constituencies. Independent candidates can, however, be elected if they win 10 per cent of the vote in the province from which they are running.

Seeing itself as the guardian of the secular, unitary nature of the republic, the military, which has a long tradition of involvement in the country's politics and economy, still plays a considerable role. Parties considered to be anti-secular or separatist by the judiciary have been banned, and the military has played a determining role in influencing this. The religious Welfare Party, removed from government in 1997, and more recently the Kurdish nationalist People's Democracy Party (HADEP) are two examples of this.

The **Justice and Development Party** (Adalet ve Kalkınma Partisi, AK Parti or **AKP**) is Turkey's ruling political party and has been in power since 2002. It describes itself as a centre-right conservative party, but is better known for its Islamic roots, which have proved controversial, given the commitment to secularism within the Turkish constitution. However, in practice the government's policies have only been mildly influenced by religious issues, and it has been hugely successful in introducing fundamental legislative reforms that aim at satisfying the criteria for Turkey to be allowed to join the EU and stabilising the Turkish economy. As a result, the government, led by prime minister **Recep Tayyip Erdoğan**, won the elections again in July 2007, taking 341 of the seats with 46.76 per cent of the total votes, increasing the AKP government's electoral share by more than 12 per cent.

The AKP extended its influence and success in August 2007 with the appointment of one of its founder members and foreign minister, **Abdullah Gul**, to the post of president. The appointment caused considerable consternation in the military and among opposition groups and brought millions of protesters onto the streets. At issue were Gul's Islamic beliefs and the fear that these would conflict with and override Turkey's secularism. The wearing of a headscarf by the president's wife was particularly contentious, as the headscarf has long been a symbol of the anti-secular, and is prohibited in all of Turkey's government buildings. Gul's appointment meant that, for the first time, prayer mats and headscarves entered the presidential palace. Aware of the potent symbolism, Mr Gul assured the world of his commitment to Turkey's secularism – 'As long as I am in office, I will embrace all our citizens without bias' – while at the same time asserting his right to his own Muslim beliefs. All this has the potential to become one of Turkey's defining moments; and Gul's appointment certainly marks a victory for the governing Muslim democrats over the military and bureaucratic élite that has controlled the country since its modern foundation in 1923.

The AKP's flimsy opposition is based around the **Republican People's Party** (**CHP**, Cumhuriyet Halk Partisi), which won 110 seats in 2007 with only 20.64 per cent of the total vote, and the far-right **Nationalist Movement Party** (**MHP**, Milliyetçi Hareket Partisi), the two other main parties in the Turkish National Assembly. The rest of the seats are occupied by independent candidates.

During the war in the east and southeast of Turkey in the 1980s and 1990s, between Turkish armed forces and those of the **Kurdistan Workers' Party** (**PKK**), who campaign for the establishment of a separate socialist state of Kurdistan, tens of thousands of people, the majority of them PKK militants, died. In 1999, PKK leader **Abdullah Öcalan**, who had been living in Syria in exile, was detained and sentenced to death. However, the sentence was converted to life imprisonment after three years because of the abolition of the death penalty. In 1999 the PKK announced a unilateral ceasefire and declared its intention to switch to peaceful struggle. The organisation, which is still outlawed in Turkey, has since changed its name to the **Congress for Freedom and Democracy in Kurdistan** (KADEK) and subsequently to **Kongra-Gel**. The ceasefire became increasingly ragged, so that by the end of 2004 it had broken down completely, and recent years have seen an increase in Kurdish militant activity, partly feeding off the troubles over its Iraqi border, which has led to calls by the Turkish army for action against Kurdish training camps in northern Iraq. As of summer 2007, the Turkish government has started seriously considering the option of a military operation into northern Iraq.

The Economy

Turkey has a dynamic economy that is a complex mix of modern industry and commerce along with traditional village agriculture and crafts. It has a strong and rapidly growing private sector, yet the state still plays a major role in basic industry, banking, transport and communication. Many of these public firms are inefficient and poorly managed, but its most important industry – and largest export – is textiles and clothing, which is almost entirely in private hands.

The economic situation in recent years has been marked by erratic, but increasingly steady, economic growth; despite serious imbalances, the growth rate remains high. In the 1980s Turkey began a series of reforms designed to shift the economy to a neo-liberal, market-based model. The reforms stimulated growth that was interrupted by recessions and financial crises in 1994, 1999 and 2001. Turkey's failure to pursue additional reforms, combined with large and growing public sector deficits, resulted in high inflation, increasing macro-economic volatility and a weak banking sector. A much disputed economic recovery programme was agreed with the IMF in 2002 after years of growing economic difficulties. The government has made progress with tax reforms, privatisation and cutting back in the public sector. It has been much heralded by the IMF for its determination and success.

Economic disparities among the population today are very pronounced. The difference between the cities and the countryside is significant and there is no functioning social security system. Around 40 per cent of the population still earn their living in agriculture, though this is fast changing with the erosion of the agricultural sector. The share of agriculture in the GNP is around 12 per cent. Fields are family-owned and people grow cotton, wheat, barley, tobacco, fruit, nuts and oil seeds. The southeast and eastern provinces remain underdeveloped and impoverished despite the Southeast Anatolian Project (GAP), which is aimed at economic development in that region.

Tourism is a very important source of foreign currency for the country. The most important tourist areas are the Aegean and Mediterranean coasts; every year approximately 19 million tourists visit Turkey, seven million of whom visit Antalya. In addition to the beach and city holidays on offer, Turkey has developed new attractions like rafting, hiking, snow festivals, birdwatching and numerous activity holidays. Faith tours are made to Konya, and there are other tours following the Silk Road from İzmir to Kayseri.

Turkey and the European Union

EU Membership

EU membership has been a goal continuously pursued by Turkish governments for over 40 years. Finally, with the beginning of formal negotiations for membership in October 2005, Turkey appears to have its foot in the door. Admittedly these negotiations have since run into roadblocks on both sides, including the firm opposition of France's new president, Nicolas Sarkozy. But talks about EU membership are, at least formally, still continuing.

To get into this position the country has had to make huge steps towards the development of full democracy: modernising its constitution; shaking up its judiciary; updating the penal code; fighting corruption; and starting to nudge the army towards civilian control. Most significantly, the death penalty has been abolished; and there have been great reforms to Kurdish cultural rights, including the freedom to teach of the Kurdish language in private schools, and the broadcasting of Kurdish-language programmes on state television.

The position of Turkey within the European Union (EU) is of fundamental concern to most Turks, and to many foreigners thinking of buying property there. The Turks see their membership of the EU as important for many reasons, and money is not the most significant. Turkey already enjoys the benefit of a special status with regard to trade with the EU, so the vast majority of its commercial activity is tariff-free. The EU had invested a substantial amount of development money in Turkey even before it was a candidate for membership. Throughout Turkey there are projects bearing the familiar EU logo. For business people, the main interest in joining the EU appears to be a feeling that recognition of Turkey as an EU member would widen their markets *outside* the EU, because Turkey would be recognised as a modern, competitive society.

It is this sense of wanting to be recognised that, more than anything else, seems also to drive private citizens' wish to join the Union. It would be naïve not to recognise that in a relatively poor country the prospect of free movement throughout Europe, further EU investment and EU spending in Turkey are all important considerations too.

From the point of view of the person buying a holiday or retirement property in Turkey, the main advantage of Turkey joining the EU would be political and economic stability. From the point of view of a person buying an investment property in Turkey, it is just a question of money. The overwhelming evidence from all other countries admitted to membership of the European Union is that the economy booms and property prices rise substantially once the country has joined. In many other places, the possibility of future entry to the European Union has already been factored into the prices of real estate, but in Turkey this has not yet happened.

Application History and Current Status

Since 1963 Turkey has been an associate member of the EU, and since 1995 it has had an exclusive customs union agreement with the EU. Under this agreement, trade in most industrial products between Turkey and the EU takes place on the same basis as inter-EU trade. In 1999, at the EU Helsinki summit, Turkey was accepted as a candidate country for full EU membership.

In December 2002, at the European Council meeting in Copenhagen, the European Union recognised that Turkey was 'a candidate state destined to join the union on the basis of the rules applied to other candidate states'. It resolved that 'if the European Council in December 2004, on the basis of a report and a recommendation from the Commission, decides that Turkey fulfils the Copenhagen political criteria, the European Union will open accession negotiations with Turkey without delay'.

In 2004 the European Commission made an official recommendation for the opening of EU accession negotiations with Turkey, and in 2005 formal membership negotiations started. This decision was, at least on paper, based on the progress made by Turkish leaders in the area of individual liberties and the respect of human rights as well as the other membership criteria set out in Copenhagen. Some of these have occasioned constitutional amendments to bring Turkey closer to EU standards of democracy.

The announcement of the start of formal membership negotiations has been long awaited; nevertheless, debate continues both in the EU and within Turkey. Among the topics are: will Turkey be a Trojan horse allowing poor Muslim nations into the union? Is Turkey too Asian, not European enough? Will Turkey become a bulwark against the influence of Islam in Europe? Will membership improve Turkey's huge market for European goods? Will Turkey's large and low-paid working population destabilise European labour markets? Will the European Union threaten Islam in Turkey? Will its policies betray the interests of Turkey and Turkish independence?

Whatever the speculative answers to these questions are, as an official candidate state Turkey's progress towards fulfilling all the strict criteria for EU membership is now being closely monitored over several years. Once reports show sufficient progress on a raft of new legislation and adaptive measures, then a date for annexation to the Union should be proposed. It is dangerous to make predictions, but it is possible that admission would take place after about 2014. But to some extent it is important to remember that, even if this entry is postponed or even cancelled, the massive steps that Turkey has made as a country by attempting to fall in line with EU standards has markedly improved its stability and democratic apparatus, enforced a commitment to human rights and substantially improved its economy. All these factors should be massively encouraging to anyone looking to invest or even live in the country, whatever the eventual outcome of EU negotiations.

Turkey and Islam

As already mentioned, Turkey has a predominantly Muslim population, but constitutionally Turkey is a secular state. The position of its non-Muslim minorities is legally protected and, recently, the Supreme Court ruled against a proposal to introduce certain aspects of Islamic teaching into Turkey's schools.

Islam is a more demanding religion than Christianity in its effect on its adherents' day-to-day lives. There are more strictly religious Muslims than there are devout Christians. One is reminded of the fervent religious activity of mid-Victorian England. Despite this, there are many Muslims who are Muslim in little more than name. They attend the mosque about as frequently as many Church of England members go to church. They follow the teachings in their own and a rather vague way in the same way that many Christians and non-Christians vaguely follow the broad principles of the Christian religion.

Thus it is important to stress that Turkey is not a fundamentalist Islamic state. This is not Afghanistan or Saudi Arabia. Women have the right to vote and many have paid employment. Alcohol is tolerated and consumed, especially in Istanbul and on the southern coast. Relationships between the sexes can be open and affectionate.

Yet Islam remains a very important element in Turkish society. It is as much an intellectual as a religious cornerstone. The influential *Turkish Policy Quarterly* back in spring 2004, in a special issue on religion and politics, contained the following articles: 'The Quest of Islamic Migrants and of Turkey to Become European'; 'The Directorate of Religious Affairs in Turkey'; 'Political Islam, Governments and Democracy'; 'The Compatibility of Islam and Democracy'; 'Non-Muslim Minorities in Turkey'; 'AKP and the Paradox of Islamic Europe Europhilia'; 'The Role of Religion in Turkish Reactions to Balkan Conflicts'; 'The Failure of Political Islamic in Turkey'; 'Re-socialising Religion; Can Religion Heal America's Disadvantaged?'; and 'The Unique Role of Religion in Middle Eastern

Case Study: The Wedding

In 2003 the writer was lucky enough to be invited to a wedding in Istanbul. The sister of a Turkish friend was marrying. As is often the case in Istanbul, both families' roots lay in the villages of inland Turkey. The groom was a hairdresser, the bride a teacher. The wedding was attended by around six hundred of their family and friends.

The cross-section of people present was extraordinary. There were simple village people of all ages, some traditional and religious. There were young friends from Istanbul, the girls dressed in crop tops and hot pants. There were businessmen in suits. There were foreigners. There was a priest and there were politicians. The majority of the people present were Muslim but there was a smattering of Christians, Jews, atheists and agnostics.

There was drinking of champagne, beer and spirits. There was a discotheque, there was traditional village music and there was a belly dancer! The guests danced and some of the younger ones kissed on the dance floor.

And nobody minded. Everybody had a good time. This is modern Turkey.

Ethnic Conflict'. These are thoughtful and fascinating articles, and give an insight into the typical thinking of at least a section of the political class, although these are not the concerns of the average man in the street.

Turkish Law

Few English people understand anything about Turkish law. Some people are worried that the legal system might be 'exotic' or primitive, which deters them from buying property there. To complicate matters further, there are very few materials about Turkish law written in English – or at least in intelligible English. For this reason, and rather strangely for a book of this kind, we are going to set out a brief description of some key parts of Turkish law.

Obviously, any person who buys a house in Turkey will have to deal with the Turkish legal system from time to time. Normally their dealings with it will be almost unconscious; it will be a mere backdrop to their activities in Turkey. Occasionally, however, they might have to take active steps to enforce or defend their rights using the law and the Turkish legal system.

Turkey is developing very quickly. As discussed earlier in this chapter, it has ambitions to join the European Union, and many of the country's laws are being changed so as to be fully compliant with the requirements of the European Union. The effect of this is that the statements made in this book, although accurate at the time it is being written, are likely to become out of date over the course of the next couple of years in certain important aspects.

The law is a complicated subject, and a textbook on Turkish law would run to many hundreds if not thousands of pages. Therefore this very brief guide should be treated as no more than that – it is not intended to be used as the basis for making any decisions about action to be taken or not to be taken in any given set of circumstances. For that you will need to consult lawyers.

Sources and History of the Law

Ever since human beings began to gather together in social groups ten thousand years or more ago, there have been rules or laws. Such communities cannot function in the absence of law. If there is no law there is chaos and constant dispute.

To begin with the laws were simple and customary – in other words, they were not formalised and often not written down. Gradually these laws became more formal and were recorded in codes. With the advent of the nation state, the power to make laws became the sole province of the state, although some of the older or customary laws were either incorporated into the state's new laws or were recognised as ancillary to those laws.

Religion and the Law

Part of the earliest law – and a major part – was the rules of religion. Religion (whatever that religion might be) lays down certain principles of conduct, and those principles are often the first manifestations of law. The position of religion in Turkish society is interesting, particularly after the new Turkish state was formed in 1923. Religion has a peculiar and important place in Turkish society and so it is worth looking at this in a little more detail.

All major religions have their set of religious requirements which become religious laws. In most cases they are static – they do not develop over time. They are treated as the word or the direction of God and, therefore, as being immutable. They also have the peculiarity that they are one-sided. This means that they impose duties upon you but do not give you rights to ensure that either God or your fellow man complies with his obligations.

When the Republic of Turkey was formed in 1923, religion had been a major issue. The Republic was formed after a war of independence from the Ottoman Empire, which had, at its peak in the 16th and 17th centuries, been absolutely vast, extending all the way to Algeria and Vienna. In its later years it had decayed into a mere shadow of its former self but still had a strong cultural and religious identity. It was partly against that identity that Mustafa Kemal Atatürk, the founder of modern Turkey, and his colleagues rebelled.

As a consequence partly of this and partly of the times in general, the new Turkish Republic was set up on the basis of being a secular state where the influence of religion was severely limited by the constitution.

The Basis of Turkish Law

Although we still talk about the Turkish constitution and the Turkish state's being founded in 1923, in fact there were a number of earlier constitutions that greatly influenced the 'new' 1923 constitution. The 1923 Constitution of the new Republic of Turkey specifically states that it is based on the earlier constitutions, and it came into effect as a modification of those constitutions.

The first Turkish constitution of modern times goes back to 1839, a time when the whole of Europe was busy writing constitutions on the French model. It was amended in 1876, at which time it still embodied the monarchist and theocratic ideals of the Ottoman Empire and, in particular, declared that the person of the Sultan was both sacred and above the law. This constitution did, however, recognise that Muslim and non-Muslim citizens were to be treated equally within Turkey.

The constitution was further revised in 1921 and then substantially revised, as a result of the War of Independence, in 1923. This new constitution originally declared the official religion of the state to be Islam but, by amendments of 1928 and 1937, cancelled that provision and made it clear that religion was to be entirely separated from the affairs of the state. It also set out the powers of the various branches of the state and the fundamental rights and freedoms to be enjoyed by the systems of Turkey. In short, it was remarkably like most other constitutions built on the classic 19th-century French '*liberté, égalité, fraternité*' model – though in this case the major influence was, in fact, the Swiss constitution, which had, in its turn, been based upon the French model.

A second republican constitution was implemented in 1961, after a further revolution, and a third was implemented in 1982 after a military coup. That 1982 constitution has been subject to further amendment over the years, but is the basis of the Turkish state today. After their recent election success, the ruling AKP party has commissioned a new constitution, which is expected to be completed by the beginning of 2008.

Sources of Law

In Turkey, law is recognised as having a number of distinct sources, which are arranged in a hierarchy. Any rules directly applicable to your situation in a high level source override any rules that may conflict with that rule in a lower-level source.

The primary source is the **Turkish constitution**. Below that (and in descending status) are the **Civil Code** – laws passed by parliament; **ordinances** – laws passed by the Executive; **regulations** – rules made under the provisions of a general power in a particular code; **by-laws** – rules made at a local level in order to enforce a code; and the **'unified' decisions** of the Supreme Court. These unified decisions are published officially and acquire the same legal power as statutes.

They are decisions that have been made in the various parts of the Supreme Court of Appeal and which are either all to the same effect or, where there have been differences of opinion, where those differences have been reconciled and one version has been declared to be the correct interpretation of the law.

The Courts

The courts in Turkey are divided into various sections. The **constitutional court** deals with the interpretation of the constitution; **criminal courts** deal with criminal cases; **administrative courts** deal with administrative law; **financial courts** deal with financial law; and **civil courts** deal with anything that is not dealt with in any of the other parts of the court system.

Each of those groups of courts has a **central (supreme) court** and **local courts**. Local courts deal with all cases for the first hearing. The supreme courts, with few exceptions, deal with cases on appeal. There is generally only one level of appeal, rather than two as in Britain and many other countries.

The courts are required to apply the law. Article 1 of the Turkish Civil Code states that the Code must be applied in all cases that fall within it. If no provision exists about a particular set of circumstances, the judge dealing with the case must decide it as if he himself were the legislator making the law and do so in accordance with legal doctrine and case law.

This means that the judge will apply the direct instructions of the constitution, the rules in the Civil Code, the direct instructions of other written sources of law (statutes, regulations and so on) in descending order of importance, and only if none of those covers the situation (which is highly unlikely) does he fall to considering any of the old customary law.

Constitutional Law

The 1982 constitution is interesting in a number of respects. It is based on the principle of 'popular sovereignty'.

Grand National Assembly

The supreme governing entity is the Grand National Assembly. From the members of that Assembly are appointed a Council of Ministers and the Prime Minister. The Grand National Assembly comprises 550 members. Members must be aged at least 30 and must have been through at least primary school education and have completed their compulsory military service. They cannot be elected to the membership of the Assembly if they have been convicted of serious criminal offences. They sit for five years. They are directly elected by the voters.

Turkey has universal suffrage, enjoyed by all citizens over the edge of 18 years who do not suffer from a very limited number of specified disabilities. The Grand National Assembly's main job is to make and pass laws.

Executive Branch

In common with most common continental constitutions there is also a separate Executive.

President

The Executive is headed by the president of the Republic. He is elected by the Grand National Assembly for seven years. He can only serve for one term of office. The person elected must be at least 40 years old and have an education up to at least degree level.

The functions of the president are to represent the state and to appoint diplomatic representatives. He or she 'signs off' laws passed by the Grand National Assembly and has the power to reject those laws once and to send them back for reconsideration. The president also appoints the prime minister and presides over the Council of Ministers.

Council of Ministers

The Council of Ministers is elected from the members of the Grand National Assembly. It carries out much of the day-to-day government and law-making.

Prime Minister

The prime minister is appointed by the president and has the power to appoint limited numbers of ministers other than from the Assembly.

Articles of the Constitution

Turkey is declared to be a democratic and secular state in which everybody has the freedom of conscience, religious belief and opinion (Article 24). It is also proclaimed as a social state. This concept recognises a state that has obligations to provide for the social security of its people as well as the right to expect the people to uphold the interests of the state (Article 2). Some progress has been made in this direction but there is a lot more work to be done.

The Republic is a state governed by the law. The state must respect human rights (Article 12). This is an area in which Turkey has been subject to a lot of criticism. Various modifications were made to the constitution in 1995 with a view to addressing some of those criticisms, and much work is currently being undertaken to improve Turkey's performance in human rights. That has recently been monitored by the European Commission as a condition of Turkey's being considered for admission to the European Union, and the reports of the European Commission (*see* their website, **www.ec.europa.eu/enlargement/turkey/index_en.htm**) indicate the progress that has been made over the last few years in this respect. The situation at the time of writing is summarised in the opening paragraph of their 2006 progress report: 'Turkey [...] has continued political reforms. However the pace has slowed during the past year. Significant further efforts are needed in particular on freedom of expression. Further improvements are also needed on the rights of non-Muslim religious communities, women's rights, trade union rights and on civilian control of the military.' Some of these issues clearly relate to the way in which the law is exercised, but many still pertain to underlying issues within the constitution and administrative law (*see* below).

Administrative Law

Administrative law is something that we do not have in profusion in the English legal system. It is the body of law that governs the conduct of the government – that is the same in the UK. However, the conduct of the government in Turkey reaches into many more places than it does in the UK, and so the impact and the importance of administrative law is much greater under the continental civil law system (as adopted in Turkey).

Administrative law is one of the least satisfactory aspects of Turkish law because it has not yet been fully codified. More is comprised of principles, drafted by the law-makers, and case law, established by the administrative courts in their decisions.

Administrative law is not directly tied into other aspects of the law; it is an entirely independent system of law and not bound by the decisions of the other courts. Thus, for example, if a term is defined in the context of civil law then that does not mean that the same term will have the same definition in the context of administrative law. Administrative law developed later than other aspects of Turkish law and is still in a state of continuous development.

There are some key elements to Turkish administrative law that we cover in some detail because they are *aspects of the law that are likely to be of direct application to foreigners owning property in Turkey*: they govern the actions of the authorities that indirectly or directly affect foreigners, and if foreigners have any problems with the authorities it is this aspect of the law that they will become involved in.

The main principle of administrative law is the recognition of the concept that **the state is subject to the law**. In other words, any action of the state can be challenged via the legal system. This supremacy of the law is exemplified by the right of the citizen to go to the administrative courts to protect their human rights, to protect their entitlements to benefit under the 'social state' and to enforce their constitutional rights to equal treatment in a secular – i.e. non-religious – state.

Any action of an administrative authority (including the signing of contracts, the making of decisions and the performance of its public duties) is an 'administrative act'. Some of those actions are treated on the basis that the administration has such overwhelming power that the individual has to be protected from the abuse of that power.

Other administrative acts – including business contracts – are treated on the basis that the administration and the person entering the contract on behalf of the business have agreed to do so on free and equal terms. In other words, contracts where the government is deemed to have excess power are subject to administrative law; contracts deemed to be between equal parties are subject to ordinary private law (*see* below).

Administrative acts can be challenged by the individual on a number of bases: because they have been taken without legal justification; because they have been taken without legal authority; and because they are not in the right form. If they are challenged they can be declared null and void – as if they had never happened – or they can be cancelled but remain in effect until the moment they were cancelled.

Any actions in respect of administrative acts are made through the **administrative courts**. The first hearing is at regional level and, on appeal, goes to the **state administrative court**. Below the state level of administration but subject to roughly the same rules are the provincial and local administrations. Each central government department has a provincial sub-department and there is local administration (elected for five years) at provincial, municipal and village level. The provincial 'local' administration is basically there to deal with the money collected by the province for its own benefit as opposed to the money collected by central government and delegated to the province.

Municipal public administration exists in all districts that have a population of more than about two thousand people. They have certain powers delegated to them from the central administration.

Village administration applies in towns and villages with a population of less than two thousand people. It then has a general village meeting (which is the supreme deciding body) which, in turn, votes for the mayor (*muhtar*) and the executive board of the village. The board automatically also comprises as members the village priest and the village teacher.

Public Property

An important concept in Turkey is that of public property. This can be land, buildings or 'movable' property. Any property that is in public service for the public benefit is deemed as public property. Some of it is public property at the national level and some is public property at the local level.

At the national level public property includes, most importantly, any property without an owner. Some categories of property are deemed not suitable for private ownership and, as a consequence, automatically belong to the state. The land that is the property of the state includes all land that is unsuitable for agriculture (mountainous areas and rocky or marshy areas), the sea shore, forests (other than a few private forests) and historical, cultural and similar buildings or sights. In addition, the state also owns the so called 'common property', which is property designed to be used by everybody, for example, roads, market squares and cemeteries. Anyone who damages public property is punished more severely than those damaging private property.

Public property cannot usually pass into private ownership, and most public property cannot be registered at the land registry. However, occasionally the state authorises the private sale of part of this property, and this has given rise to a lot of development on the coast in recent years.

This issue is particularly important if you are thinking of acquiring land or a building built on land that has been in public ownership but which has now been passed into private ownership. It is necessary to make sure that that passing of ownership has been properly undertaken. Alternatively, and more frequently, land that is in public ownership will not pass into private ownership but will be leased to a private operator for a period of, usually, 60 years. Thus if you buy a property on such leased land, at the end of the 60-year period your property will revert to the government.

Private Law

Private law is the law that applies to the private individual and includes everything that does not fall within constitutional or administrative law. It includes the law that applies to individuals dealing with the state in circumstances where the administrative law says, for example, that their contract has to be dealt with as a private act.

Civil Law

Civil law is the main part of private law. It is set out mainly in the Civil Code, updated in 2002. It was originally based on the Swiss Civil Code but has since drifted away from it in certain respects. It is divided into sections on some general principles: the law relating to people (persons), family law, the law of succession and the law of property.

Article 1 of the Code lays down the various sources of law referred to above.

Article 2 states that a person must act in good faith and that the law does not protect the person who abuses rights and unjustly inflicts harm upon others. This concept of abusive rights is important in Turkish law and can overturn otherwise clear principles or rules. For example, the owner of a property must use his property in such a way as not to interfere with the rights of others (Article 737). A house owner cannot, therefore, build a wall around his or her garden that interrupts the view of the sea previously enjoyed by his or her neighbours; the neighbours will be entitled to go to the courts for the demolition of the wall. This concept obviously involves a balancing of the interests of the two parties.

Article 6 of the Civil Code says that the burden of proof is always upon the person who alleges something.

Capacity

This is divided into two parts. There is the legal capacity to enjoy rights and be subject to obligations, and there is the capacity to act in any particular set of circumstances.

All persons are deemed to have **full legal capacity**. All persons are deemed to be equal. This includes foreigners. The rights of foreigners are, however, in some ways restricted on the basis that they have the same rights as each other but not necessarily the same rights as a person of Turkish nationality. This book will look in some detail at some of those restrictions.

Capacity to act is determined by a number of factors, one of which is age. The age of majority is 18 and only a person aged over 18 has the full capacity to act. (In certain circumstances majority can arise earlier than 18.) Also, a person only has capacity to act if they have the maturity of judgement to know the difference between right and wrong. Mental illness, drunkenness and fever can eliminate or suspend the capacity to act.

The capacity to act can be taken away from you by order of the court. For example, if you have been in prison for more than one year you lose some of your legal rights. If you are a profligate spender or you behave badly in your private life, some aspects of your life can be constrained.

Capacity to act is recognised in all contracts and is an important preliminary to the effectiveness of the contract. People of full capacity can enter transactions on their own and be fully legally bound by the transaction.

Some people have a **limited legal capacity**. For example, a married couple only has limited capacity on their own to dispose of the assets that belong to them both. Again, this is important if you are dealing with a contract of sale from a married couple where only one of the parties is proposed as the signatory to that contract.

Family Law

Women have exactly the same legal rights as men.

A UK citizen who marries or cohabits with a Turkish person will be subject to Turkish family law, and his or her position is governed by the third book of the Civil Code.

Turkish family law is based upon the notion of the authority of the chief of the family and – at first sight in contradiction to the principle of equality of treatment – the husband is deemed to be the chief of the family.

The minimum age of **marriage** is 17. Parties under 18 can only marry with the consent of their parents or guardian. In 'necessary circumstances' parties can marry at the age of 16 with the order of the court – this is normally when the woman is pregnant.

Turkish law provides only for monogamous marriage; you can, therefore, not marry somebody else until your first or former marriage has been brought to an end by death, divorce or nullity. A woman cannot remarry within 300 days of her divorce or widowhood unless she can prove that she is not pregnant or is incapable of being pregnant. **Same sex marriages** are not permitted.

Divorce is permitted in Turkey and covered by Articles 161–166 of the Civil Code. Grounds for divorce are:

- **adultery.**
- **if a spouse makes an attempt against his or her partner's life.**
- **extreme cruelty by spouse.**
- **if spouse commits a felony (serious crime).**
- **if spouse leads a lifestyle that offends against public morals; the usual example of this is homosexuality.**
- **desertion for more than six months.**
- **incurable insanity.**
- **severe incompatibility – partner has to show that the prospects of future happiness have been lost completely.**

Divorce by mutual consent is permitted if the parties have been married for at least one year providing they have agreed the legal consequences of their divorce, such as the division of property.

Succession

Succession is covered by the fourth book in the Civil Code. For Turkish people the law lays down who has to inherit what. If the deceased did not make a will, she or he will be considered intestate.

There is mandatory heirship in Turkish law, but foreigners are bound by the law of their own nationality rather than by Turkish law – in the case of British people, there are very few constraints on what they can do on their death and, therefore, in effect, they can leave their property in Turkey to whomsoever they please. This is only the case, however, if they do not die intestate, therefore we highly recommend that you make a Turkish will, to eliminate the possibility of your estate passing to someone against your wishes who is nominated as a mandatory heir by the law. Please note that your English will will not cover

Turkish property, though it will cover your movable assets such as the money in a Turkish bank account.

The general principle of succession is that of 'universal succession'. This means that you take not only the assets but also the liabilities. It also means that all of the deceased person's rights pass by succession.

We recommend you use a UK-based law firm with Turkish expertise for inheritance issues, which will have the ability to cover both jurisdictions should you have any specific questions or concerns.

Property Law

The law of property deals with rights and obligations relating to land and buildings, which are known as **real rights** or rights *in rem*. These are contrasted with **personal rights** or rights *in personam*, which arise in the case of, for example, the possession of a car or stocks and shares.

Real rights are enforceable against everybody, even somebody who is not party to the transaction. For example, a right of way passing over a property is enforceable by anybody against the owner of that property.

Letting contracts are not real rights. A tenant only has a right against the person who granted the tenancy. If the land is sold then the tenant will not have any rights against the new owner of the land – subject to one or two exceptions.

Real rights are divided into two groups: absolute real rights and (more limited) real rights. An absolute real right gives the person the complete freedom to use, dispose of or deal with the property (*mulkiyethakki*). More limited real rights include mortgages over property, servitudes (such as rights of way) over property or encumbrances of property.

Real rights are not brought to an end by the passage of time, however long that time might be. Lesser rights are. Real rights are only fully effective if registered at the land registry.

The real rights in respect of property are broken into three parts. They will sometimes pass together and at other times can be separated. They are:

- **the right to use the property (*usus*).**
- **the right to enjoy the benefit of the property (*fructus*).**
- **the right to sell or dispose of the property.**

It is possible and, in some cases, advantageous to convey the ownership to one person and the right to enjoy the property to another. For example, your son could have the legal ownership of the property but you might have the right to enjoy it for your lifetime. This would, in some circumstances, significantly reduce your tax bills.

Foreigners cannot enjoy absolute real rights over property in Turkey without the permission of the Turkish authorities. The process is called a **military**

clearance application. The rationale behind this is that the military in Turkey happens to be the authority who keeps a record of the total land being purchased by foreigners. There is a limit to the total land that can be purchased by a foreigner, which is currently 2.5 hectares, though this can in exceptional cases be raised to 30 hectares by application to the Council of Ministers.

The limited real rights referred to above may be enjoyed by foreigners without permission. The first of those limited rights is the **servitude**. This is the right to enjoy at most two of the three components of full real ownership. So, for example, the right to use the property or the right to enjoy the property are both servitudes. A person could have either the right to use or the right to enjoy, or both. They could equally have the right to use and the right to sell but not the right to enjoy and it would still remain a servitude. As soon as all three rights are untied in the same hands, it ceases to be a servitude and becomes a real right of ownership.

Mortgages are a separate category of limited real right. The detail of rules as to the content of mortgages are complicated and must be complied with strictly. The mortgage right can be registered. Other encumbrances can also give rise to limited real rights, for example, a charge put on the property to secure compliance with some obligation.

Although rights in respect of real property last forever, this is subject to the provision that prescription (limitation) applies in connection with the acquisition of real property. If a person acquires a movable property (for example a car) from a usual place of business and holds it for at least five years without dispute, he or she becomes the owner of it. If a person acquires real property from another person who is the overt owner of that property and continues in possession of it for 10 years without interruption or dispute, he or she becomes the valid owner of the property. There are some limitations to this doctrine.

The ownership of land carries with it the ownership of things under the land down to a reasonable depth and the airspace above the land up to a reasonable height. It also carries with it the ownership of anything attached to the property as a component part, so, for example, fitted wardrobes will pass with the land. Anything that can be separated from the property without giving rise to harm or significant damage to the property is permitted to be removed.

Unless otherwise agreed, a spring on land gives the person who owns the land ownership of the water coming out of it.

The Law of Obligations

The law of obligations breaks down into three parts:

- **the law of contract (the most commonly applied part).**
- **the law of tort (actions giving rise to consequences for another person).**
- **the law of unjust enrichment.**

In Turkish law, obligations between private individuals or between a private individual and the administration, where the two parties are deemed to be equal participants in the venture, are governed by this law. The parties have the freedom to decide how they wish the transaction to proceed. Thus, within certain limits, they can decide on the terms of their contract, the court that should deal with any dispute relating to it and the legal system that should apply to it.

This is not an absolute freedom, however; there are certain limits imposed by the law. If a transaction violates those legal limits then it will be null and void. Some transactions are deemed illegal. A contract to perform a criminal or immoral act, for example, would be illegal and therefore null and void. Similarly, a contract for the transfer of ownership of land must be made before the land registry for it to have legal effect.

Pre-imposed upon whatever the parties may have agreed is the concept of equity. If, for example, one of the parties to a contract does not specify a clause to cover a particular situation, the court will decide what is fair and reasonable in the circumstances. This, of course, is not a substitute for having a proper clause in the first place, as the outcome of that deliberation can never be guaranteed.

Obligations are normally enforceable through the courts.

Contracts

Legal transactions are generally, but not always, bilateral transactions, that is to say, transactions in which two or more people agree to take a particular course of action. In these transactions the interests of the two parties are essentially opposed: I have the obligation to pay the price of the property to you; you have the duty to deliver the property to me. These bilateral contracts are enforceable through the courts.

They are enforceable in two principal ways: by an order that the person do what he or she contracted to do (execution), or by an order that the person pay compensation.

The validity of a contract in Turkey is governed by much the same principles as apply to the question of the validity of a contract in England. There must be an offer and a corresponding acceptance. This contrasts with the situation in most continental countries where offer and acceptance are not required but other formalities are.

A verbal offer lapses immediately if it is not accepted. A written offer lapses, if not otherwise stipulated, within a reasonable period or when it is rejected.

This is important if you are putting in an offer to buy a property. Generally, however, any such offer should be drafted carefully by your lawyers, because you would not want to rely upon a general provision of this kind. Contracts are considered in terms of debtors and creditors even where the performance of the contract does not involve the payment of money. Thus the person who has to do something is the debtor and the person to whom the obligation is owed is the creditor. A contract where each party has an obligation to the other and receives and gives something (such as the purchase of a house) is called a 'syanallagmatic contract'. This is an important distinction because if one of the parties does not perform his or her obligation, the other party is entitled to suspend performance of his or her related obligation. If one party only partially performs his or her obligation the other party is entitled to respond reasonably. This is the sort of contract with which we will deal most of the time.

When two or more people enter a contract as either the seller or the buyer, unless stipulated to the contrary, they are liable in equal shares to perform their obligations. So if one person fails to perform because, for example, he goes bankrupt, you will only have the right to collect half of the money from the other person. This can be varied by making both parties jointly and severally liable for performance of the contract, in which case you can recover the full amount from either party – but, of course, not from both. Contracts become effective the moment that they have been agreed, unless the contrary is stipulated.

Contracts can be suspended until a certain action has taken place. These **suspensive conditions** are very useful if, for example, a person wishes to buy a property and make sure that it is in good condition by way of a survey before finally committing himself.

If a contract imposes a condition that is a **penalty condition** that punishes non-performance of the contract, a judge can vary the terms of that penalty if he considers it to be unfair.

Certain types of contract have special formalities, for example contracts of sale, contracts of exchange (*trampa*), contracts of employment and contracts of rental.

Non-contractual obligations are obligations that arise other than by way of a contract.

Torts

Torts are wrongful or unfair acts causing injury or damage to another person. They are governed by Article 41 of the code of obligations. Most result from the wilful intention or negligence of the person committing the damage.

A tort only arises in circumstances where there is no contractual relationship between the parties, and the action that gives rise to the tort can be either positive or negative. A positive action would be when you did something that positively caused damage – for example, breaking a window. A negative action is when you remain inactive in circumstances where you should have taken some action to prevent harm – for example, taking no action to help a victim of a road accident.

A tort is only going to give rise to a claim for compensation or other remedy if the action taken is not authorised by the law and if damage was caused. Damage may not be physical damage but could be financial or emotional damage. The action will only give rise to a claim for compensation if the action caused the damage. This is defined in several ways and the definitions generally follow common sense. You will see that the law of tort in Turkey is very similar in concept to the law of tort in Britain. It is unusually close for a continental legal system.

Unjust Enrichment

The concept of unjust enrichment gives a person who has suffered loss as a result of the actions of another person who acted unreasonably or unlawfully the right to seek compensation. If a person wilfully sells something to another at four times its true value and conceals the status from the buyer then this could give rise to a claim. If a person seeks compensation for the payment of a debt and is paid twice, that would be unjust enrichment. If a bank accidentally takes the money twice from someone's bank account then it would have to return the excess taken because otherwise there would be unjust enrichment.

Criminal Law

Crimes are actions that are specifically stated to be crimes and to which a penalty attaches. This distinguishes them from actions that, although considered to be wrong (for example, unjust enrichment), are not stigmatised – called crimes. Crimes differ from torts. Crime is almost always the result of an intentional act rather than a negligent act.

In Turkey there are some basic concepts associated with criminal law.

- **Nobody can be punished for something that was not a criminal offence at the time when he or she did it.**
- **The penalty imposed can only be that laid down by the law.**
- **Nobody is guilty of a crime until his or her guilt has been determined by a court.**
- **Nobody can be compelled to incriminate him or herself by statement.**
- **Nobody can be tried for something done by somebody else.**

Crimes are divided into categories under the Criminal Code.

- **Crimes against the state – including the embezzlement of public funds or damage to public property.**
- **Crimes against society – including forgery.**
- **Crimes against public order, including inciting someone to commit a crime.**
- **Crimes against public safety – including, for example, arson or negligence causing an accident with an aeroplane.**
- **Crimes against public decency – including rape, indecent assault and, until recently, adultery (now declared by the constitutional court to be invalid and law has not since been re-drafted and re-introduced).**
- **Crimes against a person – including assault and murder.**

- **Crimes against property – including fraud, theft and – interestingly – kidnapping for ransom.**

Under the Turkish Penal Code there are various categories of punishment. Capital punishment was abolished in 2004. The nature of the penalty depends upon the nature of the offence. Some offences are defined as serious offences (felonies) and they are punished as follows:

- **Heavy imprisonment – imprisonment until the death of the person concerned.**
- **Imprisonment – imprisonment up to 20 years.**
- **A heavy fine – fine up to an amount specified from time to time by the system.**
- **Disqualification from public service.**

Lesser offences (what we would call misdemeanours) are punishable by imprisonment for up to two years, a small fine or a disqualification from exercising some trade or profession.

The punishments can generally be applied either individually or together.

Private International Law

As in all other countries, Turkey has rules about what should happen if two systems of law clash. Private international law covers what happens when a private individual is involved in a situation where he or she can potentially be covered by the law of two countries. It is an immensely complex subject.

The Turkish Code of Private International Law dates back to 1982. It covers the rules of private international law and the ways in which those rules should be enforced internationally. It has some general principles.

The applicable law is generally determined by the place where the action took place. Unless the parties have agreed to the contrary, a Turkish person and a French person who enter into a contract in England will be governed by English law. A person granting a power of attorney in England to sign a document in Turkey will have the document validated in accordance with English law and not Turkish law.

Torts are dealt with in accordance with the laws of the place where they were committed.

Personal matters are usually dealt with by the law of your nationality. So, for example, the capacity to marry or to inherit is dealt with in accordance with the law of the country of which the person in question is a citizen. This is why, generally, British people can leave their assets in Turkey to whoever they please on their death, which is not the case for Turkish people.

There is one possible exception to this rule and that is the transmission of real estate (land and building) located in Turkey where the Turkish law applies. There are, however, indications that, as English law will govern part of the inheritance (the other assets apart from land owned in Turkey), the principle of unity of the inheritance should mean that all will be dealt with together and in those circumstances English law should apply. Because so few people have ever owned land in Turkey in the past, this position is not entirely clear.

Family relationships are dealt with, ideally, in accordance with the national law of both of the parties. However, where a marriage is celebrated in Turkey it is governed by Turkish law. If the marriage is celebrated in another country between parties of differing nationalities, the situation gets a little complex.

Profiles of the Regions

03

This chapter summarises the main areas where property is sold to foreign buyers, and gives an indication of the character of each place, local sights and attractions, and public transport links (mostly bus or shared taxi, the latter known locally as *dolmuş*, but also ferry and train connections where appropriate; pretty much all the resorts also offer boat trips in the tourist season).

Currently your best options are largely concentrated on the Mediterranean and Aegean coasts (the southwest corner of which is known as the Turquoise Coast), which have the advantages of a good climate, relative accessibility from Britain, a superb coastline and a developed tourist infrastructure. In certain areas such as around Fethiye there are large expatriate communities. This is one of the most popular places for British buyers, particularly the resorts of Çalış, Hisarönü and Ovacık. Other property hotspots are currently Kuşadası, Altınkum, the Bodrum Peninsula, Dalaman and, to the east, Side, Alanya and the golfing centre of Belek.

There are also working expatriate communities in the major cities of Istanbul, Ankara and İzmir, but only the first of these is really a tourist destination, and, even there, buying property for holiday lets is unusual.

Inland Turkey, though beautiful and rewarding to explore, is only briefly covered in this book – to give a hint of what lies in store should you wish to spend time travelling around the country. Cappadocia is the main focus as far as property-buying is concerned.

Because of its inaccessibility and relatively poor climate, the northern Black Sea Coast is visited by few tourists, and the property market has barely been exploited by foreign buyers, although it's an interesting area to visit.

The Aegean Coast

The resorts may have arrived in force, but the Aegean – Turkey's intricate western coast – still harbours a remarkable amount of gloriously unspoilt, rugged coastal scenery, where the pine forests slope down steeply to clear turquoise waters and secretive coves. This area once lay at the very heart of the ancient Greek Mycenaean empire, and there are more Classical sites than in Greece itself – among them Ephesus, Troy and Pergamon. The numerous islands provide an extra attraction, and it's an easy ferry hop to some of the Greek islands from the Turkish mainland.

Generally it's a little cooler here than on the Mediterranean, with bearable temperatures in June and September, although July and August tend to be extremely hot. Large sandy beaches are not very common – many but by no means all the beaches are of coarse grey sand – so, if swimming is important to you, you may prefer to confine your searches to properties with a pool. In resort centres it can get very noisy, so you may need to weigh the advantages of a central location and convenience against tranquillity and inaccessibility.

Çeşme is one of the quieter larger resorts, while Bodrum still has plenty of character; both make good bases for trips inland, to atmospheric hill towns and archaeological sites. Airports serving the Aegean, all with flights direct from the UK, at least in the summer months, are at İzmir, Bodrum and Dalaman (the latter being just east of Marmaris).

This section looks at the main areas for property for sale, arranged from north to south. These are:

- **Çeşme**
- **Kuşadası**
- **Altınkum**
- **Bodrum**
- **Marmaris**

The Northern Aegean

Between the Sea of Marmara and the Gulf of İzmir the coastline is far less touristy than it is further south. Access is more difficult here – there is no major airport – and the sea is noticeably cooler. **Çanakkale** is the main jumping-off point for visiting the First World War landing and battlefield sites across the water at **Gelibolu** (Gallipoli). Further south is **Troy**, perhaps Turkey's most famous archaeological site but by no means its most spectacular. Most of what survives is Roman, although the gigantic wooden horse of Greek legend fame – a modern replica – is the most photographed feature.

Foça

Just north of the mouth of the Gulf of İzmir, the seaside town of Foça – the modern town of **ancient Phocaea** – stands on two curving bays, known as Big Sea and Little Sea, divided by a headland capped by a Genoese castle. There's a busy fishing industry here, and you can taste the results at virtually any of the restaurants that are strung out along the cobbled promenade. The town has a good sandy beach, and for more isolation there are unspoilt coves within easy range; İzmir is a short drive away – hence Foça's popularity as a bolthole from the city, with many locals from there and Manisa owning or renting out apartments in Foça itself. Despite that, the town is still far from frenetic.

Foça has mosques and a functioning *hamam* (Turkish bath), and you can take boat trips from May to September to nearby islands. The route west to the main road is served by *dolmuş* and there are frequent buses to İzmir.

To the northeast, the ancient city of **Pergamon** is within day-trip range (though you need longer to do the site justice), and accessible by car or bus. Although it's not on the same scale as Ephesus, it is every bit as enthralling, a mighty citadel perched high above the surrounding plain. The two principal sites are the Acropolis, with its theatre and library, and the Asklepeion, the medical centre in ancient times.

İzmir

Although it is finely set on a gulf with a fine mountain backdrop, İzmir is a large, functional, modern city of two million inhabitants – Turkey's third largest town – so perhaps not ideal for enjoying the best of the Aegean, although it is very handy for the airport.

The city's roots go back to around 3000 BC, but much of İzmir was destroyed during the First World War. The rebuilding was scarcely inspiring, consisting of high-rise blocks along wide, tree-lined boulevards. However, you may wish to be near İzmir for its facilities, which include a British consulate, a railway station, car hire places, hospitals and an outstanding bazaar. Buses to Adnan Menderes airport run 10 times a day, with journey times of around 20 to 30 minutes. Cultural attractions include the State Opera and Ballet, the International İzmir Festival (mid-June to early July, with some events at Ephesus and Çeşme) and the İzmir International Film Festival held in April (not annually).

East of İzmir, the modern village of **Sart** stands on the ruins of the ancient capital of Lydia, **Sardis**, which during the 7th to mid-6th century BC had the distinction of being the world's richest city – thanks mostly to the gold that was washed down in the River Pactolus from the slopes of Mount Tmolus. There's still quite a bit to see of Sardis itself, notably the Temple of Artemis, with its Ionic columns (mostly re-erected) and the Roman gymnasium and baths from the 2nd century AD.

The Çeşme Peninsula

Some 80km west of İzmir airport and blessed with a less fierce climate than much of the rest of the Aegean, the Çeşme pensinula has a string of beach resorts, villages and thermal spas – the word *çeşme* means fountain – and it's lapped by clear turquoise waters and has numerous unspoilt inlets and bays. Aniseed, artichoke and sesame fields are interspersed with fig and gum trees in the hinterland, although around Çeşme itself there is mostly barren scrub. A motorway connects Çeşme with İzmir, an 80km trip taking around an hour and a half. Despite its many attractions, Çeşme has been rather ignored by foreign buyers, and the resort is popular mostly with Turks. But, with good beaches, world-class windsurfing and attractive properties, Çeşme is likely to soon become a property hotspot for British buyers.

Çeşme

At the tip of the peninsula and facing the Greek island of Chíos, Çeşme itself is Turkey's westernmost town and pre-dates İzmir as the region's main port. A

14th-century Genoese castle overlooks its narrow streets and red-tiled roofs, and generally it's more laid-back and less flashy than many of the places further south, with a decent provision of services – banks, supermarkets, seafood restaurants and a clinic. But the old red-roofed town with its narrow streets gets packed with holidaymakers at peak times. Indeed it has something of a party atmosphere in the evening; the international song contest in July is one of Turkey's biggest music festivals. You can also hire yachts.

The beaches hereabouts are the longest in the Aegean, and although the one in town is small, there's a good one close by at Ilıca (with water sports), and other possibilities within close range at Çitftlik, Ovacık, Altınkum Plaj (not to be confused with the much more substantial resort of Altınkum; *see* p.38) and Güvercinlik, while Çark has shallow waters popular with families with small children. Alaçatı is another major water-sports centre, good for wind-surfing, sailing and water-skiing. The best of the peninsula's thermal spas are on Şifne Bay, near Ilıca, where the waters are said to relieve rheumatic pain, digestive complaints, spine marrow infections and inflammation of the joints.

Çeşme is served by plenty of buses from İzmir, and has local buses to beaches, villages and other points around the peninsula. During summer, car ferries link the town with Venice and Brindisi, and the Greek island of Chíos is accessible by ferry all year round. Chíos is easy to visit on a day trip and has a prosperous main town; you can explore the island by bicycle. Otherwise, the vicinity of Çeşme is a bit restricted if you want something over and above idling on beaches.

Around Çeşme

Just 4km north and with a frequent *dolmuş* service from Çeşme, the pretty village of **Dalyan** (not to be confused with the Dalyan on the Turquoise Coast; *see* p.43) occupies a peninsula within the peninsula, and has attracted numbers of people to build retirement and holiday homes. It's still a fishing community, however, and the beach is mediocre.

Some 20km northeast, **Ildırı** was ancient Arythrai, with some Hellenistic-era mosaics and the remains of a theatre. It has been ruthlessly quarried for its stone over the centuries, but the position and views still justify a visit.

The Southern Aegean

Kuşadası

Endowed with a yacht marina, abundant ancient attractions (notably Ephesus), easy access to İzmir airport (around an hour's drive away) and nearby beaches, Kuşadası has become one of the tourism hotspots on the Aegean, and it's not difficult to see why. Around town there are some extremely enticing spots: the **Güzelcamlı** (a national park) for instance is verdant, with mountain views and a nearby Blue Flag beach; regulations prohibit high-rise development on the shoreline.

But Kuşadası's status has dealt it a rash of high-rise developments elsewhere in the town, which won't be to everyone's taste, and its bustle can reach the point of being clamorous. The laxity of planning laws means that supply (a mixture of villas and apartments) tends to outstrip demand, and prices are comparatively low; at the time of writing, one-bedroomed furnished villas are on sale here from just £18,000, but the cheaper properties often have poor access to the town centre and low build-quality (no central heating, for instance), making them unlikely to appreciate much in value, and unsuitable for holiday lets.

The deep harbour has enabled Kuşadası to become a stopping-off point for cruise ships – when the cruisers turn up, the prices at the bazaar reputedly go up. Aptly named Long Beach, 7km from the town, is one of the bay's several excellent white sandy beaches with plenty of opportunities for water sports. More tranquil coastal spots can be found in **Dilek Peninsula National Park**, also known as Milli Park, some 28km out of town, which has a number of idyllic little inlets.

Bus connections from Kuşadası are excellent, and Selçuk near Ephesus is on the rail network, with train services to İzmir taking around 1hr 40mins. Additionally, regular daily ferries make the short crossing to the Greek island of Sámos, where the main attraction is Pythagoria, with the ruins of Hera's temple and a remarkable kilometre-long tunnel built in the 6th century BC.

Around Kuşadası

The ancient sites of Priene, Miletus, Didyma (or Didim) and Herakleia each lie within day-trip distance, but nearby **Ephesus** (Efes), the most visited ancient site in Turkey, eclipses them all. In the days of the Roman Empire, this was the finest city in all Asia Minor, with a population of nigh on half a million; enough of it survives to evoke its halcyon days. The main street, the so-called Marble Road, extends for a kilometre, with remains of baths, fountains, a splendid theatre, temples and other civic buildings dotted around. Chariot ruts are visible in the paving stones, and an undercover section displays a wealth of frescoes and mosaics. Many of the other finds, including two famous statues of Artemis and some choice carved ivory furniture, are on show in the outstanding archaeological museum in the nearby modern town of **Selçuk**, within strolling distance from the main site itself. There's a great number of other ancient sites within day-trip range, some of them little-frequented: at **Belevi** (16km northeast of Selçuk), for example, are two monumental tombs of the 3rd century BC.

Further inland, about 120km east, lies **Pamukkale**, a wonderland of petrified springs where you can bathe in the warm waters, and the site of Aphrodisias, dating from the 6th century BC, which includes a stadium and Temple of

Case Study: Not Buying through an Agent

Helen (39) and her Turkish husband Metin (45) bought a four-bedroomed villa with a garden in the national park area of Güzelcamlı, a 20-minute bus ride from Kuşadası, with shops and restaurants en route. They like being close enough to Kuşadası to take advantage of the facilities of the busy, thriving resort, which has something for everybody, but also a quiet and picturesque location, and a clean and safe beach. They wanted their villa to be a base in Turkey for visiting relations, and hope to retire there for at least part of the year in the distant future. 'As Metin is Turkish we knew exactly what we were looking for, and we have had a lot of help from family, friends and acquaintances both in terms of recommending workmen, volunteering services, supervision of building work and general upkeep of the house,' Helen says, although decoration and installing a new kitchen and two bathrooms meant they ended up spending more than they had planned.

Helen and Metin also want to let out the property, but the first year was a struggle. As time progressed they got more emotionally attached to the house. 'This influenced how we tried to market it, as we wanted control over who rented it – in particular we were looking for families or older couples – and believe me, word of mouth really doesn't work. We bought the house in January, and completed building and furnishing in April in time for a provisional booking in May, which then never happened. Lesson learnt – beware.' Helen had not asked for a rental agreement or contract, so received no money. 'This showed quite a lot of naïveté on our part but we were too embarrassed to ask for a deposit. After not marketing ourselves widely enough I am now becoming more business-minded about the property and have stopped thinking of it as my second home! If buying to let, don't expect to make loads of money or for it to happen overnight.'

Helen continues to be enthusiastic about Turkey and is very happy with her purchase. 'Turkey is a lovely country, unspoilt, and the people are not yet cynical or unwelcoming of holidaymakers. In particular children are very welcome everywhere and are not seen as an added inconvenience as sometimes happens in restaurants in England. Older people are particularly treated with respect and the local people usually can't do enough for you.'

Helen is sure that she saved money by not buying through an estate agent. 'On my last visit in April, I noticed for the first time loads of estate agencies appearing, and these are exploiting British and German buyers as the prices are expensive in comparison to us buying directly from a vendor. We would not have found a property like this for this price except through word of mouth – a friend of my mother-in-law was talking to somebody else in the local market, who knew somebody who had built the structure of a house but had then run out of money.'

Aphrodite. Heading inland northeast from Kuşadası, the valley of **Küçük Menderes** is pleasant to explore for its traditional-looking settlements such as **Birgi**, with its wooden houses, and **Tire**, where gypsies from the surrounding area come in for one of the region's most colourful markets. There are feasible bus connections via Ödemiş.

For general information on the resort and surroundings (including Çeşme), visit **www.kusadasi.net**. For a forum on the area visit **http://forum.kusadasi.biz**.

Altınkum

Meaning 'golden sand', Altınkum is just that – so much so that at peak times in summer the beach is absolutely packed. The sea is really gentle, with no surf at all, hence the resort's popularity with families with small children, and a variety of water sports are on offer. The Brits are here in large numbers, and a number of British-style eateries have sprung up to cater for them. Properties are predominantly villas. Just inland is the considerably less touristy village of **Yenihisar**, which has a wider range of shops than you will find at Altınkum. Altınkum is a couple of hours' drive from İzmir airport, and you can reach Bodrum in an hour by hydrofoil or in 2hrs by ferry. Bus services are somewhat limited.

Around Altınkum

Just 5km away, **Didyma** (Didim), served by *dolmuş* and bus from Altınkum, was thought by the Greeks to be the oldest of the 19 oracles in all Asia Minor. They rededicated it to Apollo and set about building the largest temple in the world. It took them 500 years of endeavour, yet they never finished it. They left some 120 enormous columns, ranged in a double row, some standing and others toppled over, a *cella* with 70ft-high walls, and a smaller temple to house the statue of Apollo.

To the northwest, the once-great Greek port of **Miletus** (Milet) has dwindled into comparative insignificance, but has a vast Roman theatre with arcaded sides to act as a reminder of headier days. An even more evocative ancient site awaits at **Priene**, with an intoxicating hillside location and a grid of excavated streets of a small Greek city, scattered with remnants of Ionic columns – a well-preserved theatre, municipal buildings and a Temple of Athena. Inland from Altınkum, the Byzantine ruins of **Herakleia** – including a shrine to the local shepherd Endymion – look over **Lake Bafa**, a scene of exquisite stillness. The remains are scattered around a working village.

The Bodrum Peninsula

With its low-rise, whitewashed, bougainvillaea-decked villas, Bodrum is a sophisticated, lively resort set amid some stupendous scenery, although in recent years much of the surrounding Bodrum peninsula has been much built up with Spanish-style villa development, a phenomenon that looks set to continue. The nearest beach is at the somewhat characterless water-sports resort of **Gümbet**, 3km outside town.

Virtually unlike anywhere else on the coast, **Bodrum** has a pulsating nightlife that keeps going all through the night – the nightclub strip can get rather loud. Restaurants and bars line the long waterfront promenade, while the narrow streets of the old town are full of shops selling jewellery, fabrics and leather goods, and there's a good weekly produce market. There are also plenty of health centres and hospitals with English-speaking staff.

Bodrum has kept much of its old character. In ancient times it was known as **Halicarnassus**, a Carian city colonised by the Dorians, who originated from the Peloponnese in around 1000 BC. Bodrum later came under Persian rule, but its greatest hour was in the 4th century BC when Mausolus made himself king of independent Caria and began the Mausoleum of Halicarnassus, which became one of the Seven Wonders of the World, and was dedicated to himself. This was later toppled by an earthquake and, although a few bits survive, most of the remains were recycled into the harbourside 15th-century Crusader castle of St Peter, now home to one of the most absorbing museums on the Aegean. This has a staggering collection of treasures rescued from the sea bed, including a 14th-century BC Canaanite vessel, and eye-catching Roman glass artefacts.

Bodrum airport (35km) is a 30-minute drive away, and has a shuttle bus (booking required) into town. In addition to various pleasure cruises, ferries leave for Altınkum, Datça, Knidos and Marmaris as well as the Greek islands of Kos and Rhodes. Buses get you to numerous other places along the coast. Bodrum's one-way system makes driving a bit of a chore, and parking can be an ordeal too.

The outskirts of Bodrum are not especially inspiring, with the surrounding area sprawlingly developed beside pocket-handkerchief-sized beaches, but further out along the Bodrum peninsula there is some gorgeously verdant scenery (although development tends towards the concrete style). Here you'll encounter olive orchards and citrus groves – pine forest to the north and sandy beaches and impressive crags to the south. Much of it is accessible for those without a car, as good *dolmuş* services link Bodrum itself to such resorts as **Bitez** and the tranquil village of **Gümüşlük**, with waterfront restaurants looking out to the half-sunken ruins of ancient Myndos. Both **Turgutreis** and **Yalıkavak** have yachting marinas, and are pleasantly low-key, although there's nothing much else to distinguish them. On the north coast near Gölköy, with its low-rise development and shallow strip of beach, **Türkbükü** has become a smart holiday retreat for Turks.

For further general information on Bodrum and the surrounding area, visit **www.bodrum-info.org**.

Marmaris

In character, the giant resort of Marmaris seems the double of Bodrum, and its nightlife is nearly as lively. As a yachting centre it is unequalled in Turkey, with a 700-berth marina and an annual regatta. A wide strip of coarse sand stretches several kilometres round the bay.

The magnificent harbourage of Marmaris attracted the Carians, who used it as a base to attack the Phoenicians on nearby Rhodes. Much later, in the 16th century, Süleyman the Magnificent ordered a castle to be built in the town to assist his own conquest of Rhodes. However, when he saw the building, he did not like it, exclaiming '*Mimarı as!*' – 'Hang the architect', supposedly the origin of the town's name. You might feel that way when you see the tacky concrete sprawl that prevails here. But nothing can detract from the majestic setting, beneath majestic pine-covered slopes, and there's a sweet, compact old quarter of cluttered charm around the castle, which escaped a big earthquake in 1958. The bazaar area has lots of carpet- and leather-vendors, and there's a good weekly market. Other facilities include a number of large, modern shopping centres, and several private hospitals and health centres with English-speaking staff.

Around the harbour is a row of waterside restaurants (many of them excellent, though not always cheap) and cafés. At night, the centre of the action is Hacı Mustafa Sokağı, with numerous bars and clubs, and close by an open-air cinema screens international movies in their original language with Turkish subtitles. In May, Marmaris hosts a yachting and arts festival. There's also Atlantis water park, with exciting water slides, bumper boats, an open-air swimming pool, snack bar and air-conditioned bowling alley.

Hourly buses serve Dalaman international airport, from which it's about a 90-minute drive. In summer tour boats get you out to some gorgeous spots, among them **Sedir Adası** (also known as Cleopatra's Isle), where Mark Antony and Cleopatra are said to have met, and the yacht haven of **Karacasöğüt**. You can charter motor schooners or yachts from Marmaris at a reasonable price and explore things at your own pace.

Around Marmaris

Regular ferries and hydrofoils make the crossing to the Greek island of **Rhodes** – one of the biggest playgrounds on the Med (with the consequence that hordes of day-trippers from Rhodes come over to Marmaris too). The landing point is at Rhodes town, the island's capital, which has a castle and walls built by the Knights of St John, who controlled the island for two centuries after 1306. From there it's an easy bus journey to see the superb acropolis at the island's beautiful second city, Lindos.

A few kilometres southwest of Marmaris, the much smaller purpose-built resort of **İçmeler** has a wide array of activities, including paragliding, jet-skiing, windsurfing, canoeing, sailing and bathing in thermal springs, and there's good bathing in the calm waters as well. Craft stalls line a canal in the town centre, and there are a few general stores, plus regular *dolmuş* and boat services to Marmaris. A bit further out, **Turunç** has an enviable position on an arching bay backed by steep mountains. Its comparative inaccessibility might appeal to escapists; the sheltered beach of coarse sand is good for water sports and for children, while just across the bay are the Phosphorescent Caves where the water glows when it's disturbed. From Turunç it is a 30-minute journey by *dolmuş* into Marmaris during the day.

Some 30 minutes north of Marmaris, **Akyaka** has an attractive, secluded setting, and very little traffic passes through, but the beach is mediocre. The area southwest of Marmaris includes **Orhanıye**, **Selimiye** and **Bozburun**, a trio of modestly sized yachting resorts.

For more information, go to **www.marmarisinfo.com**.

Datça

On a long, narrow peninsula that juts out towards the south coast of Kos and with views across the water to the Greek island of Sými, Datça may appeal if you are looking for somewhere uncrowded and unhurried. In scale it doesn't amount to much more than a one-street village: expansion has been limited, with a marina and a few streets of tourist accommodation, a tourist office and a handful of travel agencies and restaurants. In the centre are a number of older stone properties, and seafood restaurants cluster around the harbour. The beach is generally not overly busy, and there are several others nearby. Because of Datça's isolated position, driving anywhere means going east across tortuous, mountainous landscapes – it's absolutely exhilarating the first time you do it, but not exactly a stroll in the park.

The scope for day trips is limited, although you can reach Bodrum by ferry or hydrofoil from Körmen Limanı (9km north; shuttle bus into Datça). Other possibilities are the weekly ferries to the Greek islands of Kos and Rhodes, or to reach Marmaris and Muğla by bus or *dolmuş*, from where there are further transport connections. Further west, idyllically forgotten villages dot the groves of almond and olive trees, and the ruins of the ancient port of **Knidos**, site of the sanctuary of Aphrodite, stand at the very tip of the peninsula. Driving time to Dalaman international airport is around 3–4 hours.

The Mediterranean Coast

Backed by a mountainous hinterland for much of its length, Turkey's long southern coast has hotter weather than the Aegean, and it's here that you'll find many of the best beaches, notably at Dalyan, Ölüdeniz and Patara.

General Data on Southern Turkey (2007)

Flying time from London: 4 hours
January temperature (minimum): 3°C
July temperature (maximum): 40°C
Population: 74,877,000 (UK 60,587,300)
Size: 780,580 square km (UK 224,820 square km)
GDP: US$708.053 billion (UK US$2,121,766 billion)
GDP *per capita*: US$7,300 (UK £25,500)
Tourists per year: 19 million (1.8 million from UK)

The region subdivides into four: **Lycia**, with some of the finest coastline in all Turkey, between Fethiye and Antalya, and also known as the **Turquoise Coast** (with justification – the sea really is that colour); the level **Pamphulian coast**, with its ancient ruined cities; the pine-fragrant, little-known **Cilician coast**; and the **Hatay**, an Arab enclave bordering on Syria. Only the western part – notably Dalyan, Fethiye, Çalış, Ölüdeniz, Hisarönü, Ovacık, Kalkan, Kaş, Antalya and Alanya – really stands in the limelight as far as property-buying and mass tourism go. The two international airports for this region are Dalaman (between Dalyan and Fethiye) and Antalya. Further east, access to airports becomes difficult, though Adana has domestic flights.

The Mediterranean resorts are suitable for visits year-round, with perfect swimming in September and October. In April and May the weather is mild and the distant mountains are still snow-covered, while July and August are fiercely hot and you will need to take things very leisurely. The November to March period is relatively wet, with some storms, although it's often very pleasant in the sunshine, with bright, clear days, but it is usually too cool to swim in the sea at this time.

In ancient times, the Lycian people, natives of Anatolia, settled in Turkey's southwestern corner and left behind a host of wonderfully sited cities and monuments. The first mention of **Lycia** appears in the 13th century BC, although most of what you see, such as the region's rock tombs, which were carved into cliff faces and with temple façades, is from the 7th century BC or later. The rugged hinterland of the coast, with its steep, scrub-covered mountainous slopes, is still remote in character and largely hard to penetrate, although a recent coastal road makes access reasonably easy between Fethiye and Antalya.

For walkers, a major attraction is the long-distance **Lycian Way**, which runs from Ovacık, near Ölüdeniz, to a point near Antalya, through a magnificent variety of mountainous and coastal landscapes. In its entirety it takes about a month to complete, but one can walk stretches of it as day walks, and in many places you can use local bus or *dolmuş* services for the return leg. There is a guidebook and map to the route, and the website **www.thelycianway.com** is a useful source of information.

This section follows the coast from west to east.

Dalyan

Set between mountains on a meandering river and less than 30 minutes and under 40km from Dalaman international airport, Dalyan (not to be confused with the Dalyan on the northern Aegean coast, *see* p.35) is still largely unspoilt, with an alluring position among olive groves and beneath a cliff face cut into by ancient Lycian rock tombs.

Although new properties are still being built and the town is spreading appreciably, planning restrictions prevent anything higher than two storeys, and there is a good supply of traditional Turkish-style villas with ground-level terraces. There is plenty to do in and around town, but although the scenery and town itself are attractive, be warned that there are squadrons of persistent mosquitoes, which can make things a bit miserable.

The main street is traffic-free, and a number of restaurants are found along the banks of the river. You can walk out to the ruins of the ancient port of Kaunos, long silted up and abandoned, and effectively the dividing point between the Aegean and the Mediterranean coasts. Here survive the remains of an ancient Lycian and Carian settlement, with tombs from both cultures, as well as bits and pieces from various other eras, including a Roman fountain and a Byzantine basilica.

A 30-minute boat trip downriver takes you to a magnificent sandy beach at **İztuzu**, safeguarded against development because of its status as a nesting ground for giant loggerhead sea turtles, who lay their eggs at night. When in the 1980s beach development was proposed, this sparked a nationwide debate: the eggs were in danger of being crushed by sunbathers and sun umbrellas, and the lights from hotels and bars would disorientate the hatching turtles, who would mistake these for the gleam of the sea, crawl the wrong way and die. In 1991 the developers backed off and the conservationists won the argument. As a result no buildings will ever be erected here, and the entire beach is closed at night especially for the turtles' protection.

Organised excursions include white-water rafting on the Dalaman river, canyoning, sea kayaking, walking, mountain-biking, motocross, Jeep safaris, paragliding, horse-riding, sea-fishing and boat tours along the coast to such places as the thermal mud pools at Ilıca.

The website **www.dalyan.co.uk** has good overall coverage of the resort and its surroundings.

Fethiye and Around

In 1957 an earthquake effectively destroyed the old town of Fethiye, but although it is a modern place it has a pleasantly relaxed ambience, and a setting beneath yet more pine-clad mountains. Yachts and *gülets* are moored along the waterfront promenade, itself lined with waterside cafés and seafood restaurants. The population of Fethiye has risen to around 60,000 as its importance as one of the major holiday and retirement areas of the Aegean has grown and grown, and development has spread along the coastal plain. Accordingly, there's a very wide choice of property for sale, as well as a sizeable expatriate community – more than 2,500 Brits in the area at the last count – but the town still clings on to its Turkish character. You can find all the facilities of a major resort here, including Internet cafés, a modern private hospital, a Turkish bath, car and motorcycle hire and banks. There are some small supermarkets, but much more interesting are the weekly street market and the food market and bazaar district in the town centre.

The nearest beach is 5km north of town at the suburb of **Çalış**, which has become one of the main areas for property-buying and -building in recent years. It is served by regular buses and a boat *dolmuş* service from Fethiye itself. Beachfront apartments have glorious views across the Gulf of Fethiye and the beach itself is about 12km long, with coarse sand and shingle. There is a Sunday market. With excellent letting potential, Çalış is popular with the British and Dutch, many of whom have retired here and found it a very friendly community. It is more obviously a resort than Fethiye and can feel overrun with tourists at peak times. West of town is the leafy suburb of **Karagoz** with its villas and

Case Study: Buying as an Investment

In 2004 Maria (45) and Shaun (52) made a cash purchase of a one-bedroomed flat in Çalış, close to the sea, as a holiday home for letting. They had taken holidays in the area about 30 times since 1989 and wish they had taken the plunge earlier. 'The resort was very different from how it is now. Over the last few years we have seen the sprouting of both new housing developments and estate agents and, frankly, felt we'd missed out. There is a certain charm about Çalış that I can't articulate. Although the hotels and restaurants aren't the smartest, the view is beautiful and the sunsets are spectacular – and the people are wonderful. The Fethiye area generally is ideal for those wanting a relaxing base with a choice of nightlife. There are many places round and about to visit and even after all these years we're discovering new things to do.

'Our chosen property meets all our requirements as an investment: good location, easy to manage and maintain, good price and marketable. We have no intention of using it – instead we stay in a hotel on the beach with unobscured views. We pay such a low rate per night that it's cheaper to stay there and let our place out.'

Profiles of the Regions

1 Ülü cami, Bursa
2 Ephesus
3 Carpet shop, Marmaris

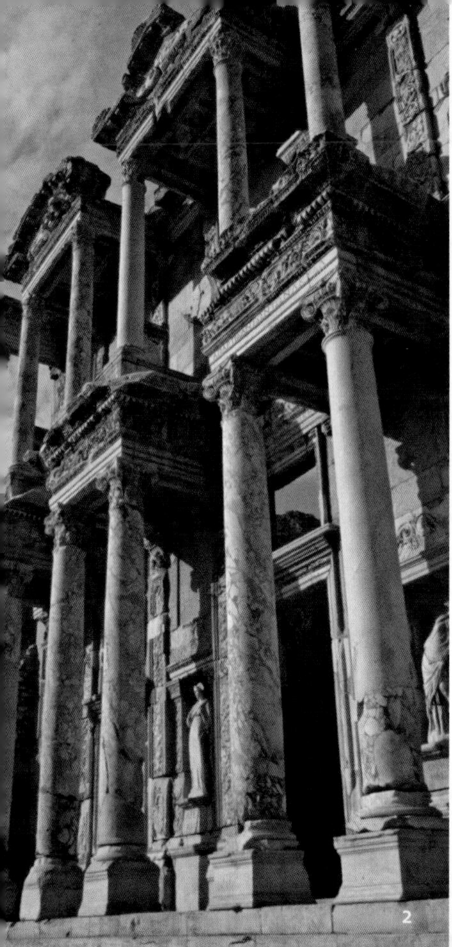

2

The Aegean

Almost impossibly intricate and endowed with clear blue waters that look too good to be true, Turkey's south-western corner shelters a sequence of rocky headlands and secretive little coves, more easily explored by boat than by car. Beyond the distinctly expanded, exuberant and cosmopolitan package resorts of Bodrum and Marmaris lie beguiling smaller centres based around tranquil fishing villages, while little-frequented beaches cluster beneath olive groves and pine forests. Along the coast and just inland, the huge number of classical remains, including such celebrated sites as Ephesus and Pergamon as well as many lesser gems, are as hauntingly evocative as anything else in the ancient world. In the Aegean interior, the Ottoman rule left a wealth of mosques and domestic architecture.

3

The Mediterranean Coast

Long, hot summers and generously sized sandy beaches have made the south Turkish coast one of the great playgrounds of the Med. At its western end, foreign property-buyers have colonised idylls on the aptly named Turquoise Coast, such as Dalyan, Kaş, Ölüdeniz and Fethiye, while giant loggerhead sea turtles quietly go about their own business. Mixed in with ancient Greek ruins such as Termessos are astonishing Lycian sites, including citadel-like honeycombs of rock tombs cut high into the cliffs. Alluring seafood is on the menu, trinket-sellers carry on a brisk trade, and tourists flop on the beaches of Antalya and Alanya. Yet in the distance the mountains, dusted with snow for much of the year, promise something very different. The Lycian Way provides an exhilarating walker's route through some of the choicest scenery.

1 Harbour, Kaş
2 Patara beach, Kaş
3 Carpets, Antalya

4

4 Harbour, Antalya
5 Private residence, Antalya
6 Restaurant, Kaş
7 Mediterranean Sea
8 Ottoman house, Antalya

5

Ezme Hot Chili Salad
Mixed or Green Salad
Humus
Stuffed Aubergine
Green or Dry Bean Salad
Soup of the Day
Zeytin Yağlı Mezeler
Seafood Starters
Cheese or Olive Salad

6

8

7

1

Central Turkey

An immense region that seems more like several countries than part of one, Turkey's interior is an explorer's terrain. In the northwest, the land of whirling dervishes, donkey carts, carpet-weavers and lonely shepherds, austere and empty plains give way to mountains and lush pastures, while European-style Ankara performs its role as capital. Further east, the staggering emptiness has an austere beauty, the great mountains merging into the steppes of Georgia, Armenia and Iran. The lunar volcanic landscape that is Cappadocia presents a formidably exotic landscape of underground cities and rock churches, and is witnessing central Turkey's most appreciable influx of property-buyers. Meanwhile, the parched southeast, peopled by Kurds, Turks and Arabs, has its foot firmly in the Middle East.

1 Üçhisar, Cappadocia
2 Near Göreme, Cappadocia

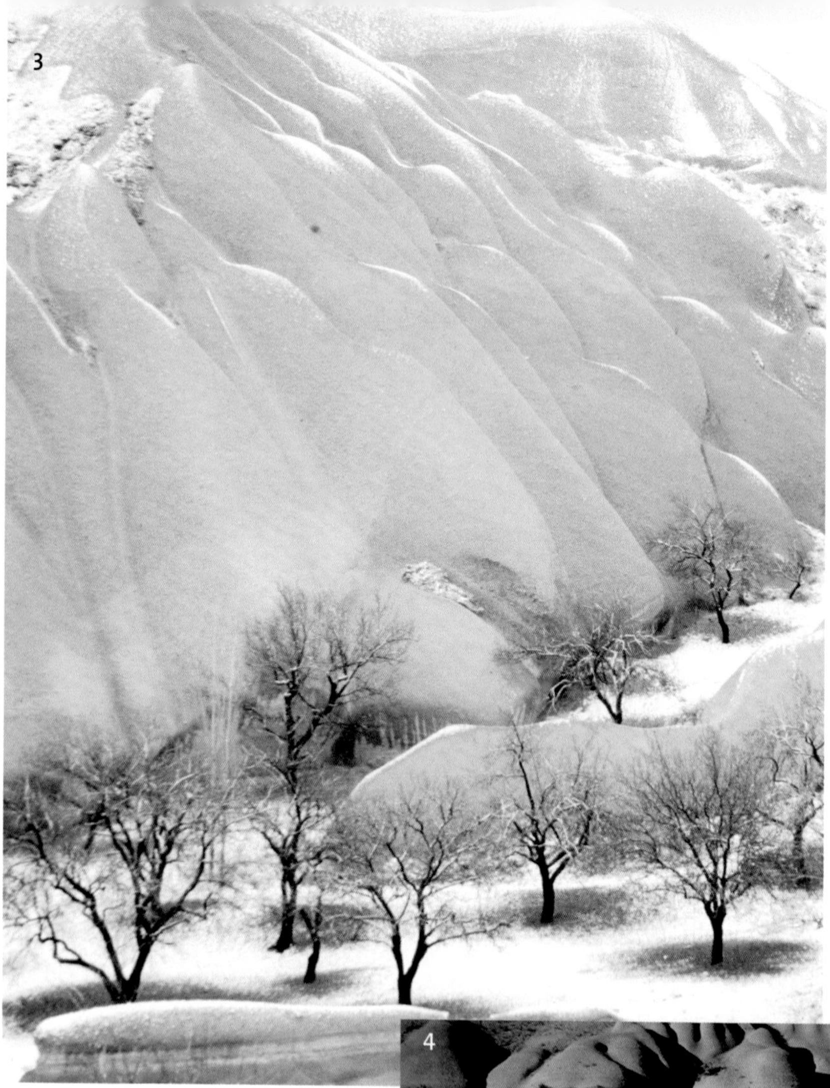

3 Near Üçhisar
4 Near Göreme
5 Church of Three Crosses, Cappadocia

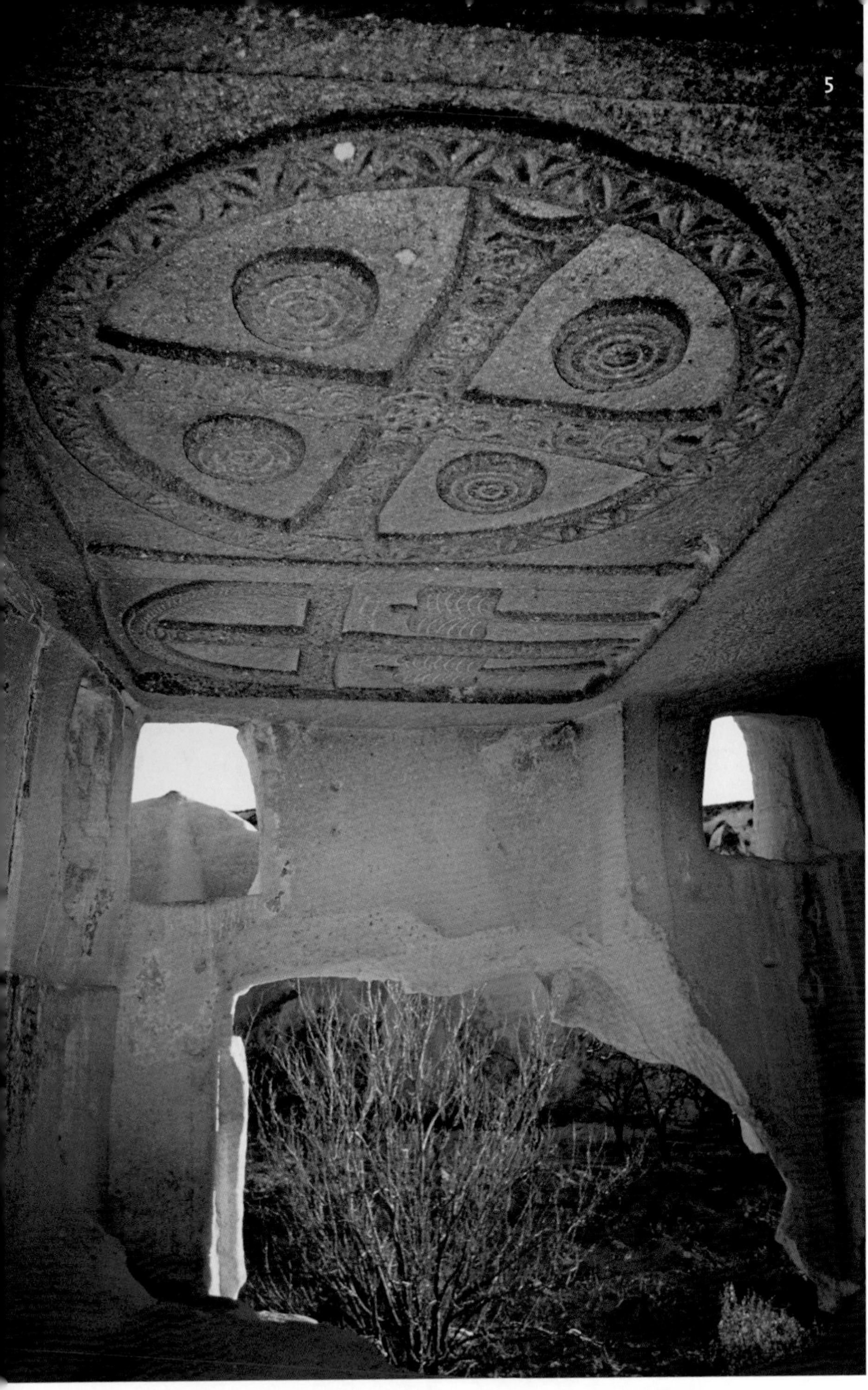
5

1

2

3

4

5

Istanbul and Around

Minarets and domes contribute to one of the world's most distinctive skylines. Byzantium, Constantinople and then Istanbul – Turkey's cultural epicentre has changed its persona many times. The best ferry trip in the world plies the great waterway between two continents. Vibrant and demanding, this city presents a kaleidoscope of impressions, from the wholesome whiff of the Spice Bazaar to the gorgeous splendour of Topkapı Palace, from the haggling carpet-sellers to the shoeshine boys touting for business. Southwards beyond the Sea of Marmara, the old Ottoman capital of Bursa conjures up an air of gracious refinement in its mosques and old houses. To the east and abutted by soaring, forest-clad mountains, the rainy, verdant Black Sea coast is Turkey's longest.

1 Doorway, Safranbolu
2 Sunrise on the Black Sea
3 Divan Edebiyati Muzesi, Istanbul
4 Divan Yolu, Istanbul
5 Aya Sofya, Istanbul

6

7

11

10

6 Restored house, Safranbolu
7 Sunset over Istanbul
8 Mısır Çarşısı (Egyptian Bazaar), Istanbul
9 Tea plantations above Rize
10 Near Perşembe, Black Sea coast
11 Sumela Monastery, near Trabzon

8

9

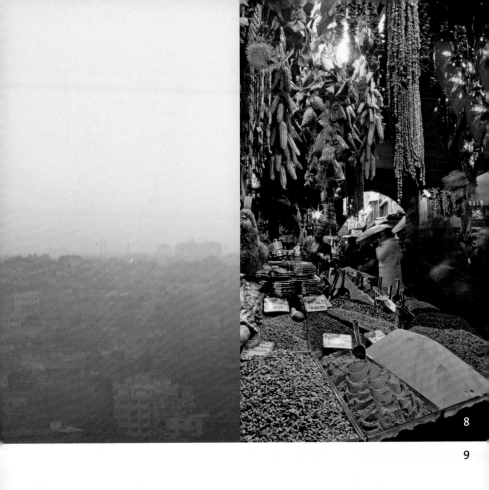

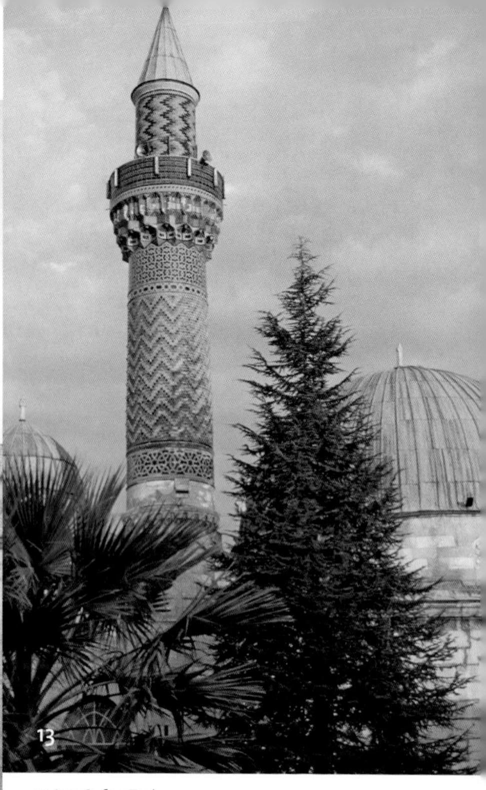

12 Aya Sofya, Trabzon
13 Yeşil Cami, İznik
14 Kariye Church, Istanbul

apartments looking over the recently built marina. Çalış also has a nesting area of protected sea turtles where in June and July you can see females arriving, and in September watch the hatchlings leave.

Boat trips take you out to some remote, rugged spots and unspoilt coves: the Gulf of Fethiye contains 12 islets, with plenty of possibilities for escaping from the bustle of the town itself. To make the most of it, you could plan to hire your own boat and spend several days exploring the area. A new ski resort is being developed in the mountains close to Fethiye, which may lengthen the tourist season substantially.

Fethiye makes an excellent base for visiting local Lycian sites, many of which date back to the 7th century BC. The Lycians left remarkable rock tombs carved with elaborate temple-like façades; the cliff face immediately above the town itself is the site of ancient **Telmessos**, including the magnificent Ionic Tomb of Amyntas, cut in the 4th century BC. You will stumble across ancient sarcophagi dotted around the town – there is one carved from a single block of stone next to the post office. Fethiye also possesses a 6,000-seater amphitheatre from the late Hellenistic period.

Well away from the tourist mainstream but easily reached from Fethiye are three other Lycian cities that are remote and usually unfrequented by visitors. To the east and off the coastal road towards Xanthos, the overgrown remains at **Pınara** feature Lycian rock tombs, a Greek theatre and a Roman odeon; while, near Yeşil Üzümlü and northeast of Fethiye, **Kadyanda** has a Doric temple, baths and a theatre. The area's most spectacularly sited Lycian city is 48km east of Fethiye at **Tlos**. This remained inhabited during Byzantine times and was home to a notorious pirate in the 19th century; rock tombs, a fortress, a Roman stadium, a necropolis, a theatre, baths and a Byzantine church have survived.

Transport links from Fethiye are comprehensive, with good bus connections to Dalaman international airport (about 50km away; currently a 45-minute drive, but a tunnel is proposed that would cut the journey time); outlying suburbs can be reached by bus, boat or *dolmuş*, and there are buses to local beaches such as Ölüdeniz and the historic sites of the Xanthos Valley. Antalya airport is more than 3hrs by car or more than 4hrs by bus – though in winter snow often blocks the mountain road and it's often better to go along the coast via Kaya, which takes at least 5hrs).

A useful website for Fethiye, Ölüdeniz and surroundings is **www.fethiye.net**. For a forum on Çalış and its surroundings, visit **www.calis-beach.co.uk/forum**.

Ölüdeniz

Some 20km south of Fethiye, much-photographed, massively visited and almost impossibly perfect-looking, Ölüdeniz stands by an idyllic lagoon with clear waters and a tempting sandy beach dotted with sun-loungers, paragliders launching themselves from the mountain immediately above, and kayaks

Case Study: An Unexpected Second Home

George (54) and his wife Chris (53) are a widely travelled couple who visited Turkey for the first time in 2002 and fell for it immediately. 'My mental picture was of somewhere dirty, unsafe and full of people who will con and steal from you. The travel agent showed us the standard picture of Ölüdeniz and rather reluctantly we agreed to give it a go. After we arrived my reservations immediately evaporated: the people were fantastic and I think the most helpful we have come across, the food lovely, the scenery was stunning and really green, not at all how I imagined, and cleanliness was of the highest standard. We picked up the local English paper called *Land of Lights* over a cold drink at the marina and started to read some of the property adverts; the prices were remarkably low, and all of a sudden our place in the sun looked like being a real prospect, as we just could not afford the sort of prices being asked in Spain and Portugal. We returned to the UK and researched on the Internet; the time to reflect proved to be invaluable. We did consider shared ownership with friends or family but we talked to others who had done this and discovered a number of downsides and tensions that can occur with this method.

'We have far from let go of our desire to see new places, but at the moment the novelty of owning a second home and the charm of a relatively unspoilt Turkey is too much of a magnet to allow us to consider going elsewhere. Out of season it is a completely different place; after October 31st, lots of places are closed, the weather can be really wet one day and then hot the next and it can get really cold, especially at night. We often fly into Antalya, as Dalaman has few flights in the winter. A tourist complex we have seen buzzing in the summer was a deserted ghost town in the winter and some homes were damp and not really up to winter living conditions. However on November 5th we were the only people sitting on Ölüdeniz beach in 23 degrees: heaven!'

dotting the ocean. The resort itself is low-rise, set a kilometre or so away, with more spreading up the mountain. The restaurants tend towards the overpriced, while the nightlife is fairly noisy. There's anchorage for visiting yachts, but a charge for using the beach.

Hisarönü and Ovacık

On the road between Fethiye and Ölüdeniz, the recently developed resort villages of Hisarönü and Ovacık virtually merge into one another, and both offer opportunities for foreign buyers. These places are away from the coast, but have the benefit of an airy setting among pine and almond forests, with choice views and scope for country walks; each village has a decent supply of bars and places to eat, although they are more limited in that respect than Fethiye.

A short trip west from Hisarönü leads to the historic and remarkably poignant medieval ghost village of **Kaya Köyü**, which was abandoned by its Greek

Orthodox inhabitants during the Turko-Greek war in 1920–22, when they were forcibly exiled to Greece, a country in which they had never resided. Around a thousand dwellings survive in various states of ruin, and a preservation order has been applied to prevent development. This site can also be reached on foot by a delightful path climbing up from Ölüdeniz.

Göcek

Northwest of Fethiye (from which it is linked by a handful of *dolmuş* services each day) and endowed with four marinas, the compact sailing resort of Göcek has become a major stopover points for yachts and *gület* tours. The town is slick and sophisticated, and packed with eateries, shops and cafés in its largely pedestrianised town centre. It does not possess a beach, but has plenty of appeal for its water sports, including diving and fishing. The yacht club organises regattas and social events.

Patara

Patara, east of Fethiye and safeguarded against development thanks to the summertime presence of giant loggerhead turtles, has a gloriously long sandy beach, which, in the turtles' interests, is closed at night from May to October. The quiet modern resort here is **Gelemiş**, lying a couple of kilometres inland from the beach. **Ancient Patara** is one of the great sites of Lycia, with fine tombs, Roman baths built by Vespasian, a splendid theatre and a Christian basilica. The ancient sites of **Xanthos** (fine mosaics in the acropolis) and **Pınara** (less to see but atmospherically set in the mountains) are also in this region, should you have visitors who want to explore the historic sites.

Kalkan

Kalkan has streets sloping steeply down to its fishing harbour and a backdrop of hills. Many houses here are built of traditional stone, with wooden carved balconies, and mostly with superb views of the bay. Upmarket boutiques, bars and a remarkable number of restaurants (well over a hundred) cater for tourists, but the nearest sandy beach is well out of town at **Kaputaş** (Kalkan itself has a pebble beach), and free water taxis take you to beach clubs; Patara beach is a 20-minute ride by *dolmuş*. Nightlife is low-key, and building regulations have prevented the invasion of mass tourism here, although there has been recent development either side of the centre.

Kaş

Meaning 'eyebrow' – denoting the curved bay on which it stands – Kaş was once one of the great secrets of the Aegean, an idyllic little port in a superlative position beneath towering summits. It's been comprehensively discovered, with crowds and noisy nightlife to match, but expansion has been restrained and the narrow cobbled streets and harbour retain a great deal of charm. Overall the atmosphere is relaxed and villagey, making it perhaps the best base in the vicinity for this prized section of coast. It's pretty much without equal as a centre for diving, both for the clarity of the water and the rich variety of underwater life, and Professional Association of Dive Instructors (PADI) diving courses (essential for anyone intending to dive) are available locally. However, the beaches are stony (which probably explains why the town has been saved from overdevelopment) – the nearest sands are 16km west at Kaputaş.

To the Lycians Kaş was Habesa, and to the Greeks Antiphellos – there are remains from both periods in and around town, including Lycian rock tombs cut into the cliff and a remarkably complete 1st-century AD theatre.

North and inland from Kaş extends a sizeable arable plain, where **Elmalı** has traditional wood-framed houses and a delightful tiled 17th-century mosque.

Boat trips from Kaş include Patara (*see* p.47) and **Kekova Island**, where underwater remains of a long-abandoned city submerged by earthquake can be seen by kayak, and close by is the ancient town of **Aperlae**. Providing there's enough demand, boats also go out periodically to the uninhabited nearby Greek island of Kastellórizo. The area around Kaş has some exciting gorges, and canyoning is big business. There's also scope for paragliding.

Kaş is roughly midway between the international airports at Antalya and Dalaman, and about 2hrs' drive from both. Bus services are characteristically thorough, with frequent services to Fethiye (2hrs 15mins), and a few buses a day to Antalya (4hrs) and Marmaris (5hrs), as well as a daily bus to Bodrum (6hrs).

Kale

A short way east, and reached by ferry from Üçağız as it is inaccessible by road, Kale is a marvellous hideaway of a village – it has no beach, no traffic, no new buildings, a choice of eateries, a ruined castle of the Knights of St John, and the chance to snorkel over the ruins of a submerged ancient city. The name Kale is also the alternative name of Demre, a modern town on a farmland plain to the east, and the home in the 4th century of St Nicholas – St Nick or Santa Claus. It is worth a detour for **St Nicholas Church**; dating from the 5th century and enlarged during the 11th century, it is thought to be the oldest church in Turkey. On the outskirts of the town, more than 20 rock tombs are cut into a cliff at the site of **ancient Myra**, which also has a Roman theatre.

Kemer

Kemer's advantages are its natural ones: the plunging, forested mountain slopes and a fine beach of white sand have tempted the developers. Facilities include water sports, banks, a supermarket and a modern private hospital. However, the resort looks uninspiringly functional, with concrete shopping arcades and a yacht harbour overlooking a crowded beach. Frequent buses make the 40km trip into Antalya, and you can reach **ancient Phaselis** by *dolmuş*, with its substantial remains of harbours and a Roman aqueduct. Antalya international airport is an hour's drive away.

Further south, and within easy day-trip range of Antalya, are the ancient sites around **Olympos**, itself sporting a Byzantine aqueduct. To the north, near the shingle beach at the resort of **Çıralı**, the **Chimaera** spouts a natural eternal flame. Further north still, the ancient port of **Phaselis**, one of the most important cities in Lycia, has good views of its three harbours from the shore, and there are tombs, a theatre and an aqueduct dating from Roman times. Sections of the **Lycian Way** (*see* pp.42–3) hereabouts make for great walking.

Antalya

Antalya is the name for a region, a bay and a city. With around 300 sunny days a year, this is very much a hub of tourism, together with the pine-clad Toros (Taurus) Mountains. The long coastal plain begins here, with the Lycian mountains forming an impressive backdrop; eastwards the land is flat, covered with citrus groves and banana plantations for much of the way as you carry on to Side. The outskirts of the city spread some way, with many new properties appearing each year; there is an increasing number of Russians visiting and living in the city.

Antalya city, with a population exceeding half a million, sprawls hugely and is now Turkey's most prosperous city, as well as one of the most rapidly expanding ones. It has been continuously occupied since ancient times, but there's not much to show for the passage of history, though by the harbour it retains a likeable maze-like old quarter known as Kaleiçi. Here there are numerous balconied, wooden, Ottoman-style houses, many now converted to small hotels and galleries, others serving as bars and clubs and often sporting delightful gardens or rooftop terraces. There is a triple-arched Hadrian's Gate of AD 133 and a tower built into the old walls and overlooked by the Yivli Minare, or 'Fluted Minaret'. Filled with yachts and tour boats, the harbour itself buzzes with vendors and general bustle, and is pleasantly animated in the evening when townspeople come out to stroll, and clubs, bars and discos keep going well into the night. The Archaeological Museum, one of Turkey's best such collections, has a wealth of items from the ancient world, including statues from Perge and a reassembled Pantheon.

The city has an eclectic range of restaurants and an excellent food market with fresh local produce; there are also several supermarkets and modern shopping centres.

Antalya has a small beach where you can have a cool dip, although most people head for the long sandy beach at **Lara**, a relaxed seaside suburb 10km from the centre (with plenty of *dolmuş* services from Antalya). Here the Düden waterfalls tumble into the sea. Buses also take the 18km trip to the **Kurşunlu waterfalls**, where there is a pleasant walking trail through the forest. Local companies offer white-water rafting in the **Köprülü canyon**.

There's an abundance of sporting activities in and around Antalya, including windsurfing, water-skiing, sailing, mountain-climbing and caving. In March and April it is possible (if you time it right – the snow's not that reliable) to ski in the mountains of Saklıkent and swim in the Mediterranean on the same day.

Around Antalya

Two of Turkey's finest ancient sites lie inland, and *dolmuş* and bus services mean you can get there without a car. The city of **Perge**, 15km east, is second only to Ephesus in scale. Founded around 1000 BC and impressively preserved, it has a huge theatre, and a colonnaded street leading to a nymphaeum and acropolis. **Termessos** (30km northwest), wonderfully set on a mountain with valleys plunging either side, seems to have been abandoned after an earthquake in AD 243, but the romantically overgrown fortifications are still formidable. It takes time to find them, but scattered here and there among the scrub is a remarkable number of tombs, some carved out of the rocks as façades in the Lycian manner, others freestanding sarcophagi. After these come the lesser sites of **Sillyon** (8km east), which is particularly atmospheric when there's no one else around, and **Aspendos**, with an impressively intact theatre that hosts an opera and ballet festival during the summer season.

Also within easy reach of Antalya are the sunken city of **Simena** and ancient Lycian cities such as **Apollonia**, **Letoön**, **Myra**, **Patara** and **Xanthos**, as well as **Aqualand Water Park** near Konyaaltı. To the east, another expanding resort out of town and with properties for sale is **Belek**, spread along an uninterrupted expanse of white sand, backed by pine forests. This is the foremost golf centre in Turkey, with four top-quality 18-hole golf courses.

Transport connections to Antalya include eight buses a day to Adana, Ankara, Mersin and Silifke, plus four a day to Istanbul (taking a gruelling 18 hours). Antalya international airport lies 10km east of the city centre, and has regular charter flights direct to the UK, as well as daily scheduled Turkish Airlines services via Istanbul.

For further information, visit **www.antalya-ws.com**.

Side

Within an hour's drive of Antalya airport, Side stands on a headland flanked on both sides by long, white sandy beaches and culminating with the romantic temples of Apollo and Athena. It's an attractive place, though very densely developed for tourism, while on the inland side the modern town merges into ancient Side, which features a fine amphitheatre and the Roman walls pierced by the city gate. A frequent *dolmuş* service leads to Sorgun beach, quieter than the bathing spots closer to town, while other excursions reached by public transport include waterfalls and gorges around **Manavgat**.

Alanya

Some 135km east of Antalya, Alanya has some of the biggest beaches on the south coast, though these are not necessarily the cleanest and it's certainly been discovered by mass tourism. The central feature is a dramatic rocky promontory topped by the castle, looming high over wooden houses and the citadel walls. From here the view sweeps along the coast with its abundant citrus orchards and banana plantations. Far below, the 13th-century Red Tower guards the harbour, and there's a colourful Friday market.

The town has spread out a lot in recent years, and there are several large supermarkets as well as scores of package hotels. Nightlife is mostly confined to the larger hotels, though in the centre there are plenty of eating places as well as a handful of discos, bars and clubs. West of town is the newer resort of **İncekum**, where the sands are backed by pine forests.

Boat trips to nearby sea caves feature a phosphorescent cave and a 'pirate's cave', and Damlataş Cave with an eye-catching array of stalactites and stalagmites. By car or a combination of *dolmuş* and walking, you can eat fresh trout and swim in the cool Dimçay river before heading on up to the unspoilt villages of the high plateau (known as *yayla*) of the Taurus Mountains, where villagers go to spend the summer.

Case Study: Buying for all Seasons

George and Gail are retired. After spending a few holidays in the south of Turkey they decided to buy a property there. They chose Alanya because although it was a holiday town it had a life in winter as well as summer. 'The natural setting is very nice here, so are the local people. Communication was not a problem at all, as the staff around you speak about three languages each. We think we made a good choice for the location.'

The couple bought a two-bedroomed apartment with a living room, bathroom and two balconies for £25,000. As the property was five years old, they had to make some slight repairs. They found the cost of getting jobs done reasonable but that it can be hard to get people to complete things at the time they promise.

'Our apartment is on the top floor. We see now that it would be better to pay more if necessary and have it on a lower floor, because when you are at the top, air-conditioning costs increase considerably.'

There are passenger-only ferries to Girne in Cyprus (3hrs 30mins); the coast and area inland to Konya is served by *dolmuş*, which ply along the waterfront. The bus station is a mile outside the town, connected to the town centre by *dolmuş*. Bus services include Antalya (2hrs), Istanbul (18hrs) and Mersin (9hrs).

East of Alanya

As you proceed further eastwards, property-buying options dry out rapidly, and public transport isn't as good either. There are still good beaches here and there, and some resort developments, but it's all some way from Antalya airport. **Gazipaşa**, 50km east of Alanya, has a yacht marina and lies beside the ruins of ancient Selinus. Anamur holds little to shout about, although its suburb of İskele, blessed with good beaches, is a busy little resort popular with Turks. **Kızkalesi**, overlooked by the Kızkalesi ('Maiden's Castle), which gives the town its name, has a good family beach and sizeable resort development, with bus connections to **Mersin** (**İçel**), the large modern port city just to the east.

This region is a favourite holiday place for the Turks, which in itself might be a reason for choosing it over areas more dominated by the influx of foreigners. Some 40km further east from Mersin, **Adana** is Turkey's fourth-largest city, with domestic flights, but is not really a place to linger in.

Central Turkey

Foreign property-buyers have penetrated little into this region, with the notable exception of Cappadocia (Kapadokya), and the huge distances from the coast mean that things are likely to stay that way. However, the charms of inland Turkey are many, and, even if you intend to base yourself on the Aegean or Mediterranean, the chances are that some day you may consider a trip to explore the dauntingly vast expanses of the interior.

While the effects of mass tourism and creeping Westernisation are ever-apparent on much of the coast, inland Turkey is unmistakably Asian. The astonishingly empty eastern plateau is part of the great central Asian steppe land, with Iran, Armenia and Georgia just across the border; however, parts of the far east of Turkey, towards Lake Van and Mount Ararat, are currently unsafe areas in which to travel, and you should check for latest conditions before going there. The vast region of central Anatolia, at the geographical heart of Turkey, spreads from Eskişehir and Konya in the west to Sivas in the east. It has vast, arid plains punctuated by the extraordinary moonscape of Cappadocia and its awe-inspiring underground cities and rock churches.

Amaysa in north-central Anatolia is a narrow river valley with ancient rock tombs carved into the cliffs by the kings of Pontus and some gorgeous Selçuk and Ottoman architecture and 19th-century wooden houses. Southwest of here is the modern village of **Boğazkale**; the ancient walled city of **Hattuşaş** was the

Hittites' religious centre from around 1375 BC and became known as the 'city of temples' – there were originally 70 of them. Devastated in 1180 BC by the Phrygians, it nevertheless retains superb ruins, notably the great temple (Büyük Mabet) to the storm god Teshuba and the sun goddess Hebut.

High above the town of **Doğubeyazıt** in the southeast, and strategically positioned to control traffic on the Silk Route, perches **İshak Paşa Sarayı**, a 366-room palace built between 1685 and 1784 in an intriguing blend of Ottoman, Persian and Selçuk styles.

Ankara

Ankara is the Turkish capital and the country's second-largest city. It is in the northern part of central Anatolia, 454km from Istanbul, 545km from Antalya and 580km from İzmir. This prosperous city of eastern Europe was founded in around 1200 BC by the Hittites, then ruled by the Phrygians, who named it Ankyra. The Romans took it for their Empire, but the city was then under the control of Turkish-Muslim states for centuries before coming under the control of the Ottoman Empire in the 14th century. In 1923 the city was elevated to capital status when Atatürk selected it for its central location, preferred over that of Istanbul. German and Austrian town planners were employed to instil a new sense of order but the city population soon swelled well above the numbers they envisaged, and is now around 3.5 million.

Ankara is a major transport hub, with bus and rail services, and an international airport served by buses to the airline terminal next to the rail station. Although it lacks the major attractions of Istanbul, Ankara is a busy modern city with a growing expatriate population (a number of whom work in language schools, embassies and elsewhere), a range of cultural activities, a university and other educational establishments.

There are still remnants of the ancient city beneath the modern veneer. The Hisar, a 1,300-year-old Byzantine citadel giving far-ranging views, stands close to relics of the Roman city (notably the Temple of Augustus and Rome) and the city's bazaar. Ankara's other major attractions are the Mausoleum of Atatürk and the Museum of Anatolian Civilisations, with a peerless accumulation of Hittite artefacts from the region. The Hittites ruled this area from around 2000 to 1180 BC, and the surroundings of Ankara harbours numerous archaeological sites from the period.

Ankara is home to the Turkish State Opera and Ballet and the Presidential Symphony Orchestra, and foreign films are shown in their original language with Turkish subtitles. There isn't, as yet, much of a clubbing scene.

Trains get you to Istanbul in around 8 to 9 hours, and to İzmir in 15 hours. There are plans to speed up journey times. The bus network fans out from here to most parts of Turkey and beyond. Generally, internal flights to places such as Antalya, Bodrum, Istanbul and İzmir are far preferable to travelling overland.

Cappadocia (Kapadokya)

Quite unlike anywhere else in the world, this extraordinary geological wonderland of rocky pyramids in central Anatolia has become firmly ensconced on many visitors' itineraries as one of the most interesting areas of Turkey, although you should be aware of the great distances to anywhere else on the tourist circuit, especially the coastal resorts. Almost uniquely in the country's interior, Cappadocia is now an area where foreigners – Germans, Britons, French and Americans in particular – are buying up accommodation for holiday lets or for their own use. In a few settlements, the cave houses are still inhabited (and not just by newcomers).

In Byzantine times, early Christian settlers on the run from religious persecutors carved out a subterranean world here among the natural rock pinnacles (known as 'fairy chimneys'). More than two hundred underground churches and entire underground cities were gouged out as places of refuge from the summer heat and from times of war. Cappadocia is still a deeply traditional region, where wine has been produced since Hittite times, and horses and donkeys are used by farmers and for transport.

Some cave houses that are for sale date back a thousand years or so, but most have electricity and water installed. Living in one may be more comfortable than it sounds: the temperature is stable, keeping them reasonably snug in winter and cool in summer, and they stay dry all year round, with the vaulted ceilings providing sufficient air movement. Sizes vary enormously, from a few rooms to a couple of dozen. Some conversions have been known to be fancy, including Jacuzzis and the like.

Nevşehir

The main town in the area is the unprepossessing modern settlement of Nevşehir, the principal point for transport connections (with good services to Ankara, Konya and Kayseri), supermarkets, banks, ATM machines and a substantial weekly market. Avanos and Göreme on the other hand have developed themselves for tourism. Quite a bit of property has come on to the market in such places, most of it requiring refurbishment or wholesale restoration, and there are still bargains to be had. Inevitably the tourist trade brings pluses and minuses: some good restaurants, but some eyesore hotels around the peripheries of the villages.

Göreme

Right in the middle of the Cappadocia region and a short bus ride from Nevşehir, Göreme represents the epicentre of the area's troglodyte phenomenon, with white cliffs surrounding a basin of weathered rock cones. Within are any number of churches and homes with vaulted rooms, some adorned with remarkably fresh-looking frescoes, some dating back to the 8th century, others dating from around the 10th to 13th centuries – though, sadly, local developers have destroyed some choice examples in recent years. One complex of underground churches and monasteries has been designated the Göreme Open Air Museum, with some of the finest examples of frescoes.

Üçhisar

Smaller and distinctly sleepier, Üçhisar crouches beneath a huge rock, riddled with more cave houses, and with superb views; the Club Med pool is open to non-residents for a small charge. A few minutes' drive away from Göreme, **Çavuşin** is still largely unspoilt and peaceful, with cave houses built into the cliff. From here, paths lead through valleys studded with secretive cave churches. Life in the traditional village of **Ortahisar** focuses on a main square lined with teahouses and dominated by a pillar of rock (which you can climb up), which is cut with passages and chambers. There are a few shops here, with more just up the road at **Ürgüp**, itself a pleasant base for the area with a good balance of tourist facilities and plenty of local colour.

Other Areas of Cappadocia

You may well be attracted to the possibility of living in Cappadocia if you get a buzz from the idea of living in a historic cave house and the surrounding countryside appeals to you. There is, in fact, much to discover in the lesser-known spots, and the area of interest extends for some 80km, though the bulk of its attractions lie within an area about 13km square. Walking can be wonderfully rewarding, along peaceful alleyways and paths between villages, with lots of opportunities for spotting wildlife and enjoying natural spectacles. One area not to miss is the **Valley of Ihlara**, an astonishing red canyon near Aksaray and some 70km southwest of Göreme, with the backdrop of 3,000-metre summits close by. It is full of ecclesiastical treasures, including the Snake Church, which has frescoes of sinners facing the Last Judgement and some nasty serpentine tortures. Cappadocia is also a rewarding area for horse-riding and cycling. Rock-climbers and serious mountain-walkers have the **Taurus Mountains** within striking distance, some 100km away. East of Cappadocia there's skiing within easy day-trip reach at Erciyes (*see* box, overleaf), 104km from Nevşehir.

Exotic and fascinating as Cappadocia is, it is something of an expatriate and tourist oasis in the middle of Turkey, some 280km from the nearest stretch of the Mediterranean coast. About 500km to the west, far beyond the desert-like terrain around the vast lake of Tuz Gölü, there's the little-visited **Lake District** that offers some exhilarating walks, winter sports and wildlife experiences in the stunning mountains above Eğirdir. Further west, **Konya**, the old Selçuk capital, is a Muslim pilgrimage centre and was where the order of the Whirling

Winter Sports

There is enough snow cover in winter to provide decent conditions for downhill skiing in the mountains of inland Turkey, with snow depths of up to 3m and skiing often feasible for some 120 days a year (generally from late December to late March). While ski areas are limited in size and number, there's enough here for some enjoyable days out for beginners and intermediates in particular, as well as scope for heli-skiing and cross-country skiing. Equipment hire, accommodation and tuition are available. Access from the Aegean and Mediterranean coasts is a problem, though – on the whole, you are out of day-trip range, as you need to head a long way east or north.

Uludağ, near Bursa and within 150km of Istanbul, is a well-equipped resort (Turkey's biggest) with a cable car, five chair lifts and seven T-bars, and a maximum drop of 460m (1,509ft), with the skiing area 1,750–2,543m (5,741–8,343ft) high. Mist can be a problem here, however, and after February the piste tends to be slushy and slow most years. In the mountains south of the Black Sea Coast, **Kartalkaya** (near Bolu and 220km northwest of Ankara airport) has slopes of 1,800–2,220m (5,906–7,283ft) altitude, with three chair lifts and seven T-bars. **Erciyes** (east of Cappadocia and 25km south of Kayseri) has a longer ski season, running from 20 November to 20 April, with 2m of snowfall typical; there's a small ski area with a couple of chair lifts and T-bars. Way out east, near Erzurum, **Palandöken** rises to 3,176m (10,420ft) and has the longest season and best snow conditions of any Turkish resort.

Closer to the Aegean and Mediterranean coasts, the options for skiing are very limited as snow cover simply isn't reliable. There's a little skiing area at Saklıkent near Antalya, and another is being planned near Fethiye.

Dervishes was founded by the great poet Mevlâna in the 13th century. One of the most traditionally Turkish of cities, it can seem austere, but has some impressive Selçuk and Ottoman architecture. The Mevlâna festival, featuring the Whirling Dervishes, takes place in December.

The nearest airports for the region are in Kayseri (about 50km from the north-east corner of the region, with twice daily flights to Istanbul) and Nevşehir (two flights a week to Istanbul). By road from Nevşehir it is 276km to Ankara, 538km to Antalya, 729km to Istanbul and 763km to İzmir.

Istanbul and Around

Istanbul

Make no mistake, Istanbul is a giant of a city, far greater than London, with a population of over 12 million and growing. More than a third of the nation's industry is based here. Both the spiritual and cultural heart of Turkey, the city famously has the unique distinction of straddling two continents, as the Bosphorus divides Europe from Asia. The European side itself is split by an inlet known as the Golden Horn, or Haliç.

The contrasts are exhilarating: on one hand there's a distinctly European look to the city's tree-lined boulevards and modern shopping centres; on the other it is vibrantly exotic with its skyline of minarets and domes. Istanbul is noisy and hectic, with appalling traffic jams, street vendors greeting you everywhere, and noises and smells assaulting the senses. However, the city is not universally claustrophobia-inducing thanks to its wide, watery spaces, hilliness and spacious parks. The medieval street pattern looks daunting on a map, but walking around the pleasantly compact centre and riding the ferries are two of Istanbul's great pleasures. A hour-long cruise along the Bosphorus by the daily Bosphorus Tour gets choice waterfront vistas.

Some expatriates working in the city have bought their own properties, but the sale of real estate to foreigners here is insignificant compared with what is happening on the Aegean and Mediterranean coasts. Nevertheless, there is potential for buying to let – for example letting flats to foreign workers employed here short- or medium-term; also Istanbul is a leading city-break destination, and many visitors spend a few days in the city before venturing elsewhere in the country.

The ancient Greeks knew Istanbul as **Byzantium**, but during Roman times Emperor Constantine renamed it **Constantinople** and, in AD 330, relocated his capital here from Rome (like Rome, it was supposedly built on seven hills, though identifying all of them requires creative effort). With the fall of the Roman Empire in the west, the remnants of 'Rome' carried on for a further thousand years until falling to the Ottoman Sultan Mehmet II in 1453. As the Ottoman Empire expanded, the city became the capital of an even greater empire that extended from the Danube to the Red Sea. Its pervasive cosmopolitan character echoes those heady days, when the city was as much Greek, Armenian and Balkan as Turkish. It gained the name Istanbul in 1930, when it was renamed by Kemal Atatürk, father of modern Turkey. For centuries Istanbul was a world centre of art and learning, and even today it remains a strikingly multicultural city.

The city's rich heritage makes Istanbul a place to return to again and again to make new discoveries. The list of attractions is extremely long, though the majority of the historic tourist sights are in Sultanahmet, south of the Golden Horn, on the European side. Here the central tree-lined square known as the Hippodrome makes an obvious starting point: within it are a bronze pillar known as the Serpentine Column of 479 BC, brought by Constantine from Delphi. Flanking the Hippodrome are the Museum of Turkish and Islamic Arts, with its priceless collection of carpets, tiles and calligraphic art, and the Basilica Cistern, an underground reservoir constructed by the Roman emperor Justinian. On the north side of the Hippodrome, Ayasofya Museum has its origins as the

Basilica of Aya Sofya (Haghia Sophia – Holy Wisdom), founded by Justinian in AD 347; this served as Constantinople's cathedral until 1453, when it was converted into a mosque. It displays magnificent mosaics and Christian frescoes. A stroll away, Topkapı Palace, seat of the Ottoman sultans from the 15th to the 19th centuries, has an eye-popping collection of Imperial treasures as well as an extensive harem; the wealth of the Ottoman court is illustrated by the sumptuous array of objects in the treasury and Hall of Costumes. The Baghdad Kiosk is an especially exquisite pavilion, beautifully tiled and inlaid with mother-of-pearl. Close by stands the harmonious Blue Mosque (Sultanahmet Camii), constructed in 1616 and so called because of its blue and white tiles. Some of the superb mosaics from the once-vast Palace of the Byzantine Emperors can be seen in the Mosaic Museum.

The city's thriving nightlife caters to a range of tastes, from clubs aiming at urban, rich yuppies to the largely all-male *rakı*-drinking taverns known as *meyhane*. Major nightlife areas are İstiklâl Caddesi, in the Beyoğlu area, Ortaköy and the classier European-side suburbs, and in summer there are good night clubs by the Bosphorus. Taksim is the heart of the city's gay scene. Cinemas are found all over the city, with foreign films shown in the original language, with Turkish subtitles, so it's easy to catch the latest Hollywood releases. *Time Out Istanbul* (**www.timeoutistanbul.com**) is an indispensable source of listings, published monthly in Turkish with an English supplement inside.

Shopping is one of the great Istanbul pastimes, with luxury shopping malls as well as more idiosyncratic establishments. The positively labyrinthine Grand Bazaar (Kapalı Çarşi) is large enough to get lost in, while the rather more manageable Spice Bazaar sells spices, confections and much more. İstiklâl Caddesi in Beyoğlu has the main concentration of chainstores, as well as market stalls selling CDs, second-hand books, fake designer clothes and the like.

Istanbul has a comprehensive arts scene, with very inexpensive (thanks to generous government subsidies) performances of theatre, opera and ballet. The Cemal Reşit Rey Hall hosts classical music performances, including a number of special festivals. There's also a busy events calendar, which you can check at **www.iksv.org**. During April to October the city hosts a number of international festivals. In April there is the International Film Festival, with films from around the world (including Turkey, of course), or see the best of Turkish drama at the International Theatre Festival. The International Istanbul Music and Arts Festival takes place in June and July, with top orchestras and classical musicians from round the world. This is followed in July and August by the International Jazz Festival, which extends over a couple of weeks. Held in odd-numbered years, the International Istanbul Biennial (in and around October) is the city's biggest art event.

For more information go to **www.Istanbullife.org**, which has plenty on living and staying in Istanbul, with links to property for sale as well.

Around Istanbul

Istanbul makes an excellent base for exploring the rewarding surroundings of the city (a region known as Thrace) – the **islands of the Sea of Marmara** (a 40-minute boat trip from Istanbul), and the battlefields and war cemeteries of **Gallipoli** (Gelibolu), the sobering scene of the fatally flawed ANZAC landing in 1915. These are quite a distance away and justify a full-day excursion. Kilyos and Şile have the nearest beaches to Istanbul, and take about an hour to reach.

Two outstanding old Ottoman cities are Edirne and Bursa. **Edirne**, tucked up in Turkey's northwestern corner and close to the Greek and Bulgarian borders, has some magnificent monuments, notably Selimiye Camii mosque, designed in 1569. In June or July, the Kırkpınar festival just outside town features the most prestigious oil-wrestling tournament in Turkey, in which contestants are lubricated with olive oil before the bouts. **Bursa**, the Ottoman capital before Istanbul was captured, is hectically noisy but full of history. It has a wealth of traditional wooden houses and fine mosques including the sublime Green Mosque (Yeşil Camii) with its ornate carving and coloured tiles. The covered market ranks second only to Istanbul's, and to escape all the commotion there are thermal baths and a cable car up to the 8,300-foot summit of Uludağ, often snow-covered in summer, and Turkey's major area for winter sports.

The southern shores of the Sea of Marmara are heavily industrialised for much of the way, and not a patch on the Aegean further south.

The Black Sea Coast

All but cut off from the rest of Turkey by a long range of mountains, the green, extremely lush northern coast of Turkey has extensive dairy pastures, cherry orchards and tea and hazelnut plantations. This coast is craggy and steep, with interesting fishing villages, wooden houses and many sandy beaches. Many of the mountains just inland are quite spectacular, but the area's appeal is limited because its wet climate can be depressing. The summer season is far shorter than further south, with reliable hot weather largely confined to July and August, when it's subtropically humid. Another detraction, once you're away from the area close to Istanbul in the far west, is the lack of access to airports; in the east the only options are the domestic airports at Samsun and Trabzon. Consequently the Black Sea coast is considerably less crowded than the Mediterranean and Aegean coasts, and the property market to overseas buyers has yet to take off (if it ever will).

Highlights include **Sinop**, beautifully set with its harbour backed by mountains, and miles of beaches nearby, and **Trabzon**, with superb frescoes in the monastic church of Aya Sofya, the little-changed Byzantine citadel, and 45km south of town the remarkable 14th-century Sumela Monastery, built into the cliff. Inland are outstanding opportunities (particularly from June to September) for mountain-hiking, white-water rafting and wildlife-spotting in the Kaçkar Dağlari range.

Selecting a Property

04

The Need for Preparation

At the moment we are in a property 'boom'. In most popular areas, not just Turkey, it is a seller's market. Property – and, in particular, attractive, well-located and well-priced property – sells very quickly. A few years ago it was fairly simple to go to Turkey, look around, see a few properties and then come back to England to ponder which to buy. Today someone doing this would be likely to find that the house they wanted to make an offer on had been sold to someone else in the few days since they had seen it.

As a result of this, people who are serious about buying property in Turkey should do some research and make some preparations *before* they go on a visit to look at property. When they go on a visit they should do so with the intention that, if they see something that they really like, they will make an offer and commit themselves (at least in principle) to the purchase while they are still in the area.

What Preparation Should You Make?

Understand the System

The system of buying and selling property in Turkey is, not surprisingly, different from the system of buying property in England, Wales or Scotland. On balance, neither better nor worse – just different. It has many superficial similarities, which can lull you into a false sense of familiarity and overconfidence. *The most important thing to remember is that buying a home in Turkey can be just as safe as buying a home in the UK – provided that you take the right professional advice and precautions when doing so.* If you do not take such advice, there are many expensive traps for the unwary.

Select an Area

You cannot scour the whole of Turkey looking for a property. It is just too big. Turkey is more than four times bigger than the UK. Those who do not narrow down the scope of their search fairly early on tend to go round and round in ever-decreasing circles and never buy a property. No area is perfect. No area has the best climate or the finest beaches or the best food or the cheapest prices or the friendliest locals. It is all a question of personal preference. Yet there is, behind it all, a logical process of selection that, if used sensibly, can help you choose an area – or, more likely, eliminate others.

Read the previous chapter, **Profiles of the Regions**, if you need to identify some starting points. Then *see* pp.74–80, 'Choosing an Area'.

Make a Preliminary Selection of a Type of Property

This is not always as obvious as you might first think. Once again common sense can help inform your decision but the human spirit often ignores such considerations. If you, or your spouse, falls in love with a farmhouse (*çiftlik evi*) in the middle of the countryside, then, although reason will tell you that you ought to be looking for an apartment near an airport, you will probably buy the *çiftlik evi*. And possibly enjoy every minute of owning it.

This does not mean, however, that it isn't worth spending a little time thinking about the type of property that would suit you best *before* you travel to Turkey to look at buildings. Buying an inappropriate property can prove very expensive and, worse still, can put you off the whole idea of owning property abroad.

As well as helping you to focus your ideas, thinking about these issues will help you give estate agents a clear brief as to what you are looking for. This will help them to help you and ought to prevent them from wasting your time by showing you totally inappropriate properties. Always discuss your requirements with the local agents who are helping you rather than dictating those requirements to them. They may well say that what you are asking for is not obtainable in their area – but that something very similar is, and at a reasonable cost.

Don't be afraid to change your mind. It is quite common for people to start off looking at older rural properties for restoration and to end up deciding that, for them, a new property is a better bet. Or, of course, the other way round. If you do change your mind you *must* tell the estate agents you are working with. Better still, you should be discussing your developing views with them and getting their confirmation that what you want is possible.

Some of the issues to think about are discussed in more detail on pp.80–93, 'Choosing a Property'.

Fix a Budget

Fix a budget for the operation. What is the maximum that you are prepared to spend to end up with a house ready to let, live in or holiday in? Include the cost of purchase, any essential repairs or improvements and taxes and fees payable.

If you are buying a new property or one that does not need major repair, this is fairly simple. If you are buying a house in need of repair, fixing a budget is clearly more difficult. You will always underestimate the cost of the repairs. No job ever finishes exactly on budget! That is as true in Turkey as it is in England. Buyers, however, create a rod for their own backs by making unrealistic costings.

If you are buying a property that needs major work, do not commit yourself until you have had a survey and builders' estimates for the work shown to be necessary.

If you are told that there is no time for this and that you will lose the property if you can't sign today/this week/before Easter, walk away.

Turkey has the advantage of much lower labour costs than the UK. Repair costs *can* be much cheaper than the UK. This is up to you. Owing to the process of negotiating in Turkey – haggling is a more accurate term – you can, if you are inexperienced, end up paying UK repair or renovation levels *or more* if you are not careful.

Make sure that you get estimates from reliable people. There are a lot of 'part-time' builders in Turkey. They may do odd jobs during the winter season and work in the tourist industry or in agriculture during the summer. The quality of their work can be very poor and you will have no effective redress if they do a bad job. Always get recommendations before asking for a quote. The estate agent who sells the property or the lawyer who does the conveyancing should be able to point you in the right direction. It might also be useful if they become involved in negotiating the price – because they are local and Turkish-speakers, they will probably get a much better deal than you would. But make sure that whoever is negotiating for you does not see it as a legitimate opportunity to take a sizeable commission.

Unless you are in the happy position that money is no object, do not exceed your budget. It is too easy, after a good lunch and in the company of a silver-tongued estate agent, to throw your financial plans to the wind. 'Only another £30,000' is a statement you may later come to regret.

See a Lawyer

It will save you a lot of time and trouble – as well as a lot of money – if you see your lawyer *before* you find a property. There are a number of preliminary issues that can best be discussed in the relative calm before you find the house of your dreams rather than once you are under pressure to sign some document to commit yourself to the purchase. These will include:

- **Who should own the property?**
- **Whether to consider mortgage finance and, if so, how best to arrange it.**
- **Whether to have the property surveyed.**
- **What to do about buying the currency needed to pay for the property.**
- **If you are going to be living in Turkey, sorting out the tax and investment issues that will need to be dealt with *before your move* if you are to get the best out of both systems.**
- **What will the process involve? Should you sign a reservation contract? Should you sign a preliminary contract? Should you sign a notarised agreement? Should you buy in the name of a Turkish company? Should you give power of attorney to the agent?**

UK lawyers who specialise in dealing with Turkey are the best people to help you fully. Your normal English solicitor will know little or nothing of the issues of Turkish law, and a Turkish lawyer is likely to know little or nothing about the British tax system or the issues of English or Scots law that will affect the way the transaction should be arranged. The lawyer may also be able to recommend estate agents, architects, surveyors, banks, mortgage lenders and other contacts in the area where you are looking.

A physical meeting is still the best way to start an important relationship. It has a number of advantages. It allows you to show and be shown documents and for the conversation to wander off more easily on to related topics. Most importantly, it is usually easier to make certain that you have each understood the other in a face-to-face meeting. But if this is impractical, these days, 'seeing' your lawyer does not need to involve an actual meeting; contact can be made by telephone conference call, by video conference or over the Internet.

Decide on Ownership

Who should be the owner of your new home? This is the most important decision you will have to make when buying a property. Because of the combination of the Turkish and British tax systems, getting the ownership wrong can be a very expensive mistake indeed. It can lead to unnecessary tax during your lifetime and on your death. Even on a modest property this can amount to tens of thousands of pounds.

This subject is dealt with more fully later (*see* **Making the Purchase**, 'Who Should Own the Property', pp.113–18).

Get an Offer of Mortgage or Other Finance

These days, with very low interest rates, more and more people will borrow at least part of the money they need to buy their home in Turkey. Even if they don't need to, for many it makes good business or investment sense. And if you want to borrow money to finance your purchase it is better to get clearance *before* you start looking at property.

Turkish mortgages are at the moment quite new for non-resident foreigners purchasing property in Turkey, though they can be available for certain foreign residents, and finance can sometimes be available for Turkish companies buying property in Turkey. The most common method of raising mortgage finance for Turkish property purchase is therefore through the remortgage of a property in the UK. However, this situation is likely to change soon as several banks are starting to offer mortgage finance to non-resident foreigners buying holiday or investment property in Turkey.

See 'Raising Finance to Buy a Property in Turkey', pp.106–13.

Think about How You Will Pay a Deposit

If you are going shopping for property you will need to have access to some money to pay for it. As we will see later (in **Making the Purchase**, 'Initial Contracts', pp.133–9), you will normally need to put down either a reserve deposit of £2,000–3,000 or a preliminary deposit of 10 per cent or more of the price of the property. Think about how you will make this payment.

Some estate agencies, particularly those operating from Britain, will ask you to take out a bankers' draft for the likely amount of any deposit. Avoid this if you can because, although it is ideal for the estate agent and the seller, it can put the buyer under subtle but unnecessary pressure to spend the money on *something*. Happily, the usual way of paying the deposit is still via a British cheque for the sterling equivalent of the amount needed. This is a simple and effective method of payment.

There is, however, a further option that people are increasingly using. This is for purchasers to leave the amount likely to be needed as a deposit with their specialist lawyer in the UK, if they are using one. Then, when they have found the right property and the estate agent is asking them to sign some form of contract, they can tell the agent that their lawyer has the money and that they will sign the contract as soon as he or she has approved it. Lawyers are usually able to look over a contract faxed to them while purchasers wait, and can tell them whether its terms appear reasonable, and check that any necessary special clauses have been included. The lawyer can also advise on the nature of the contract (whether formal offer, reservation, option or full contract) and explain, briefly, its legal effects. If all is acceptable, the lawyer transfers the funds into the estate agent's bank account by electronic transfer.

This method has a number of advantages. It can take a lot of pressure off you. It makes it very hard for the agent to persuade you to sign a document that could have – in every case – far-reaching consequences if it is not checked properly. Agents benefit because they receive the cleared funds within a couple of days rather than the two or three weeks it can take for a British cheque to pass through the banking system and be cleared into their account. Be aware, though, that this preliminary check by lawyers, though useful, is limited. They will not have seen proof of title or planning consents, inspected documentation about the construction of a new building, or been able to carry out any checks on the property. But it is a great deal better than nothing.

Again, this is another reason for making contact with your lawyer before you go to look at properties, to enable them to understand something about your circumstances.

Travelling to Turkey

A major factor in most people's decision-making process is the question of how easy it is to get to the property you are thinking of buying. How will you travel there? How will your family and friends travel to visit you? How will you get about while visiting? There is interesting research in the tourist industry that suggests that if visitors have a journey of more than one hour by road at either end of their flight, 25 per cent will not bother to travel. More than one and a half hours and 50 per cent won't bother. This may not worry you personally, but it is worth bearing in mind as far as family and friends are concerned. It is even more relevant if you are thinking of letting your property.

Although it is theoretically possible to travel to Turkey by land or by a combination of land and sea, the vast majority of people arrive by air. Air travel to Turkey is relatively cheap and the most common way of travelling to Turkey from the UK. Many UK airports service Dalaman, Bodrum, Antalya and İzmir with charter flights. Many also fly to Istanbul. Most of these services are best booked online.

By Air

Not all places in Britain are equally served when it comes to flying to Turkey. and not all places in Turkey are readily accessible. However, there are now regular flights to Turkey from Birmingham, Manchester, Teesside, Cardiff, Edinburgh, Glasgow, Newcastle, Bristol, Aberdeen, Belfast and all the main London airports.

Fares to Turkey vary considerably. Flights in summer typically cost around £150 return, but it is possible to pay less, or up to four times as much. There are also cheaper deals for those under 26 and over 60. Beware those cheap fares that are not always so cheap! Sometimes, particularly if you need to travel at a particular time and cannot arrange your travel a long way in advance or right at the last minute, BA and Turkish Airlines (THY) can offer more competitive prices and take you to more mainstream destinations than the low-cost airlines.

The largest airport in Turkey is **Atatürk Havalimanı** in Istanbul, with flight connections across the globe as well as to domestic airports in Turkey. The other major international gateways are **Bodrum** and **Dalaman**, on the Aegean, and **Antalya** on the Mediterranean coast. **İzmir** also has international scheduled and charter flights. There are more services in summer (particularly charters).

Scheduled Flights

Several airlines offer scheduled flights: **British Airways** and **Turkish Airlines** fly daily from Heathrow to Istanbul, and Turkish Airlines also operates five flights a week from Manchester to Istanbul. **Cyprus Turkish Airlines** run scheduled flights throughout the year from London Heathrow, London Gatwick, London Stansted, Belfast, Glasgow and Manchester to Antalya, Dalaman and İzmir, then continuing to Northern Cyprus.

It can work out cheaper to make indirect flights than take the journey in one trip, changing in continental Europe and travelling with an airline such as **Air France**, **Alitalia**, **Lufthansa** or **Austrian**. There are also bargains to be had by flying to Istanbul, which can cost less than £200, from where you can get return internal flights to a local airport with Turkish Airlines for around £100.

You should check the fare and availability of flights for different times in the year, though note that Turkish Airlines fares to Istanbul do not vary greatly. The most expensive fares are at peak times such as Easter and June to early September, while the shoulder seasons are April and May and late September and October; November to March is the cheaper time, although prices go up again at Christmas and New Year.

Direct flight times from the UK to the major resorts are around 5–6hrs.

- **Air France (t** 0870 142 4343, **www.airfrance.co.uk).**
- **Alitalia (t** (020) 8814 7744, **www.alitalia.co.uk).**
- **Austrian Airlines (t** 0870 1242625, **www.aua.com).**
- **British Airways (t** 0870 850 9850, **www.ba.com).**
- **Cyprus Turkish Airlines (t** (020) 7839 8097, **www.kthy.net).**
- **Turkish Airlines (t** 0844 800 6666, **www.thy.com).**

Charter Flights

Charter flights from various UK airports operate mostly from May to October, though some are year-round. These flights can be cheaper than scheduled ones but are not necessarily so, and you are usually restricted to fixed return dates, often with a maximum stay of two weeks. Most charter departures are from Gatwick, Birmingham and Manchester, but other regional airports – notably Belfast, Bristol, Cardiff, East Midlands and Edinburgh – also have summer departures. The main charter airlines that fly to Turkey are listed below.

- **Avro (www.avro.co.uk).**
- **Cosmos (www.cosmos.co.uk).**
- **Excel Airways (www.xl.com).**
- **First Choice Airways (www.firstchoice.co.uk/flights).**
- **Holidays 4U (www.h4u.co.uk).**
- **MyTravel Airways (www.mytravel.com).**
- **Pegasus (www.pegasusair.com).**
- **Sun Express (www.sunexpress.com.tr).**
- **Thomas Cook Airlines (www.thomascook.com).**

No-frills, Low-cost and Cheap Deals

Turkey, alas, is out of range for no-frills flights for the time being at least, although there are some extra-cheap deals from Europe, notably from Germany – see **www.germanwings.com**.

You can find cheap deals over the Internet or through specialist flight agents who act as consolidators by buying up blocks of tickets at a discount from major airlines. Turkish travel agencies in London are another good place to look for the cheapest tickets and other options.

A good website with links to bargain flights and budget airlines is **www.whichbudget.com**. This has a search facility showing which cities in Turkey you can get to from where, and links to budget and charter airline sites for online fare information and booking. Useful on-line booking agents include:

- **www.cheapflights.com**
- **www.kayak.co.uk**
- **www.lastminute.com**
- **www.skyscanner.net**
- **www.travelocity.co.uk**
- **www.travelsupermarket.com**

Air Travel to Turkey in Winter

Travel to southern Turkey during the winter is more complicated than in summer, since there is little demand for flights outside the May to October peak tourist season. This means far fewer charter flights ply the route, so you may end up using a scheduled service via Istanbul which will be more expensive and time-consuming, particularly if you have to stay overnight in Istanbul.

At present the only budget winter flights are with **Holidays 4U** from London Gatwick and Manchester to Dalaman and Bodrum, and **Sun Express**, who link London Stansted to Antalya and İzmir (see left for websites). More companies are likely to join these two in the near future as the numbers of resident foreigners in Turkey increases and as its tourist season is gradually extended by the opening of new, high-quality 'resort hotels', with year-round facilities.

By Rail

If you have around three days to spare you can take a fascinating train journey across Europe to Turkey, but it is neither cheap nor convenient; although it may be an exciting one-off experience, the journey is not something you are likely to want to take frequently. You can get unlimited travel across Europe with Inter-Rail passes (**www.raileurope.co.uk/inter-rail**); there's no age restriction, though it is more expensive if you are over 26. Note that you will need to pay extra on supplements for certain express trains, and reservation fees. Inter-rail passes are available to European residents only.

Perhaps the best site for information about travelling to and around Turkey by train can be found at The Man in Seat Sixty One (**www.seat61.com**); the German Railways website (**www.bahn.de**) also has an excellent search facility giving fares and times for all major European rail journeys, although it will only get you as far east as Istanbul. The North Wales-based rail travel specialists **Ffestiniog Travel** (Porthmadog, Gwynnedd, LL49 9NF, **t** (01766) 51240, **www.festtravel.co.uk**) deals with tickets to Europe.

By Road and Sea

It is a good idea to have an **international driving licence** if you are going to drive in Turkey, or else at least carry a translation of your UK licence. If you want to drive all the way from the UK it will take you three to four days minimum to cover the 3,000 kilometres. The fastest way of crossing the English Channel is to take the **Eurotunnel** (**t** 08705 353535, **www.eurotunnel.com**). If you prefer to go by sea, for ferry fares and times go to **www.ferrybooker.com**.

There are essentially two main routes from the UK. Either drive through Belgium, Germany, Austria, Hungary, Romania or Serbia and Bulgaria to reach the Turkish border at Edirne. Or go further south through France and Italy, and take a car ferry from Italy (from Brindisi or Bari) to Greece then on by road, or take the ferry to the Turkish port of Çeşme or İzmir on the Aegean coast. Ferries are not exactly the quick option: for example, travelling from Venice to İzmir takes 63 hours; Brindisi to İzmir takes 32 hours.

There is also the option of crossing the water from Greece (**www.ferries.gr**). There are ferries and hydrofoils from the Greek islands of Rhodes, Kos, Chíos and Lésbos to the Turkish ports of Ayvalık, Bodrum, Çeşme, Fethiye, Kuşadası and Marmaris. You can also travel by ferry to the Mediterranean coast (Mersin, Silifke, Taşucu) from Cyprus, or to Marmaris on the Aegean coast from Rhodes.

For more information and reservations for ferries contact **Alternative Travel & Holidays** (UK agents for Turkish Maritime Lines) at **www.alternativeturkey.com**.

To register as a foreign driver, contact the **Turkish Touring and Automobile Club** (**www.turing.org.tr/eng**). *See* **Settling In**, pp.208–209, for more on bringing your own vehicle into Turkey.

Travelling around Turkey

Travelling between A and B in a car or bus in Turkey – especially on the south coast – always takes a lot longer than you would expect in Britain. Most of the roads are single-carriageway. Many are twisty. All have slow traffic, including animal-drawn vehicles. The result is that average speeds are low.

Public transport in major Turkish cities is non-existent or extremely poor, but in holiday destinations there are more plentiful buses and ample cheap taxis.

Distances

The transfer time, rather than the distance, from the airport to your property is what is important. Even if it's a pleasant drive or bus journey the first time you do it, the novelty may well wear off. Also, letting out your property to holiday-makers will be tricky, however nice your property is, if getting there involves a long trip from the airport. Always check the seasonal availability of flights. You cannot fly direct to certain airports in winter – so you may have to change to a domestic flight at Istanbul or Antalya.

Turkey stretches for more than 2,000km if you travel by road. For example, from Edirne, in the far northwest, to Hakkari, tucked in the southeastern corner, it's a formidable 2,046km. Not that you would ever want to make that journey, but it does illustrate the country's size.

By Car

Whether you're travelling around house-hunting or thinking ahead to the time when you will actually be ensconced somewhere in Turkey, cars have the edge because of their sheer flexibility. It is easy enough to hire a car from airport and city locations; rates are similar to those found in much of the rest of Europe from the likes of Avis (**www.avis.com**), Hertz (**www.hertz-europe.com**) and Budget (**www.budget.co.uk**). You can shop around and save quite a bit, especially if you book in the UK, but should be able to find something for around £16 a day. Make sure that you are covered adequately for damage to the vehicle (your own travel insurance might include this), and you won't face a huge bill if you return the vehicle with a tiny bump or scratch.

Some hire companies have lower age restrictions than others. You do not need to have an **international driving permit** to drive in Turkey, although it's a good idea; you can obtain one through the RAC or AA in the UK; alternatively, carry a translation of your UK licence. You can, for a fee payable to the DVLA in Swansea, exchange your old-style photo-less British driving licence for a new one with a photo: pick up an application form in any larger post office.

Filling stations are easy to find, stay open most hours, and most have unleaded petrol. Mechanics are plentiful, too, and generally competent, though it is safest to use mechanics who have been personally recommended.

Turkish **driving conditions** are not much fun. Driving on the right is likely to be the least of your problems. The accident rate is high, and some Turkish drivers tend be horn-happy and pushy, overtaking on the inside, signalling erratically and seldom taking much notice of speed limits. On top of that, there are live-stock, tractors and bikes all doing their own thing, and a daunting number of unlit vehicles at night. You also have to contend with poor signposting, few street signs, tricky parking in cities and resorts, and bumpy, uneven dirt tracks that maps misrepresent as minor roads. Then, in winter, the mountain roads close to Aegean and Mediterranean resorts often get blocked by snow and you may need to use the more tortuous coastal roads.

Istanbul is one of the most frightening cities in the world to drive, with constant, high-density traffic. Drivers appear not to follow any rules. The man or woman who shows fear is lost. Where else in the world could one be passed in the fast lane of a dual carriageway by someone in a (hand-powered) wheelchair? Conditions in other towns and cities are much better and should not put off the average driver. Just be extra careful – and don't expect signals!

However, it's not all doom and gloom: outside the major centres of population the traffic is often very light, and driving around can be a real pleasure.

Speed limits are 120kph on highways, 90kph in the country and 50kph in built-up areas unless otherwise indicated.

You can bring your own motorised vehicle into Turkey for up to six months. You need an **international green card** from your insurers and a document showing proof of your ownership of the vehicle. If the staying period has to be extended, apply before the end of the period declared to the **Turkish Touring and Automobile Club** (**Türkiye Turing ve Otomobil Kurumu**; **www.turing.org.tr/eng**) or to the **General Directorate of Customs** (**Gümrükler Genel Müdürlüğü**), Ulus Ankara, **t** 0312 310 38 80/18, **f** 0312 311 13 46. *See* **Settling In**, pp.208–209.

By Train

Turkish State Railways (TCDD) has some 8,000 kilometres of lines, but they won't necessarily go to the places you want to go, and tend to keep well away from the coast, with the chief exceptions of Istanbul and İzmir. Trains tend to be old and slow, and the routes scenic and meandering rather than convenient. However, you can travel first-class and with air-conditioning in reasonable comfort. The project to build a high-speed rail link between Istanbul and Ankara was put on hold after the railway accident outside Istanbul in July 2004. For train times it is usually best to check information given at stations rather than printed sources, or see the Turkish State Railways website (**www.tcdd.gov.tr**; in Turkish only), which also gives fares.

Istanbul has two main train stations: for the European side use Sirkeci station, for the Asian side Haydarpaşa station. Both are close to ports.

By Bus and *Dolmuş*

Buses are more convenient and connect far more places than trains. They are fine for all but the really long routes (when you will be much more comfortable on a plane or train if there's the option). In fact travelling on buses is part of the

Turkish experience. For the most part they work admirably well; most are air-conditioned and set up with coffee, tea and snacks en route, with rest stops every 90 minutes or so. Smoking is prohibited on most public buses. Fares are cheap and buses are very frequent. Except during holiday periods you don't need advance reservations to travel by bus.

Most buses will drop you off at a bus station (*terminal* or *otogar* – a corruption of the French *auto* + *gare*), often somewhere away from the town centre.

At the bus station there is usually a shuttle bus service or minibus taxi (***dolmuş***) that provides an efficient link between the long-distance bus station and the town centre, as well as an important form of transport within cities. A *dolmuş* generally waits around the bus station and goes when it's full of passengers. You can hail one anywhere en route and you can alight anywhere where it's feasible to stop. Destinations are posted in the windscreen, and in summer in resort areas services continue until midnight.

The two major bus companies have websites with routes, times and ticket details (*see* **www.varan.com.tr** and **www.ulusoy.com.tr**). There are other companies that are less expensive than these two and their service may not be much inferior. For more local timetables, contact the tourist information office for the area that you are interested in.

By Domestic Flight

Turkish Airlines (**www.turkishairlines.com**) operates regular flights from Istanbul or Ankara to all of Turkey's regional and provincial airports.

Two cheap no-frills domestic operators also offer good value fares: **Onur Air** (**www.onurair.com.tr**) flies daily from Istanbul to Antalya, Erzurum, İzmir, Kayseri and Trabzon; and **Flyair** (**www.flyair.com.tr**) has flights from Istanbul to Ankara and Trabzon.

By Ferry

For online timetables, ticket prices and reservations for Istanbul and the Sea of Marmara go to **www.ido.com.tr**. This area is served by **catamarans** and **car ferries** from Istanbul to Yalova, Bandırma and other towns around the Sea of Marmara. These can be useful for Bursa and the Aegean coast.

Other domestic services are run by **Turkish Maritime Lines** (Türkiye Denizcilik İşletmesi; online booking and timetables at **www.tdi.com.tr**). It runs a weekly service during the summer along the Black Sea coast, starting from Istanbul on Monday evening and calling at the ports of Sinop, Samsun, Trabzon and Rize. The same company operates the weekly night ferry from Istanbul to İzmir (18 hours), departing on Friday evening from Istanbul and arriving in İzmir the next day; the return leg leaves İzmir on Sunday evening, arriving in Istanbul the next morning.

General Considerations

These are some general considerations to think about concerning transport:

- **If buying a home for retirement, is it in a place that will still be accessible in 20 or 30 years' time? Will you be comfortable driving up the twisting mountain access road at age 85?**
- **Is there any public transport? There will be times when you will need it. Your car may need repair. You may have broken a leg. You may (with luck!) be invited to a boozy party.**
- **How will your visitors get to you? Will they have to – and be able to – hire a car? Will you be an unpaid taxi service for the duration of their visit?**
- **The 4hr flight from the UK to the south of Turkey generally precludes the use of Turkish holiday homes for just the weekend, though stays of five or six days are viable. For some people this is an important consideration.**
- **Do you want to rent or own a car? It is worth making a careful price comparison. Surprisingly, the cost of insuring, taxing and maintaining your local car plus airport parking and the depreciation of its value can often amount to nearly as much as – or more than – hiring a new, clean car on each visit. Renting also means you can have different cars depending on your needs – if granny is coming, hire a car with lots of leg room and easy rear seat access. Have a look at cheap, local car hire companies as well as the big names; they sometimes have surprisingly good deals available.**

Choosing an Area

In the end, the choice of location and type of property is down to personal preference. You are probably buying a home in Turkey because you have been reasonably successful in life. One of the rewards of such success should be the ability to do as you please. It is too easy to forget, as you become immersed in the detailed planning for the purchase, that this whole exercise is supposed to be *fun*. If you want to throw reason to the wind and buy the house of your dreams there is nothing wrong with doing so – provided you understand that this is what you are doing. After all, who really *needs* a villa overlooking the Mediterranean?

Having said that, approaching the choice of area and type of property rationally means that you are less likely to buy entirely the wrong property in entirely the wrong place. It is amazing how often the obvious is not obvious in the heat of battle or at the peak of your enthusiasm to buy that 'bargain' run-down cottage in the middle of nowhere.

Case Study: The Theatregoers

Peter and Alice Hodge were in their 50s and wanted to retire abroad. They had both been successful in business and had a busy social life in London; they enjoyed the theatre and opera. Their dream had been to retire to the country in Turkey. Neither spoke the language. Neither had any do-it-yourself skills, but they fell in love with a rural property in a spectacular location with amazing views. Unfortunately, it needed substantial repair (the unkind would say rebuilding). Eventually, after 18 months and way over budget, the building work was finished. But once the Hodges had moved they noticed that they had no friends. No other English people lived in the area. No other foreigners lived in the area. In fact, nobody lived in the area. This was truly a rural location and they didn't speak the language in any case. The couple were surprised that there were no village social groups, amateur dramatics and the like. They were also surprised that the nearby towns (each of them over an hour away) did not have theatres, still less English-language theatres. Mr and Mrs Hodge felt disappointed and let down. In fact, they had broken the cardinal rule of thinking thoroughly before buying a rural property. Written down like this, it seems obvious. It didn't at the time.

If you are buying a property that is going to involve a substantial change in your lifestyle, stop. Think again. Think again. Take advice. Only then should you buy.

Getting to Know Turkey

The way that is most fun – and undoubtedly the best – is to travel extensively and to get to know different areas of Turkey in summer and in winter. The need to visit in both seasons cannot be overemphasised. Some summer resorts close down almost completely in the winter months. The climate, which was so agreeable in June, can be awful in January. The place that was a tranquil 20-minute drive from town in May might well involve a two-hour nose-to-tail ordeal in August.

Very few people know the whole of Turkey well. It is so huge that it is unreasonable to expect someone buying a holiday or even a retirement home to do so. In a sense it is unnecessary. If you like a particular place and would like a home there, does it matter that somewhere else there might be a place you like just as much or even better? Most people, therefore, select the area to live from the areas they already know plus, perhaps, another couple that they have read about and decide to visit before making their final decision.

A fair substitute for an initial visit is a bit of reading. General guides to Turkey, as well as our chapter **Profiles of the Regions**, can give you a reasonable feel for what a place will be like. Follow that up with some more specific reading about the areas that interest you, watch television programmes and so on, and you will be ready for a productive exploratory visit. Libraries, the Internet and the Turkish Ministry of Tourism are good sources of information.

Most people know within a few minutes of arriving in a town whether it is somewhere they would like to live. A two-week self-drive holiday, using some of Turkey's wonderful inexpensive small hotels, can therefore cover a lot of ground. Take a large-scale map or motoring atlas. Be a vandal: write your comments about the places you visit on the page, otherwise you will never remember which was which. Buy some postcards to remind you of the scenery or take a video camera or a digital camera. Pick up a copy of the local paper for each area; even if you do not speak Turkish, it will give you some idea of what goes on in the area and also supply details of local estate agents. Visit the local tourist office, if there is one, for more information about the area and to get a sense of what goes on throughout the year. Look in estate agents' windows and make a note of the sort of prices you will have to pay for property of the type that interests you. *But don't go inside.* Make it an absolute rule that you will not look at any properties. If you do, you will be caught in the classic trap of focusing on bricks and mortar rather than the area. What matters most at this stage is the area where you are going to live. There are nice houses in every area.

Provided the initial look at prices doesn't make you faint, if you like the town mark it with a big ✔ and move on to the next place. If it is not for you, mark the map with a big ✗ and, likewise, move on. Once you have short-listed your two or three most likely places, visit them in summer and winter. Spend a little time there. Make contact with estate agents and now look at property to your heart's content.

Generally, when going to see property you will be accompanied by the estate agent. If you are dealing with a private seller (someone who is not using an agent), when you do finally go looking at property, take a mobile phone. If you don't have one, buy one. Property in rural Turkey can be nearly impossible to find and it can save much gnashing of teeth if you can phone and ask for directions. It is also courteous to telephone if you are delayed en route.

Do You Want to Let the Property?

There are two types of people who decide to let out their home in Turkey. There are those who see the property as mainly, or even exclusively, an investment proposition, and those who are buying what is predominantly a holiday home but who wish to cover all or part of the cost of ownership from rental income.

For the first group this is a business, and, just as in any business, the decisions they take about where and what to buy, how to restore the property and what facilities to provide will be governed by the wish to maximise profit. The second group will have to bear in mind most of the same considerations, but will be prepared to compromise (and so reduce potential income) in order to maximise their own enjoyment of the property as a holiday home. Just where they draw the line will be determined by their need to produce income from the property. The choice of the right area is vital if you want to let your property successfully.

Whichever group you fall in, you are most unlikely to cover all of your expenses and capital and interest repayments on a large mortgage from letting your property, however efficiently you do so.

See also **Letting your Property**, pp.227–42.

Facilities

Your future happiness with the home you buy will depend on the facilities in the area. Each person will have different requirements. For instance, golf might be important to you. If so, just one or two golf courses in the vicinity are unlikely to satisfy you for long. Are you thinking of retiring to the area? If so, you will need a major shopping centre within an hour or so by car. Do you visit the theatre or opera? What is available? Are you sociable? Is this an area where you will find 'your kind of (English-speaking?) people'? Do you expect your teenage children to visit? If so, is there anything for them in the area? The local bowls club might not cut it!

Most people prefer a property within about an hour's drive of a city or substantial town.

Terrain

Each of us has our own preferences as far as the countryside is concerned. Is this really what you want, or is it a place that is beautiful but, ultimately, unsatisfying?

Much of Turkey is hilly. Do you have any health conditions that will make using the property difficult? Will it still be accessible in a few years' time when you may be less mobile than you are now? Will you be comfortable about driving along the mountainous access roads as you grow older?

Price Guide

There are various ways of keeping your eye on Turkish property prices generally: look at property magazines such as *Homes Overseas*, search the Internet, and go to property shows – particularly the larger events.

Once you know the area you are interested in, make contact with several estate agents in the area. Similar-sounding properties can differ widely in price because of factors not known to you, such as the property's state of repair, location, views and convenience.

Remember that this is a rapidly developing market, so old certainties as to the value of property are much more difficult to apply. Five years ago it was relatively simple. There was, more or less, a 'going rate'. In any area there was a recognised retail price per square metre for any particular category of property, which would give you a very good guide to the price you should pay. These guideline figures still apply to a certain extent, but there are much greater variations than used to be the case, sometimes with good reason. Be alert. If you are not absolutely sure that you are getting good value it can be a good idea to seek a second opinion about the value of the property.

Property in prime locations can be *much* more expensive, however. The table below shows typical prices for comparable properties in four popular areas.

Typical Prices for Properties

Location and Type of Property	**Typical Prices**
Alanya – 2-bedroom apartment (100 sq m)	£55,000
Alanya – 3-bedroom detached house (150 sq m)	£160,000
Fethiye – 2-bedroom apartment (100 sq m)	£62,000
Fethiye – 3-bedroom detached house (150 sq m)	£120,000
Dalaman – 2-bedroom apartment (100 sq m)	£50,000
Dalaman – 3-bedroom detached house (150 sq m)	£85,000
Bodrum – 2-bedroom apartment (100 sq m)	£70,000
Bodrum – 3-bedroom detached house (150 sq m)	£135,000

The Climate

Most British people buying in Turkey are motivated, in large measure, by the thought of a better climate. What is 'better' depends on your personal perspective. Remember that temperature and rainfall charts (*see* the tables in **References**, pp.265–6) do not tell the whole story. Wind, lack of shelter, altitude and other factors can greatly influence your perception of the climate, which is what really matters. A place where it rains for 200 days per year will seem wetter than a place with the same amount of annual rainfall in millimetres but where it only rains for 60 days. Figures can also conceal substantial daily variations. Despite its southerly position, Turkey does have very distinctive seasons, ranging from stupefyingly hot to bitingly cold, depending on place and time of year. Turkey is so huge that there are marked climate differences from one region to another. But the climate scores high for reliability. On the southern coasts, blue skies and warm weather are virtual certainties, though in winter there's been some heavy rainfall and flooding in recent years.

Overall, the best weather is from April to mid-June when the daylight hours are long and the temperatures like those in a good British summer – although early spring can be wet – and mid-September to October, when the weather is

Online Weather Forecasts

For five-day forecasts go to www.bbc.co.uk/weather, which has a search facility for the weather forecast for many cities and resorts in Turkey. Follow the links for World Weather and then Europe.

Earthquakes

Turkey lies on the boundary of tectonic plates, and seismic activity has for centuries been a fact of life, as numerous ruined cities dotted across the country testify; in fact about 92 per cent of the country lies in an earthquake zone. The massive earthquake on 18 August 1999 measured 7.4 on the Richter scale and devastated much of northwestern Turkey, killing or injuring some 40,000 people and destroying or damaging thousands of buildings. This was Turkey's worst natural disaster – although the epicentre was at İzmit, the shock waves were felt as far as 440km away in Ankara. This was the seventh quake in the past 60 years to rock the North Anatolian Fault, a great crack in the Earth's crust that allows movement between plates. Lamentable standards of building construction certainly exacerbated the toll of destruction, underlining the need to ensure that buildings in the future will be able to face up to earthquakes better. Self-constructed masonry houses have been particularly singled out for blame – but 45 per cent of buildings in Turkey's four largest cities are of a masonry construction.

You *must* have earthquake cover as part of your property insurance. Earthquake threats, and the need for peace of mind, may be the defining factor of your choice of a low-rise development as opposed to a high-rise one. The buildings most at risk are rickety blocks of flats built on the cheap. It is worth trying to find out as much as you can about the strengths and weaknesses of any area that you are interested in, the quality of the houses and the possible effects of the earthquake risk on house prices and insurance costs.

agreeably warm without being hot. Summer, from mid-June to mid-September, brings temperatures frequently in the 30s Centigrade (90s Fahrenheit), and air-conditioning is pretty much essential. To summarise: April–mid-June and September–October are best, mid-June–August is less good and November–March least good. For more detail, *see* **References**, pp.265–6.

The hot summers may not suit you. Elderly people in particular may suffer health problems in extreme heat, and this, in itself, may be an important factor to weigh up in deciding whether you wish to retire to Turkey.

Region by Region

Geographically the most accommodating climate is found on the Aegean and Mediterranean coastlines. Here it is warm enough to bathe in the sea from early April to mid-October and, although it does rain in winter, it's generally quite tolerable during the winter months, though not necessarily idyllic – and mountain roads can get blocked by snow in winter. Temperatures warm up as you proceed south into the Aegean. İzmir, Bodrum, Marmaris and Fethiye are sunny and hot but pleasantly green, and this is a favourite area of many Turks. It is even hotter east from Antalya, through Adana to Hatay, with the sea warm enough to swim in during October.

The swimming season gets shorter the further north you go: in the Sea of Marmara and the northern Aegean the sea is warm enough from June to September, but during April, May and October it's distinctly chilly. In Istanbul and Marmara the climate is moderate, with shortish, warm summers, fairly warm springs and autumns and pretty miserable winters from November to February, with prolonged bouts of gloomy, damp weather.

The Black Sea coast is hot and dry during July and August, though about 10°C cooler than the southern coast, and is otherwise susceptible to rain at any time – overall it is the dampest and most humid part of Turkey. Central Anatolia (including Cappadocia) has a steppe climate, with hot, dry summers and cold winters, while eastern Anatolia has mild summers and bitterly cold winters with lots of snow. Southeastern Anatolia, close to Syria, is the driest part of the country and the summer sun is uncomfortably hot, to the extent that you won't want to be outside for any longer than you have to; it is wetter during the generally mild winter.

Choosing a Property

Just as the area is vital, so too is choosing the right type of property. There are no hard and fast rules. Once again, common sense and forethought will serve you well, but in the end you will make a choice based on personal preference.

Apartment or Villa?

When thinking of somewhere to live, most British people have in mind a house and garden, but most continental people think of an apartment. Do not underestimate the humble apartment. It can have lots of advantages, particularly for someone wanting a holiday home or a home in which they will live for only part of the year.

If you are not ready for such a revolutionary change to your lifestyle there are a wide variety of types of house available, from small workers' cottages to luxury villas; something will take your fancy and suit your pocket. You may also be offered small, linked villas. These share many of the characteristics of an apartment.

These are some of the advantages and disadvantages.

Apartments: Advantages

- **Someone else looks after the repairs. All major repairs to the building and major maintenance works are likely to be the responsibility of the community of which the building is a part. Of course, you have to pay your share of the expenses, but someone else will arrange it all.**

- Apartments can offer better security. You will not be on a site that is isolated and, potentially, prone to burglary or squatters. Many apartment blocks have a security guard.
- You can lock it and leave it. Apart from turning off the water and electricity, no preparations are required for arrival or departure.
- There may be attractive communal gardens and facilities.
- You may have the use of a shared large swimming pool, tennis courts and other facilities. They are a great advantage if you want to let your property.
- The upkeep cost is generally lower than the cost of maintaining a house.
- You have ready-made neighbours who can, for example, turn on the electricity before you arrive and put some milk and bread in the refrigerator.
- Apartments are generally less expensive to buy than houses.

Apartments: Drawbacks

- You will have immediate neighbours, who may be noisy. Until recently, sound insulation was not very good.
- There may not be much storage space.
- There may be no private outside area.
- You may, at best, have an underground car parking space some distance from your front door.
- You will have to pay your monthly or annual contribution to the cost of the general maintenance of the block where you live.
- There may be a shared swimming pool, tennis courts and other facilities. These cost a lot of money to run and can be prohibitively expensive for someone using their property for only a small part of the year.
- There can be 'politics' involved in the administration of your community. If people cannot agree what they want or if some people do not pay their share of the expenses, it can get complicated. Your lawyer should check out the arrangements before you buy.
- Some people view apartments as downmarket.

Villas: Advantages

- You will have more size and space.
- There may be a private garden, terrace or pool area.
- There may be a private garage.
- You might get more distance from neighbours.
- Villas have a better image, especially for British people.

Villas: Drawbacks

- **Possible lack of security.**
- **Higher maintenance costs – particularly for extensive gardens or a pool.**
- **Security issues may be more of a worry when you are not there.**

Beware of Co-operative Properties

Co-operative properties are generally part of a complex of individual houses built by a group of people. Sometimes they are even physically constructed by those people; at other times people merely contribute together to the cost of construction. In a country where it is difficult to obtain the finance for the construction of a house this allows everyone to pool their resources, either building the properties one at a time or getting a better price for the construction of all of the properties together.

There are several downsides to this. The most significant, from the point of view of a later buy-out of a co-operative property, is that those building these properties tend to cut corners in the construction process and on the legal side of the development. The cuts on the construction side are sometimes obvious. Turkish houses are seldom finished to impressive standards when looking at the small details (although some developers excel at this). At other times, the cuts and savings are less obvious. If you are thinking of buying a co-operative property, a proper survey is imperative. On the legal side the problems tend to relate to planning; the project may have been given planning authority for the construction of, say, 60 villas, and you will find that the developers have illegally constructed 70 or 80. It is then almost impossible for those who have committed to co-operative villas to obtain good individual title at the end of the construction process. The villas will therefore remain in the ownership of the co-operative as a whole, with the individual occupants having a secondary right to occupy. This gives rise to dangers if the co-operative itself gets into financial difficulty, incurs debts or simply falls apart and has to be wound up.

Special care is therefore needed if you are thinking of buying into a co-operative property. Generally, it is better to look elsewhere.

Beware of Shared Ownership

These properties are marketed as a joint venture between a local Turkish person and a foreigner. In the past this was commonplace because of the restrictions on the freedom of foreigners to own property in Turkey. Those restrictions have now, essentially, disappeared, and so the requirement for this form of ownership is questionable.

Some joint ownership schemes are still being marketed on the basis that the local person has such good contacts and is acquiring such a bargain that the project is a good investment, but this is not always the case. Sometimes the price and the breakdown of expenses is not what it appears and you find that outside investors are putting in far more than their fair share of the development costs. If this is the case it probably indicates that the person is not trustworthy and the relationship is unlikely to be successful.

If you are considering joint ownership of this kind, you should be particularly careful and seek proper advice about the financial structure of the arrangement and about the appropriate legal structures to put in place.

Nothing here should, in any way, be taken as a criticism of joint ownership schemes between, for example, members of the same family or friends or neighbours who might choose to buy a property in Turkey for their joint use. These schemes can work very well indeed and are described later in this chapter.

Buying Off-plan

In recent years the number of new builds in Turkey has rocketed, and buying something based on construction plans, or 'off-plan', has become far more popular. By committing to buying and financing a property that has yet to be built, you help cut project costs for property developers, who can then pass some of these substantial savings on to you. And, since the price is set at the outset, you will only benefit if property prices in the area rise during the period of construction. However, before you take the plunge on buying a new-build property, consider the possible disadvantages listed on pp.90–91.

The idea of buying something unseen may seem foolish, with the potential for many nasty surprises, but you can bring the risks involved down to acceptable levels by picking a company with a good track record. If at all possible, try to visit one of their previous projects personally and, even better, talk to some of their former clients. Make sure you pay a visit to the proposed site of the development, too, to see if you like the look of it, and investigate what may happen in its immediate surroundings that may affect your investment in the future.

Once you're happy with the company and the overall project, consider the details of the building itself. The developer or estate agent should provide a detailed site plan, a breakdown of all materials and all the building specifications, as well as construction and payment schedules. Check all these thoroughly and, if comparing different developments, bear in mind that there can be different ways in which things are expressed. For example, differences in measurements can occur depending on whether or not internal walls and balconies are included in the calculations.

If all this passes muster, get a copy of the contract for inspection and ideally have an independent Turkish solicitor check it, together with the builder's authority and building permissions. Be sure to establish what the service charges will be once the property is finished, and take this into account. Once you're happy with all the particulars and have signed the contract (and not before), you will be expected to put down a reservation fee of between £500 and £2,500. Subsequent payments will then be made in line with dates specified in the contract, or preferably at specific stages in the building process. The final payment should only be made once the finished property has passed inspection. After that it may be hard to get a builder to revisit their work, though Turkish law makes all construction companies provide a five-year guarantee.

For an example of what is possible, what it costs and how it all works visit the website of Property of Turkey (**www.propertyofturkey.com**), a leading developer, although bear in mind that this is not meant as a recommendation.

Decide How You Plan to Use the Property

Despite the fact that everything depends on your personal circumstances, there are some rules of thumb that are a starting point for making a decision.

Buying as a Retirement Home

First work out your likely retirement income and expenditure. You may need some advice and guidance when doing this. If the income is in excess of your likely expenditure, buy the nicest house that you can afford. This will, typically, be a detached house or villa. Make sure you have plenty of space – including storage space, good heating and air-conditioning.

If your income is likely to be a little tight, decide how much you would like to divert from your home into investments in order to supplement your income. You will probably need to take advice about this. Buy the best house you can afford with the balance. This is a question of compromising between your ongoing income and the quality of your accommodation. You will usually be

Case Study: An Investment Property Before Retiring

Andrea and her partner went to Turkey every summer for holidays and in summer 2003 decided to look for a property, not only for holidays in Alanya, but also as an investment. With the help of estate agents, Andrea and her partner found the right property after viewing four or five villas. 'We bought a duplex villa in a nice site just 100 metres from the sea, with a spectacular view. There are also three more English families living in the same site and we have become good friends. We preferred to sign a contract with the solicitor, the estate agent and the seller as we think it was more comfortable and secure. We paid 30 per cent as deposit, and paid the rest of the amount when we received the title deed; everything was prepared by the estate agent, which made it easier for us. I recommend buyers follow the same procedure… Our duplex villa seemed brand new after some renovations that cost £3,500, organised by our estate and construction agent.' Andrea and her partner have settled easily in Alanya and plan to move there after they retire.

happier with a smaller house in a suitable area rather than moving to buy a bigger house in a less suitable area.

Buy Now, Move Later?

Think about both your current and future requirements. In Britain some people move frequently. They buy a house to suit their present needs and, as those change, they sell it and buy another. This is a very expensive thing to do in some countries, but is not too dear in Turkey. The move (buying and selling) could cost you about 8 per cent of the price of your new home. The saving from having a property that has cost you less and is cheaper to run could make this worthwhile – particularly as it will have given you time to decide where you would like to live and precisely what type of property you would like to live in.

Buying as a Holiday Home

If you can afford a detached villa or have young children, try to buy a villa. For most other people an apartment makes a more sensible choice of holiday home. If you want to let the property part of the year to defray some of the expenses of your home, read the sections on letting property (*see* 'Rental Potential', pp.91–3, and **Letting Your Property**, pp.227–42) and buy accordingly. You will need to decide to what extent you are prepared to sacrifice what you are looking for in a holiday home in order to increase the letting potential of the property. In either case, where possible buy a property that has a substantial store room or cupboard in which you can lock away your possessions when you are allowing others to use the property.

Buying to Let as an Investment

When buying an investment property, decide whether you are buying with a view to a quick sale (perhaps even before the house is built) or whether you are buying to let.

If you are buying to let, read 'Rental Potential', pp.91–3, and **Letting Your Property**, pp.227–42 – and then read it again. Your choice of property is critical to the success of your venture. If you are buying a property purely as an investment, and won't be using it personally, remember that the best buy might be a property that you would not choose to live in yourself. Although this is logically true – and many people have made a lot of money following this rule – most people are more comfortable with buying what they like and most people, in any case, will use the property themselves from time to time. Choosing a property that you like means that you will be marketing it to people like you. This is likely to include your family and friends, which can make life easier. It can also provide some fun as you market by networking in new circles.

Buying for Capital Growth

If you are buying to sell, then the section on letting your property (*see* above) is still relevant. The sort of house you would buy to let is likely to sell on well.

One of the great attractions of owning a property is the potential for the asset's growing in value at the same time as you enjoy the use of it. Few would say that you get as much fun out of 10,000 shares as you do out of a flat in Bodrum! The flat is also less likely to go bust, or to be taken over and lose half its value overnight.

For some people the choice of place to buy a property – or the selection of which of several places to choose – is governed entirely by likely capital growth. The British view property as an investment as well as as a home. We expect our house to rise in value, if not year by year, at least over time. Given the high levels of inflation and the depreciation in value of the Turkish currency in recent years, the Turks also have come to view the ownership of real estate as an investment. Property has not lost its value in the same way as other assets. A home in Turkey is both a usable asset and an investment.

But not all properties go up in value. As in every country, the investment potential of your home is governed, more than anything else, by its location. Over the last three years price rises of 40 per cent have not been uncommon, but it's also possible to find places where the value has stagnated or even fallen.

Changes in Turkish law made it possible for a short while for foreigners to own land in Turkish villages as well as the big cities and the resorts; this is now once again only possible by buying via a Turkish limited company (*see* box, p.88). The potential of this market is still huge and largely untapped. Prices in these areas will be much lower than in the cities and holiday resorts. Good properties in these areas could do well in the long term.

In popular areas – especially in popular tourist areas – there have been large amounts of property inflation. This has recently been in the region of 10–20 per cent a year. How much depends on the type of property bought and, above all else, the place where it is located. There is, of course, no guarantee that property prices will continue to increase at this rate. There is an economic cycle and prices rise and fall over time. But over the mid- to long-term they generally increase.

Facilities

Space

Most people underestimate the space they will need in their home overseas. This is because they underestimate how popular they will become once they have a villa in Bodrum or Marmaris! The combination of your own accommodation needs, the needs of visitors and the requirement for storage space means that, if the budget permits, it is worth thinking of buying one more bedroom than you first contemplated.

Heating

The south of Turkey has, generally, a much warmer climate than the UK. Even here, though, there are many days in winter when it can be as rainy and cold as in Manchester. Some form of heating is essential for such days, however few they may be. Adding proper heating to the specification for a new property adds very little to the price. This is much cheaper than doing it later. If you are buying a resale property then it is much more convenient to install the heating system before you move in.

Piped gas is rare or non-existent in many areas. Bottled gas is too fiddly to be genuinely convenient. Installing large tanks for gas can be costly and problematic from a town-planning point of view. Solid fuel has all the drawbacks we forgot about in the UK 30 years ago. Solar heating – particularly solar water heating – works well in sunnier areas but cannot be relied on as the only form of heating. For many people this leaves oil and electricity as candidates. Look out for combined heating and air-conditioning units; these operate as heat pumps and can be very efficient.

Remember that in rural and small-town Turkey power cuts are commonplace, though lessening in frequency and duration. It will come as no surprise to learn that they come when you most need the electricity.

Take advice. Don't just assume that what was best in England will be best in Turkey. Whichever you choose, installing a good centrally controlled heating system will be money well spent.

See also **Settling In**, 'Home Utilities', pp.193–7.

Air-conditioning

Summertime temperatures in southern Turkey can get very high, reaching 40°C. This is relatively rare and for some reason 40°C in Turkey does not feel nearly as hot as 40°C in Spain. Nonetheless, it is seriously hot. However, air-conditioning still has the reputation of being a luxury item although it is becoming more the norm in office properties. Some people think that giving in to the heat and turning on the air-conditioning is feeble.

We recommend that everyone buying a home in southern Turkey should install at least some minimal air-conditioning. With predicted global warming, summer temperatures are likely to rise. However macho you may be, if the 2am temperature is 30°C (86°F) and you cannot sleep, it is hard to deny the value of air-conditioning. You may not need it often but, when you do, you really need it. And for people buying a home for retirement, or with elderly relatives who will visit, it is worth remembering that, as we get older, we gradually lose our ability to adjust to extremes of temperature. A temperature that is unpleasantly hot for a 55-year-old can be life-threatening for a 90-year-old. With portable units available for £300–400, buying some type of cooling makes a lot of sense.

It is also worth thinking of other types of cooling. Most people who live in Turkey do not use their air-conditioning all the time. This is partly because they get used to the higher temperatures and partly because they have:

- **through-flow ventilation – front and back windows, which can create a draught if open together.**
- **high ceilings – it is not by accident that old houses incorporate this feature.**
- **a favourable position – for instance a house a short distance inland in the hills is likely to benefit from some breezes.**
- **ceiling fans, which can often provide enough cooling in a way that is more pleasant than the use of air-conditioning.**

But, even if you benefit from some of these features, do buy some air-conditioning for use on very hot days.

Parking

If you have a nice car and want to keep it that way, secure parking is an asset. Much property in Turkey is sold without any dedicated parking space. These can cost a surprising amount if bought separately.

New or Old?

There is no right answer! Traditionally the Turkish, except for the wealthy, have scorned older, restored property in favour of new-build. There are, however, wonderful opportunities to acquire character properties in some of the interior parts of Turkey.

These areas are not on the main tourist track and will probably, at least in the short term, not perform as well in financial terms as specialist new-build developments on the coast. In the long term, though, they will give you an entirely different lifestyle and will probably perform very well financially, as such properties are relatively rare and, by definition, in shorter supply. Following a theme that Turkey today bears many similarities to Spain 20 years ago, you

Buying Rural Properties

The chance for foreign buyers to buy outside municipal areas has only existed since July 2003. Before that time, foreigners were not permitted to own property in rural areas; then in 2005–2006 property laws again restricted foreign buyers from purchasing land in rural areas, except via a loophole allowing the purchase once they have set up a Turkish company. This is a relatively straightforward process, for which a Turkish solicitor will charge about £2,200; ***see* Making the Purchase, pp.115–17.**

Case Study: Buying a New-build Villa

Debbie and her husband dreamed of buying a tailor-made villa at their favourite town in Spain for holidays and later retirement, but couldn't afford one. The couple found the type of villa they were looking for on the Internet, but it was not in Spain, it was in the south of Turkey. They became interested in the country and decided to go on holiday there.

The holiday turned into a property-hunting trip when Debbie and her husband found out about the procedure for buying property: 'Believe it or not, after deciding, it only takes half a day to finish legal issues...and to transfer the title deed into your name takes about 6–9 weeks... The most important thing at this point is to have a solicitor who will make the searches and register the title deed in your name. We found it very convenient not to have to come back to Turkey to sign any more papers as the solicitor does it for you.'

Debbie and her husband committed themselves to buying a new-build villa, finally won over after hearing about the service that would be provided. They put down a 40 per cent deposit for a freehold, four-bedroom detached villa with sea view and private pool; it cost £80,000. Hearing that the HSBC bank was to open in the resort helped them make their decision, as their retirement pension can be paid directly to their account in Turkey. 'We were told the villa would be completed in six months and the remaining amount should be paid after the villa was completed. All we had to do after that was get six photos taken, give power of attorney to our solicitor so he could manage all the legal issues for us, sign a solicitor contract, open a Turkish bank account and leave two copies of our passports.'

Since the villa has been completed Debbie and her husband have spent two summers in it and are looking forward to moving for good after they retire.

should look at the huge increase in the value of rural properties (*fincas*) in the popular parts of coastal Spain. If you are interested in this type of property you will currently find no estate agents specialising in the field and you will need the assistance of Turkish-speaking property finders.

In addition to everyday rural properties, again like Spain, in Turkey, in some places, there is a tradition of living in caves (*see* **Where in Turkey?**, 'Cappadocia', p.54). These properties are few and far between, and prices for them have already started to rise sharply. Living in a cave has many advantages in a hot climate, as the temperature underground is preserved at a constant and comfortable level.

If you are thinking of buying any kind of rural property and, as is usually the case, you wish to restore or enlarge it, you need to be very careful to check that you will be permitted to do what you want to do, especially if it involves changing the external appearance of the property. There are maximum permitted building densities, so if your plot is relatively small you may find that you will not be permitted to enlarge the house. There may also be restrictions on your right to put in a swimming pool.

The presence of vast tracts of attractive and undeveloped land on Turkey's extensive southern coast has attracted many developers, both Turkish and foreign, and there is an explosion in the construction of new property here. This is also the region where most foreigners wish to buy, and is an area where there is relatively little in the way of attractive older property, probably because there were few prosperous farms as making a living by agriculture was difficult in this rugged terrain. As a result, it is mainly relatively new properties that are for sale in this part of Turkey.

The decision between whether to buy new or older property in Turkey raises the same questions as it would in the UK. It involves considering the features of each type of property in the light of your own personal preferences and requirements. Most people are clear from the outset which they prefer.

Here are the main advantages and disadvantages of new and older property.

New Property in Turkey

Advantages

- **The technical specification and design will be better than in an older property. This is particularly so in areas such as insulation and energy-efficiency.**
- **It will have been inspected and built to known standards.**
- **Most people prefer new kitchens, which get more sophisticated each year.**
- **It will probably have a reasonable heating system.**
- **Electrical and plumbing installations will be to a superior standard.**
- **Few people will have used the bathrooms!**
- **Provision will probably have been made for car parking.**
- **You may share the cost of expensive common resources such as pools or tennis courts with other people.**
- **The building will require a lot less maintenance than an older property, certainly for the first few years.**
- **It should be cheaper to run.**
- **You can design your own property or, at least, often fine-tune the design to your special requirements.**
- **The fabric of the building will be guaranteed.**
- **If you buy 'off-plan' you may see some pre-completion growth in value.**

Disadvantages

- **The building will be new and brash, not mellow.**
- **It can be hard to envisage what you are going to get from a plan.**

- You will have to sort out all the small snags inevitable in any new building. You may spend all your holidays chasing the builder and you probably don't speak Turkish.
- You will have to sort out the garden.
- You may have to decorate.
- Although technical design may have improved, the aesthetic appeal may be less than that of an older property and the detailed workmanship less rewarding than that of a time when labour was cheap.

Older Property in Turkey

Advantages

- The property has 'character'. Its design may be classically beautiful and the detailed workmanship will probably be superior to today's product.
- The garden will be mature.
- It may occupy a better site than a newer property – on the basis that the best were often built on first.
- It may be a more attractive rental proposition than a new property.
- You will feel that you are living in a property in Turkey.
- It may be cheaper than a comparable new property.
- It will probably have more land than a comparable new property.
- What you see is what you get. You turn on the taps, there is water. You can see the room sizes and how the sun lies on the terraces. You can see the views and the distances to adjacent properties.

Disadvantages

- Older properties can need a lot of maintenance and loving care.
- It will be more expensive to heat and run.
- You may need to spend significant sums on, say, the kitchen and bathrooms to bring the property up to modern standards.

Rental Potential

There are thousands of properties in Turkey that are, commercially speaking, impossible to let. A rustic house in a rural backwater may find a few tenants during the year but they will not be anywhere near enough to generate a sensible commercial return on your investment. If you are interested in such a house you will probably have accepted this and view any rental income as a bonus that may help to defray some of the expenses of ownership.

In general terms, the rental market for privately owned villas and apartments in Turkey is still in its infancy. As tourism grows and people start to feel more comfortable about visiting Turkey, it is likely that the number renting privately will increase substantially.

At the moment, the tourist season in Turkey is still relatively short – basically, from May to mid-October. There are a number of organisations, including very high-quality resort-style hotels, that are trying to extend the tourist season and there is no reason why this should not happen. The weather is good on either side of the official season – although it is not as good as the weather in Spain, the cooler temperatures will appeal to many visitors, particularly older people.

For the time being, a sensible budgeting estimate of the potential number of weeks that a property in a tourist destination could be let during the year would be 12 to 16 weeks; it would be lower than this for a rural property far from any facilities. This compares with about 20–25 letting weeks for a similar property in Spain. However, this is not as serious as it would first appear. The price per week that you can obtain for your property in Turkey will be lower than you would obtain in Spain, but not that much lower, and the capital cost of the property should be much less. Thus the percentage return on your investment will be better than the raw data might suggest – perhaps 5 per cent net of all expenses rather than the 6 per cent you might expect in Spain. If property price rises in Turkey outstrip those in Spain for the next few years, as predicted – and whether this is so is the vital question – then the Turkish investment could still outperform a Spanish one. Assessing rental potential is a skill that takes time to acquire. Here are some good indicators of property that is likely to let well. *See* **Letting Your Property**, pp.227–42, for a fuller discussion of all these points.

- **Is it pretty?** Most people will be choosing to rent your property after seeing a small photograph in a brochure or listings guide.
- **Is it near a village or town?** Most people like to be able to walk to a village or town – ideally one with a bar and restaurant as well as a supermarket, bakery and other amenities.
- **Who is your target audience? Is it accessible for them?**
- **Are there attractions to bring people to your area?** A property miles from any attractions will appeal only to a very small clientele, however pretty the property and however lovely the countryside.
- **Does the property have all the required facilities?** The biggest question is whether to have a pool. If you are catering to a family market in rural Turkey, a pool will increase bookings, but they are expensive. It can cost £10,000 to construct a decent-sized pool and around £2,000 a year to maintain it.

Paying the Right Price

When buying a property as a business you will be concerned to pay as little as is possible for the property consistent with getting the right level of rental return. If you are only buying the property as a business proposition then this price–rental balance (or return on investment), together with your judgement of the extent to which the property will rise in value over the years, are the main criteria on which you will decide which property to buy.

If you are going to use the property not only as a rental property but also as a holiday home then there is an additional factor. This is the amount of time that you will be able to use the property yourself consistent with getting a certain level of rental return. For example, if you bought a one-bedroom property on the seafront in Marmaris for £75,000 it might be let for 45 weeks a year and produce a return after deduction of all expenses of, say, 7.5 per cent. If you bought a two-bedroom apartment in İzmir for, say, £50,000 and let that for 20 weeks a year you might also generate 7.5 per cent on your investment. Both would be performing equally well but the İzmir apartment would allow you and your family to use the property for 32 weeks a year whereas the seafront apartment would only allow you to use it for seven weeks a year. This, and the fact that it had one more bedroom, could make the old town property the more attractive proposition.

These figures are simply examples to illustrate the point rather than indications as to what is actually obtainable at any particular moment. Whatever way we look at it, paying the minimum necessary to buy the property is the key to maximising performance.

See **Letting Your Property**, pp.235–6, for predictions of rental income that might be generated for different types of properties.

How to Find Property

Estate Agents

Most British people buying a property in Turkey will use an estate agent or buy direct from a developer. A good estate agent can make the process smoother and less perplexing. A bad or unhelpful agent can make it more complicated.

Often developers will sell directly, as well as through agents. In this case it is worth checking that you are not paying any more by using the agent than you would be if you bought from the developer direct. If you want a resale property you will almost certainly use an agent.

In Turkey you will find that the same property can be advertised by many agents – often at different prices. Do not assume:

- **that the agent actually has the authority to offer the property for sale; he may well be 'flying a kite' in the hope of attracting a potential buyer whom he can tout to the seller and so negotiate a commission.**
- **that the price shown in the window is the price you will be charged; the prices may not be up to date.**
- **that there is no room for negotiation.**
- **that the property has not already been sold to someone else.**

Some agents, of course, are much better than others. They have never been properly regulated; although things are improving and they have their own chamber, it is still difficult to know the good from the bad. Personal recommendation is your best guide. At one level, of course, it doesn't matter. The agent is introducing the buyer to the seller and being paid for doing so. If there is something wrong with the property or the title, that is not something you would expect the agent to know about in Turkey any more than he would in the UK. Your lawyer is there to ensure that the property has good title and your surveyor to make sure that it is in good condition. The problem arises, however, that in Turkey many agents will offer to 'do the legal work for you' and will ask for a power of attorney to undertake various steps on your behalf.

Whichever agent you use, and wherever they are based, remember that they are being paid by the seller to sell the property – they are not being paid by you to look after your interests. However helpful and professional agents may be, if you do not sign a contract to buy then they do not receive their commission. They therefore have their own interests to look after, which broadly coincide with those of the sellers; these interests may not coincide with yours.

Despite this, estate agents can be a mine of useful information, have much knowledge about an area and offer practical help. The large majority is genuinely enthusiastic about property in Turkey and about your joining their community. Take advantage of what they have to offer, form a rapport with them, buy a property through them...but get everything checked by your legal adviser just as you would in Britain.

Some agents will tell you that you do not need to use a lawyer, that the services of the local notary public (*noter*) and the land registry officer will suffice.

Case Study: Using an Estate Agent

Paul and his wife, experienced travellers in Europe, visited Alanya in summer 2003. They became interested in the idea of buying a property there for holidays and then to retire to, in just two years. 'But we were not sure how to deal with the local property-owners, and the bureaucracy, so we decided to work with an estate agent, which we later understood was the best way to find the most convenient property for ourselves.' They explained what they wanted and an estate agent showed them properties that met their requirements, so they didn't waste time looking at inappropriate apartments.

After agreeing on the terms, they bought a 100-square-metre flat, 300 metres from the sea, with a sea and mountain view. 'The terms were suitable, as we were asked to pay 20 per cent deposit, and pay the rest when we received the title deed, which was all arranged by our estate agent – we did not think it could be that easy. I also recommend buyers to secure themselves by using a solicitor, and signing a contract with the estate agent which involves all the details of things they want in their properties so that later on there won't be any confusion.'

Ignore that advice. It is quite true that the average Turkish person would not use the services of an independent lawyer when buying a house unless there was something complex about the transaction or about their own circumstances. For a foreigner, however, this is generally not good enough. There are many issues on which you will need guidance that it is no part of the notary's or the land registry officer's duty to provide. Furthermore, your Turkish notary will almost certainly know nothing about British law, and the Turkish land registry officer will definitely know nothing about British law, and so they will be unable to give you any help as far as such vital issues as who should own the property in order to make the most of UK and Turkish inheritance tax. For the function of the notary, *see* **Making the Purchase**, 'The Notary Public', p.121.

Turkish-based Estate Agents

The role of the Turkish estate agent (*emlakçı*) is similar to that of the British estate agent. Their job is to find buyers for properties entrusted to them by a seller, but there the similarity ends. In Turkey, a person can be a plumber today and, without any qualifications or experience, set up an estate agency tomorrow. Estate agents do not have to be professionally qualified or hold a licence to practise. There is no national association of estate agents so there is no guarantee of the level of service they will provide. Quality varies from one estate agent to another.

It is normal for Turkish estate agents to charge commission equally between seller and purchaser and this commission is typically 6 per cent of the value of the property (split 3 per cent each way). The amount depends on the value of the property, whether it is new or old, and its area. On the whole, more commission is paid on cheaper properties than on more expensive ones, and properties in the main tourist areas command more commission than those in less sought-after (and generally poorer) areas. In order to protect their substantial commission, agents sometimes ask purchasers to sign a document before taking them to see the property. This is a statement saying that it is the agent who has introduced the purchaser to the property, so avoiding later arguments about who should be paid the commission due.

There are other significant differences from English practice. Generally agents are less proactive than they are in England, especially in non-tourist rural areas. You will seldom find printed property particulars or be supplied with photographs. Still less will you find plans or room dimensions in most estate agents' offices. They see their role as capturing property to sell and then showing buyers around that property. Many agents are either single operators or in small firms with a limited range of property on their books. Again, this is especially true in rural areas, but if you walk down any street in any town on the coast of Turkey you will see evidence of the large numbers of small agents offering services to the public. This can make it difficult to get a comprehensive view of what

Case Study: Using Several Agents

In 2003 Margaret and Stuart co-bought a two-bedroom semi-detached villa with friends. It was on a site with a communal pool and security. 'We had been looking to buy on the Algarve or in Spain but it was the low prices in Turkey that swung it in the end. Our main reason for buying was for holidays and investment. We do intend to let friends and family go and merely want to cover our costs.'

They arranged meetings in Turkey with three agents they had found on the Internet. 'We took quite a bit of hard cash with us so that we would have enough for a deposit if we found a property. The first meeting was a disaster as the agent did not turn up. We ended up wasting the first night of our short trip. When we returned home I had an e-mail which said he would not deal with us as we were intending to use more than one agent to view with – I'm glad we missed them in the end. Our advice to anyone else is, do your homework. Weed out the agents by visiting forums on the Internet, and pick the brains of existing owners. Use more than one agent – one agent may have the same house on offer for much less.'

is on the market. In addition, there are few local or national groupings of agents. There is no 'multi-listing service' on the US model.

You would probably do best starting to look for property by using an estate agent in the immediate vicinity of the place where you want to buy. Many rural agents will only cover an area about 40km in diameter. If you are still uncertain where precisely you intend to buy, try several adjoining agents or, if there is one in your area, one of the big chains. Local newspapers will give you an indication of which agents are advertising, and so active, in your area. Some agents also advertise in the Turkish and UK specialist property press. Estate agents also often operate as property management companies and as letting agents.

UK-based Estate Agents

There are growing numbers of agents based in the UK who sell property in Turkey, and most popular areas are covered. Although, under English law, they are entitled to call themselves estate agents, it is important to note that, in most cases, they are not licensed estate agents.

These agents very often work in association with one or more Turkish agents or developers, generally covering a wider area than a single Turkish agent or developer. They advertise or market the properties through exhibitions and other means and then act as an intermediary between the potential buyer and the Turkish estate agent or developer – who may or may not speak English. Because these agents deal with British buyers all the time they should be able to anticipate some of the common problems that can arise, and smooth the progress of the transaction. Surprisingly, only a few of them speak Turkish or have Turkish-speaking staff in their offices.

Generally UK-based agents share the commission of the Turkish agents with whom they work – who are very pleased that they can expand their potential buyer base by introducing foreign buyers – or are paid by the developer. Thus, although they can be on substantial commissions, the services of these agents should cost you nothing extra. Some agents can be very useful, particularly if you have little experience of dealing with Turkey and don't speak Turkish.

Unfortunately, it is not always as simple as that. Some UK-based agents charge substantial amounts of extra commission for their services and often do not disclose that commission to the buyer. There is nothing wrong with paying someone who is doing a useful job some commission, but you should be told that you are expected to do so. You can then decide whether the convenience of dealing with someone in Britain is worth the extra cost. Always ask for confirmation that the price you will be paying is exactly the same as you would have paid in Turkey or, if there is an extra charge, what it is.

DIY Sales

In Turkey far more property is sold 'person to person' than in the UK. Depending on area this can be between 15 and 30 per cent. As you drive around you will see a number of DIY 'for sale' signs (*satılık*), which normally give a contact telephone number. To take advantage of property offered in this way you have to be in the area and you will probably need to speak Turkish. If you do not speak Turkish it is still worth a trial phone call. You never know your luck! If the person who answers doesn't speak English there may be a local English-speaking person – perhaps in your hotel – who would make contact on your behalf. As a last resort, phone your lawyer. He should be able to find out the necessary details and, if you wish, make arrangements to view. He will charge for this work but the saving of estate agent's fees will make his charges look cheap.

Auctions

Property in Turkey can be bought at auction, just as in England. Some auctions are voluntary, others run by court order. Prices can be very attractive, though there aren't often spectacular bargains to be had. This is because, particularly in many judicial auctions, the process is intended first and foremost to recover someone's debt. Once that and the considerable costs have been covered, there is little reason to press for a higher price, even though the owner will ultimately receive the excess. Buying a property at auction is not simple for someone who does not live in the area and it is vital that you take all normal preparatory steps – including seeing a lawyer – before you embark on the process.

The procedure leading up to the auction is basically the same whether the auction is a judicial auction or a voluntary auction. First, you have to know that the auction is taking place. They are usually advertised six to eight weeks in advance. Auctions ordered by the court will be advertised by order of the court in the local press. Notices will also be posted in the area.

Second, find out what is in the auction. Brief details of the property to be sold are published, but they will probably mean nothing to you. The place could be derelict or next door to a nuclear power station – or both. You will need to inspect the property and decide whether it is of interest. This is a time-consuming and potentially costly process. Remember that you might have to inspect 20 properties to find three you might like and then be outbid on all three.

An alternative to personal inspection is to get someone to do the job for you. This is not as satisfactory but a local estate agent will, for a fee, go to look at the property and give you a description of it. If you're lucky he or she might post or e-mail you some photographs. His or her fee, about £200 if the property is close to his or her office, will probably be less than the cost of travel.

Some people buy blind. This is for real poker-players.

Third, you will need to check out the legal situation of the property before the date of the auction. Most of the steps needed in an ordinary purchase will be required.

Fourth, many properties on sale by auction are not in the best condition. You will, therefore, need to get estimates of the likely cost of repairs or improvements so as to make sure that the price you bid is not so high as to make the project non-viable.

Fifth, you will have to appoint a lawyer to act on your behalf at the auction. You would be brave or foolish not to be represented. The lawyer will explain precisely what will need to be done for this particular auction. You will have to tell him the maximum price you want to offer and pay him the bidding deposit – a refundable deposit levied by the auctioneer in order to allow you to enter a bid. You will also have to give the lawyer your personal details (marital status, occupation, nationality, passport number and so on) and a deposit of (usually) 10 per cent of the price you are offering, less the bidding deposit. The full deposit is paid at the time your bid is accepted.

You do not need to attend the auction – the lawyer will be able to do so for you. He will probably require a power of attorney for that purpose and will charge you for this work. Get an estimate. Even though you do not need to be present, an auction (especially a judicial auction) is a most interesting event, so you might want to go along.

Although the prices at auction can be very attractive, bear in mind that you will face additional costs over and above those on a normal purchase. These are likely to increase the overall costs of buying from the normal 10–11 per cent of the price to perhaps 13–15 per cent of the price paid. The extra costs include the fees paid to your lawyer for dealing with the auction.

If you are thinking of buying in this way, remember that you will probably have to kiss a lot of frogs before you find your prince. And kissing frogs – or, more accurately, checking out the frogs before you kiss them – can be an expensive business. All in all, auctions are not for the average buyer.

Other Sources of Property

Local Newspapers

Individuals place advertisements in the 'for sale' section of the local paper. Once again, the ability to speak Turkish is an advantage.

'Freesheets'

In some popular tourist areas there are free local news-sheets, similar to those in the UK, and sometimes there are specialist free property papers. All are likely to have adverts from private sellers.

Specialist Local Property Press

In some areas there are specialist magazines that exist primarily to carry advertisements from developers, estate agents and private individuals selling property. Most have just a local coverage. Browse through a couple of newspaper kiosks and see what is on offer and buy everything that is relevant. They will give you a good general guide to prices.

There are also several more 'glossy' lifestyle publications covering property (particular more expensive property) in main tourist areas such as Marmaris and Bodrum. Again, buy the lot. They will be full of useful information.

Specialist British Property Press

Developers, agents and private individuals advertise in the main specialist British property press such as *Homes Overseas*. Also try more general publications such as *Daltons Weekly* and *Exchange and Mart*, especially for cheaper property. You may also find advertisements from private sellers in the *Sunday Times*, weekend issues of the *Daily Telegraph* and the *Mail on Sunday*. Generally speaking, private sellers advertising in the British press are British.

The Internet

Many agents and developers have their own websites, many in English. There is also a huge amount of property available for private sale on the Internet. Finding it can sometimes be tricky. Remember that you should search in Turkish as well as in English. The following combinations in the Google search box will work:

+ property + 'for sale' + Turkey
+ house + 'for sale' + Turkey
+ apartment + 'for sale' + Turkey

You can further limit the geographical area by typing in the name of the place where the property is located, but this has mixed results because of the very different ways people enter the details of the property they are selling. The best bet is probably to use the province or, if you are looking in a city, the city as the delimiter:

+ apartment + 'for sale' + Fethiye
+ house + 'for sale' + Mugla

You can, of course, search in Turkish, but don't be surprised if the results come up in Turkish. This is not as much of a problem as it might at first seem, as the price and telephone number are both usually pretty obvious and you can tell whether the place is of any interest from any picture that appears on the page.

But be extra careful when buying over the Internet. Be warned: all too often you will find that the property has been sold and not removed from the site.

Property Shows

Shows are held every weekend. Most parts of the UK are serviced by the major international property shows several times a year and smaller shows much more often. Generally only the larger shows have an extensive range of property in Turkey and other 'emerging market' destinations. The smaller ones tend to deal with little more than Spain.

There are various additional facilities that may be provided at shows. Some international shows have a section where private individuals can post details of property for sale. Sometimes shows, particularly the *Homes Overseas* shows, run by *Homes Overseas* magazine, offer comprehensive seminar programmes to explain the ins and outs of buying property in the various countries they cover. They are generally held in London, Manchester, Birmingham, Glasgow, Edinburgh, Belfast, Dublin and other UK venues as well as at various continental centres at least once a year. The *Homes Overseas* website (**www.homesoverseas.co.uk**) has details.

Alternatively try World of Property or International Property shows.

On the whole, property shows fall into three categories:

- **Those that promote properties in many countries, generally large events. They usually have a number of exhibitors offering property, legal, financial and other services relating to many countries. Look out for the *Homes Overseas* shows.**
- **Those that focus on Turkey alone or on the 'emerging markets' alone. These are rare.**

- **Those that are run by a sole developer or estate agent. These occur almost every weekend and travel from one smaller city or large town to another. Turkey is poorly served by such shows.**

Even if you intend to go to Turkey and deal directly with an agent over there, a visit to these shows is well worthwhile. They are full of useful information. You will get a feeling for property prices in the various parts of Turkey. They are also an easy way to make initial contact with lawyers, mortgage brokers, currency dealers and financial advisers, and to get a feeling of whether they are the sort of people you would like to deal with.

Some shows are free. Most charge an entry fee of £4–10 per person.

Seminars

However helpful a book of this kind may be, there is no substitute for getting information in person from a knowledgeable authority, especially when you have a chance to question that person about anything you don't understand.

To meet this need, throughout the year there are various seminars – generally run by experienced lawyers or financial advisers – which will cover various topics included in this guide, often in more detail. These are sometimes run in conjunction with the major property shows, such as *Homes Overseas* and World of Property. On other occasions the lawyers or financial advisers run them themselves. Some seminars are run in conjunction with one or more developers or agents, so you can get the information and find details of property at the same time. The author's website (**www.lawoverseas.com**) has details.

These seminars are well worth a visit and can help considerably in the clarification of your thoughts about buying a home in Turkey.

Options Other than Buying

Renting First

There is a lot to be said for temporarily renting a place in the area where you are thinking of living, and it is best to do this for a full year before deciding whether to live there. Allowing for time thereafter to find and buy a property probably means a 12- to 18-month rental. Try to rent something similar to what you are thinking of buying and do not rent unseen – take a short holiday to find your rental property.

You are unlikely to commit yourself to a purchase in an area you turn out not to like if you rent, and it avoids the expensive process of having to sell a property and buy another, either in Turkey or back in England. The overall cost of moving within Turkey is likely to be about 10 per cent of the price of your new property – 5 per cent the fees on the purchase of the new property and 5 per cent the estate agents' fee for selling the old one. A move back to England would (depending on the value of the property bought) be likely to cost about 5–8 per cent sales expenses in Turkey and 3 per cent purchase expenses in England.

If you want a holiday home in Turkey it can also make sense to rent rather than buy. The biggest drawback to owning a property overseas is that you feel compelled to take all your holidays there. You are paying for it so you feel you should use it! If you invested the money you would have spent on the home it would generate a good income, which would pay for a holiday anywhere in the world. Of course, renting is never as good as owning your own home. You do not know the quality of what you will find on arrival. You won't be able to leave your clothes there and so travel light. You won't have friends there and so feel part of the community. You won't be able to offer the use of the property to family and friends. You may find that your investment of the cash saved has performed less well than the house would. These are the main drawbacks to renting:

- **Property prices in many areas have risen rapidly recently. For example, if two years ago you had been buying in Bodrum then delaying 18 months would probably have cost you around 20 per cent in increased property cost. This is a lot more than your money would have made if invested, so the delay would have cost you money.**
- **The rent you pay out is dead money. This would probably be about 5 per cent of the value of a property per annum.**
- **You want to get on with your life, especially if you have just retired.**
- **Moving is stressful. You will have to do it twice rather than once.**
- **People in temporary accommodation can feel detached from the area they are living in, and so don't commit to it and give it a fair try. You are always looking back over your shoulder at England.**
- **It can be hard to find good accommodation available on an 18-month let.**

Exchanges

Why not spend your holidays in someone else's home – free of charge? If you have an attractive property in England you may well find a Turkish family or a British family resident in Turkey who are only too pleased to leave their house in Bodrum for August to stay in your place in London – while you do the reverse. Not only do you change houses but cars and, possibly, dogs too. What about leaving the kids behind as well? No, that's a joke.

Timeshares

Timeshares are a great product, too often sold by crooks. The accommodation is almost always first class and, often, the annual usage charges are reasonable. The problem is that the purchase price is usually out of all proportion to the value of the property. But, if you buy second-hand you can pick up timeshare weeks for £750 that will enable you to swap in and out of resorts all over the world. It is not like owning your own property and it won't go up in value. But if you only have three or four weeks' overseas holiday a year, timeshares may suit you as they are very flexible.

Be *very careful* whom you buy from – where possible deal directly with a private seller. If you are going to deal with a company *only* deal with a resale company that is a member of the **Organisation for Timeshare in Europe** (OTE) and, if in any doubt, despite the low cost of the second-hand purchase, use a lawyer to protect your interests.

Good sources of resale timeshares direct from the owner include your supermarket noticeboard, *Exchange and Mart* and *Daltons Weekly*. We would strongly advise you not to deal with so called 'holiday clubs'. As yet there aren't many timeshares available in Turkey, but this is likely to change.

Part-ownership Schemes

Part-ownership schemes are those whereby several people – your children, neighbours, friends or complete strangers – buy a home for their joint use. Each party owns a percentage of the shares of the company proportionate to the agreed use of the property; the shares generally carry the right to use the property for a certain period of time.

For example, you may buy the right to use an apartment in Bodrum for two months a year. The apartment is worth £110,000 and you have paid £22,000 for the right to use it for August and £5,500 for the right to use it for November. You would own two out of twelve shares in the company. You would pay 2/12ths (16.66 per cent) of the annual running costs of the property. You would either appoint a professional manager or, if you were friends, get together with the other owners every year to decide about furnishing, repairs and other matters relating to the property. You can (subject to the rules of the group) either use the property yourself during your period of entitlement, allow friends to use it or let it out.

These schemes can work very well. You get all the holiday you need, you don't have to worry about finding tenants or the property being empty, and you only pay for what you use. You should see a long-term growth in the value of your investment as you own the house that underlies the company structure. With luck, you become friends with the other property-owners if they are not friends already, and can therefore leave items in the house and furnish it to a better standard than you would find in rental property because you trust each other.

If you are thinking about going into such a scheme you *must* take advice from a lawyer familiar with Turkish law and the law of the country where the scheme has been constituted. There are a number of tax issues arising out of this type of structure.

Sources of Help

Sources of help about administrative affairs are few and far between, and it can be difficult getting accurate information, as rules change frequently and are complex. A general explanation will not cover every set of circumstances. In countries such as Turkey, where there has previously been little 'official' contact with English people, the rules to be applied in the case of foreigners have not always been worked out in full and, even if they have, those rules may not have been passed down the line to the local administrators who actually do the work. This results in local and sometimes significant variations in practice. For example, some land registry officers allow the inspection of title without a power of attorney or the presence of the seller; others do not. Some tax offices will allow a lawyer to apply for a tax number without a power of attorney; others will not. Some places will (apparently) allow foreigners to register provisional contracts at the land registry and others will not, because they do not yet have permission to buy. The list is endless.

There are various sources of advice:

- **Read a book like this.**
- **Attend some of the seminars run up and down the country (*see* p.101).**
- **Check the Internet for official websites of major accountants, law firms and other useful bodies in English.**
- **Read the local English-language press – though it will seldom be very helpful.**
- **In major tourist areas, some town halls offer advice, usually limited to the services they provide.**
- **If you have neighbours in Turkey who are 'old hands', speak to them. For some types of information – like where to pay your electricity bills or who to deal with for your house insurance – they can be very helpful. Remember, though, the danger of the partially sighted leading the blind!**
- **For more substantial issues, it is better to take professional advice, and your lawyers are a good starting point. Though they may not deal with detailed administrative queries about buying a property themselves, they will probably be able to recommend someone who does.**
- **Most importantly, learn some Turkish! This will open up a whole raft of good-quality sources of information at low cost, including specialist books and magazines – though be aware that these sources will approach problems from the perspective of local people and that the rules and procedures that apply to foreigners could well be somewhat different.**

See **References**, 'Major Resources in Britain and Ireland', pp.244–7, and 'Major Resources in Turkey', p.248, for useful addresses.

Making the Purchase

05

Disclaimer

Although we have done our best to cover most topics of interest to the buyer of a property in Turkey, a guide of this kind cannot take into account every individual's personal circumstances, and the size of the book means that the advice cannot be comprehensive. The book is intended as a starting point that will enable people who are thinking of buying property to understand some of the issues involved and to ask the necessary questions of their professional advisers. IT IS NO SUBSTITUTE FOR PROFESSIONAL ADVICE. Neither the author nor the publishers can accept any liability for any action taken or not taken as a result of this book.

Raising Finance to Buy a Property in Turkey

In these days of low interest rates, many more people take out a mortgage in order to buy property abroad. If the property is viewed simply as an investment, a mortgage allows you to increase your benefit from the capital growth of the property by 'leveraging' the investment. If you buy a house for £200,000 and it increases in value by £50,000, that is a 25 per cent return on your investment. If you had only put in £50,000 of your own money and borrowed the other £150,000 then the increase in value represents a return of 100 per cent on your investment. If the rate of increase in the value of the property is more than the mortgage rate, you have won. In recent years, property in most popular areas has gone up in value by much more than the mortgage rate. The key questions are whether that will continue and, if so, for how long.

If you decide to take out a mortgage you can, in most cases, either mortgage (or extend the mortgage on) your existing UK property, or you can take out a mortgage on your new Turkish property.

Turkish mortgages can be obtained (often with some difficulty) by foreigners officially resident in Turkey. Mortgages or revolving credits can be obtained (again, often with some difficulty) by foreign-owned Turkish companies buying property in Turkey.

For many years mortgages for non-resident foreign buyers of property in Turkey were extremely rare, as overseas mortgage lenders did not look favourably on the perceived Turkish risk and no local Turkish banks were active in the market. However, there have been some recent developments. Most significantly, the Turkish parliament passed a 'Mortgage Law' on 21 February 2007 which came into effect on 6 March 2007. This mortgage law sets new standards for the housing finance system and introduces new capital market instruments in this respect.

The aims of the mortgage law are:

- **to aid mortgage-equivalent systems such as housing loans to find their legal ground by promoting a primary mortgage market.**
- **to establish a secondary mortgage market by introducing new legislative instruments concerning the trade of mortgage-backed securities.**
- **to provide alternative funding mechanisms to primary lenders.**

In this new mortgage law, the definition of housing finance also includes the leasing of houses as well. Essentially, 'housing finance' is defined in the mortgage law as the extension of loans to consumers:

- **to purchase houses.**
- **for the leasing of houses through finance leases.**
- **where the loans are secured by the houses that the consumer owns.**

Refinancing as well as initial loans are included within the scope of housing finance.

The mortgage law has been welcomed by foreigners and Turkish people alike. However, despite the progressive intentions of the law, there are still certain limitations that you should take into account before considering applying for a Turkish mortgage. There are two principal requirements that you as a foreign investor and your chosen property in Turkey should fulfil:

- **any income that is raised in the UK will have to be evaluated and approved by the Turkish authorities, who will then decide whether you are eligible for a mortgage.**
- **the property you wish to buy should be more than 80 per cent complete and must have been issued with a habitation certificate.**

Given the fact that the majority of properties bought by foreigners are 'off-plan', it could be argued that the law has failed to fill the gap for this. However, despite its current inadequacies, it is widely predicted that the law will soon be revised and amended in a way that will also include off-plan properties available for mortgages.

At the moment, mortgage-providers in both Turkey and UK are introducing a limited number of offers compared to those available in the UK market. It is again of vital importance that you discuss any offers with a Turkish lawyer based in the UK before you go ahead with the process.

Taking Out a Mortgage on Your UK Property

At the moment there is fierce competition to lend money and there are some excellent deals to be done, whether you choose to borrow at a variable rate, at a fixed rate or in one of the hybrid schemes now on offer. Read the Sunday papers or the specialist mortgage press to see what is on offer, or consult a broker. Perhaps most useful are mortgage brokers who can discuss the possibilities in the UK and Turkey. It is outside the scope of this book to go into detail about the procedures for obtaining a UK mortgage but these are the main advantages and disadvantages of mortgaging a UK property:

Advantages

- **The loan will probably be very cheap to set up.**

You will probably already have a mortgage. If you stay with the same lender there will be no legal fees or land registry fees for the additional loan. There may not even be an arrangement fee.

If you go to a new lender, many special deals mean that the lender will pay all fees involved.

- **The loan repayments will be in pounds sterling.**

If the funds to repay the mortgage are coming from your sterling earnings, then the amount you have to pay will not be affected by fluctuations in exchange rates between the pound and the euro or Turkish new lira.

Equally, if sterling falls in value, then your debt as a percentage of the value of the property decreases. Your property will be worth more in sterling terms but your mortgage will remain the same.

- **You will be familiar with dealing with British mortgages and all correspondence and documentation will be in English.**

- **You can take out an endowment or pension mortgage or interest-only mortgage, none of which is available in Turkey.**

Normally only repayment mortgages are available in Turkey.

- **You will probably need no extra life insurance cover.**

If you had to take out more cover, this could add considerably to the cost of the mortgage, especially if you are getting older.

Disadvantages

- **You will pay UK interest rates which, at the time of writing, are higher than euro rates but lower than Turkish new lira rates.**

Make sure you compare the overall cost of the two mortgages. Crude rates (which, in any case, may not be comparable as they are calculated differently in the two countries) do not tell the whole tale. What is the total monthly cost of each mortgage, including life insurance and all extras? What is the total amount required to repay the loan, including all fees and charges?

- **If the pound increases in value against the Turkish new lira or euro, a mortgage in liras or euros would become cheaper to pay off.**

Your loan of €60,000 (now worth about £40,000 at £1.00 = €1.50) would cost only about £30,000 to pay off if the euro rose 20 per cent.

- **If you are going to let the property, it will be difficult or impossible to get Turkish tax relief on the mortgage interest.**
- **Many people do not like the idea of mortgaging their main home – a debt they may only just have cleared after 25 years of paying off an earlier mortgage.**
- **Some academics argue that, in economic terms, debts incurred to buy assets should be secured against the asset bought and assets in one country should be funded by borrowings in that country.**

All in all, a UK mortgage is generally the better option for people who need to borrow relatively small sums and who will be repaying it out of UK income.

Taking Out a Mortgage on Your Turkish Property

You can obtain a mortgage on Turkish property from a Turkish bank that offers them, or from a British or other overseas bank that is registered and does business in Turkey. You cannot take out a mortgage on your new Turkish property from your local branch of a UK building society or high street bank.

As previously stated, however, the availability of house purchase finance for UK citizens secured by a mortgage on their Turkish property, though increasingly available and permitted by the 2007 mortgage law, is still quite restricted at present for anyone who will not be officially resident in Turkey.

Turkish Mortgages

The basic concept of a mortgage is the same in Turkey as it is in England or Scotland, except that there is the additional possibility of an 'Islamic mortgage' (*see* overleaf). The mortgage is (usually) a loan secured against land or buildings. Just as in the UK, if you don't keep up the payments the bank will repossess your property. In Turkey also, if they do this they will sell it, and you are likely to see it sold for a pittance and recover little if anything of the equity you built up in the property.

However, mortgages in Turkey are different in many respects from their English counterparts. The main differences are:

- **Turkish mortgages are almost always created on a repayment basis. That is to say, the loan and the interest on it are both gradually repaid by equal instalments over the period of the mortgage. Endowment, PEP, pension and interest-only mortgages are not known in Turkey.**
- **The formalities involved in making the application, signing the contract subject to a mortgage and completing the transaction are more complex and stricter than in the UK.**
- **Most Turkish mortgages are granted for 15 years, not 25 as in England. In fact the period can be anything from two to (in a few cases) 25 years.**

- **The maximum loan is generally 70 per cent of the value of the property. Valuations by banks tend to be conservative – they are thinking about what they might get for the property on a forced sale if they had to repossess it. As a planning guide, think of borrowing no more than two-thirds of the price you are paying.**
- **Fixed rate loans – with the rate fixed for the whole duration of the loan – are more common than in England. They are very competitively priced.**
- **The way of calculating the amount the bank will lend you is different from in England.**
- **There will usually be a minimum loan (say £20,000) and some banks will not lend to foreigners at all on property of less than a certain value. Some will not lend to foreigners in rural areas.**
- **The paperwork on completion of the mortgage is different.**

If you are thinking of taking out a Turkish mortgage, seek legal advice.

Islamic Mortgages

As it is against Islamic law to pay or receive interest, two types of mortgages have been designed that correspond with this law. The first, called a **'deferred sale finance' mortgage**, is where the bank buys your property for the price agreed with the vendor, then immediately sells it to you for a higher price than that agreed purchase price; you put in at least 20 per cent of the price and then pay the bank the rest in monthly instalments. The second, called a **'lease to own' mortgage**, requires less capital as a deposit: the bank buys the property for the price agreed with the vendor, and it is the bank which then owns the property for the term of the mortgage; it charges you monthly rent plus a monthly contribution towards buying the bank out of its share of the property.

The Exchange Rate Risk

If the funds to repay the mortgage are coming from your pound sterling earnings then the amount you have to pay will be affected by fluctuations in exchange rates between the pound sterling and the Turkish new lira, euro or other currency that you have borrowed. Do not underestimate these variations. Over the last 15 years – a typical period for a mortgage – the exchange rate for the Turkish new lira (YTL) has varied from about £1 = YTL750 to £1 = YTL2,700. Variations occur in rates for almost any currency you might think of borrowing. The same will almost certainly happen with the euro. Indeed, in the brief period since its launch, it has varied from €1 = £0.57 to €1 = £0.65. This can make a tremendous difference to your monthly mortgage repayments.

Equally, if sterling falls in value then a debt as a percentage of the value of a property increases in sterling terms. The property will be worth more in sterling terms but the mortgage will also have increased in value. This is probably not of great concern to most people.

Of course, if the pound sterling rises in value against the Turkish new lira or euro or other currency, then the situation is reversed.

Foreign Currency Mortgages

It is possible for Turkish residents to mortgage their home in Turkey but to borrow not in euros or Turkish new lira but in pounds sterling – or US dollars or Swiss francs or Japanese yen or perhaps even in Afghanis. There may be some attractions in borrowing in sterling if you are repaying out of sterling income. Interest rates will be measured in pounds sterling, not euros, which could mean paying more. Usually the rates are not as competitive as you could obtain if you were remortgaging your property in the UK, as the market is less cut-throat. You will have all the same administrative and legal costs as you would if you borrowed in euros – about 4 per cent of the amount borrowed.

This option is mainly of interest to people who either do not have sufficient equity in their UK home or intend to remain mainly resident in the UK and do not wish to mortgage the property in which they live.

Saving Money on Your Euro or Turkish New Lira Repayments

Your mortgage will usually be paid directly from your Turkish bank account. Unless you have lots of rental or other local income going into that account, you will need to send money from Britain in order to meet the payments.

Every time you send a payment to Turkey you will face two costs. The first is the price of the new liras. This, of course, depends on the exchange rate used to convert your pounds sterling. The second cost is the charges that will be made by your UK and Turkish banks to transfer the funds, which can be substantial.

There are steps that you can take to control these charges. As far as the exchange rate is concerned, you should be receiving the so-called '**commercial rate**', not the tourist rate published in the papers. The good news is that it is a much better rate. The bad news is that rates vary from second to second and so it is difficult to get alternative quotes. By the time you phone a second company the first has changed! In any case, you will probably want to set up a standing order for payment and not shop around every month. Unfortunately, even the commercial rate for transactions of a few hundred pounds is not good.

There are various organisations that can convert your pounds sterling into euros or new liras, but your bank is unlikely to give you the best exchange rate. Specialist currency dealers will normally better the bank's rate, perhaps significantly. If you decide to deal with a **currency dealer** you must deal with one that is reputable. They will be handling your money and, if they go bust with it in their possession, you could lose it. Ask your lawyer for a recommendation.

As far as the bank charges are concerned, different banks make different charges. This applies both to your UK bank and to your local Turkish bank.

Discuss their charges with them. In the case of your UK bank there is usually room for some kind of deal to be done. In the case of the Turkish bank, the level of these charges will probably – after the ability to speak English – be the most important reason for choosing one bank over another. Some Turkish lenders may offer you a facility to pay the monthly payments into their UK branch and transfer the funds free of charge. If this is offered it is a valuable feature – if it is not, ask for it. Who knows what the response might be.

If you are using a currency dealer to convert your pounds sterling into another currency, it is usually most economical to get them to send the money to Turkey as this saves an additional set of bank charges. Some dealers have negotiated special rates with local banks to reflect the high volumes of business they do. Again, if you are using a UK lawyer, ask for a recommendation.

Another possibility for saving money arises if you 'forward-buy' the currency that you are going to need for the whole year. It is possible to agree with a currency dealer that you will buy all of your Turkish new liras for the next year at a price that is, essentially, today's price. You normally pay 10 per cent down and the balance on delivery. If the currency rises in value you will gain, perhaps substantially. If the currency falls in value – too bad! The main attraction of forward-buying is not so much the possibility for gaining on the exchange rate – though at the moment this seems likely – but the certainty that the deal gives you. You will know precisely what your mortgage costs are going to be and, therefore, are not constantly worried about the effect of a collapse in the value of the pounds sterling. Only enter into these agreements with a reputable and, if possible, bonded broker.

Bearing in mind the cost of conversion and transmission of currency, it is better to make fewer rather than more payments. You will have to work out whether, taking into account loss of interest on the funds transferred but bank charges saved, it is best to send money monthly, quarterly or every six months.

The UK Tax Trap

In certain circumstances, a Turkish mortgage can give rise to a liability to UK tax. This is because, unless the paperwork complies with both UK and Turkish law, the interest charges paid to the Turkish bank can give rise to the need to pay withholding tax to the UK taxman. Worse still, the Turkish mortgage documentation may not give you the right to deduct any such tax paid. As a result, if you make the deduction you will fall into arrears. This is not a common problem, but check the position with your lawyer or accountant.

Other Loans

Many people may not need to incur the expense of mortgaging their property in Turkey. Very often buyers intend to move to Turkey permanently. They have already paid off their UK mortgage and their UK home is on sale. They have found the perfect place in Turkey and have, say, £80,000 of the £100,000 available from savings and pension lump sums. The balance will be paid from the sale of their UK home, but they are not sure whether that will take place before they are committed to the purchase of the house in Turkey in a few weeks' time.

It is probably unnecessarily complicated to mortgage the UK home for such a short period, and indeed, it could be difficult to do so if the bank knows you are selling and if you are, say, 65 years old and not working.

In this case it is often simplest to approach your bank for a short-term loan or overdraft. This might be for the £20,000 shortfall or it could be that you don't really want to sell some of your investments at this stage and so you might ask for a facility of, say, £50,000.

Some people choose to take out formal two- or three-year UK loans for, say, £15,000 each while still resident in the UK before leaving for Turkey to cover a gap such as waiting to receive a pension lump sum. Despite the high interest rates on such loans, the overall cost can be a lot less than taking a short-term mortgage on the Turkish property and paying all the fees relating to it.

Who Should Own the Property?

There are many ways of structuring the purchase of a home in Turkey, and each has significant advantages and disadvantages. The choice of the right structure can save tax and expenses during your lifetime and on your death. People in second marriages and unmarried couples should be particularly careful. The options are discussed below.

Sole Ownership

In some cases it could be sensible to put the property in the name of one person only. If your husband runs a high-risk business, or if he is 90 and you are 22, this could make sense. It is seldom a good idea from the point of view of tax or inheritance planning.

Buying 'As Individuals In Common'

If two people are buying together they will normally buy in both their names 'as individuals in common'. In most of continental Europe – but not in England and Wales – this is the usual way in which individuals buy property. It means that if, for example, a husband and wife buy a home, a part (usually half) of it will belong to the husband and the rest will belong to the wife. Your half is yours and your fellow owner's is theirs. On your death, if you have not made a will, your half of the property will (subject to the requirement of your matrimonial regime – *see* pp.132–3) be disposed of in accordance with Turkish law.

A person who owns in this way, even if they own by virtue of inheritance, can usually insist on the sale of the property. So if your stepchildren inherit from your husband they could insist on the sale of your home.

If you decide to buy together then, in certain cases, it can make sense to split the ownership other than 50–50. If, for example, you are in a second marriage and have three children and your wife has two then to secure each of those children an equal share on your death you might think about buying 60 per cent in your name and 40 per cent in your wife's name.

It is very important to seek clear advice from your lawyer about the form of ownership that will suit you best, both with regard to the consequences in Turkey and the consequences in England.

Joint Ownership

This is the system most commonly adopted in England and Wales. Under a joint ownership scheme the buyers – say husband and wife – each own the property in such a way that on their death the property *automatically* passes to the surviving owner. The transfer is generally tax free. Joint ownership (in the English sense) of property in Turkey is not possible; you can own property jointly during your lifetime that is acquired during the marriage (*see* 'The Matrimonial Regime', pp.132–3) but you will still need to make a will leaving your share property to your spouse or partner, and they may still have to pay inheritance tax on it. Confusingly, you may therefore see the phrase 'joint ownership' used in Turkey to describe the situation of owning as individuals in common.

Adding Your Children to the Title

If you give your children the money to buy part of the property and put them on the title at the time you purchase it, they may save inheritance tax. On your death you will only own (say) one-fifth of the property rather than one-half. Only that part will be subject to inheritance tax. It may be such a small value as to result in a tax-free inheritance. This only works sensibly if your children are over 18. Of course, there are drawbacks: for example, if they fall out with you they can insist on the sale of the property and that they receive their share.

Putting the Property in the Name of Your Children *Only*

If you put the property only in the name of your children (possibly reserving for yourself a life interest – *see* below) then the property is theirs. On your death there will be little or no inheritance tax and there will be no need to incur the legal expenses involved in dealing with an inheritance. This sounds attractive. Remember, however, that you have lost control. It is no longer your property. If your children divorce, their husband or wife will be able to claim a share. If they die before you without children of their own, you will end up inheriting the property back from them and having to pay inheritance tax for the privilege of doing so.

A **life interest** is the right to use the property for a lifetime. So, on your death, your rights would be extinguished but your second wife or partner, who still has a life interest, would still be able to use the property. Only on *that* person's death would the property pass in full to the people to whom you gave it years earlier. This device can not only protect your right to use the property but also save large amounts of inheritance tax, particularly if you are young, the property is valuable and you survive for many years. As ever, though, there are drawbacks, not least the fact that after making the gift you no longer own the property. If you wish to sell, you need the agreement of the 'owners', who will be entitled to their share of the proceeds of sale and who would have to agree to buy you a new house. Structure the gift carefully if you decide to do this, otherwise the property could be taxable at once in Turkey under gift tax rules.

Forming a Limited Company

For some people, owning a property via a limited company can be a very attractive option. You own the shares in a company, not a house in Turkey. There are various types of company and it could be English, Turkish or based in a tax haven.

Ownership in the form of a limited company can have a number of advantages – mainly because the company never dies and because when you sell the house you can sell the company (and so the house it owns) instead of transferring legal title to the property. These steps can save tax.

To balance against this is:

- **the cost of setting up and maintaining the company.**
- **the risk of being assessed by the British tax system as enjoying a 'benefit in kind' from the company by virtue of your right to use the property; this could be taxable at your highest British tax rate. *See* pp.116–17.**

Turkish Commercial Companies

If a property is owned via a company, the income from letting it is taxed in the way usual for companies – i.e. on the profit made – which can reduce the overall tax bill.

There can also be marginal tax advantages of land ownership through a company rather than as an individual. Taxation applies principally to two aspects of income from land: income from rental, and gains resulting from profit on re-sale of the profit – capital gains. Under Turkish tax law, individuals will be taxed on these two sources of income under the **income tax rules**. The rate of tax that applies to such income will depend on the individual's total income tax liability. Income tax rates for income sourced other than through employment range from 15–37 per cent. **Corporate tax**, however, is levied on company income at a rate of 20 per cent. The withholding tax payable on dividends means that the effective rate of corporate tax is 27 per cent. Additionally, companies may offset against their tax liability certain expenses such as start-up costs, previous year's losses, depreciation of fixed assets and certain other items that are more generous than the items permitted to individuals.

Ownership in the form of a company has other advantages – primarily the ability to buy property without obtaining the **military permission** needed by a foreign buyer (*see* pp.140–41). Some properties would not be granted permission, so buying in this way can expand the range of property available to you. On other occasions, even if permission would be available, the seller may refuse to wait the several months needed to obtain it. If you are thinking of buying through a company for this reason, seek legal advice.

The downside of ownership in the form of a company is that selling a property owned by a Turkish company is much more difficult than for an individual, as more paperwork and permissions are needed. It also gives rise to certain expenses – accountancy, filing tax returns and so on. Typically, the cost of setting up a Turkish company is about £2,200. Companies in Turkey are required to have a minimum paid-up capital, which must be deposited when the company is formed. Once the company has been formed, that capital can be used for the business of the company and so this is more a cashflow item than an overall cost. The minimum number of shareholders is two.

Owning a Turkish company can have significant tax consequences in the UK, particularly if you intend to use the property as a holiday home and you are tax resident in the UK. In these circumstances British tax law will apply to the company. Under British tax law, in most cases you will be treated as either a director or a 'shadow director' of the company. The effect is the same. If the company allows you to use its property for your own personal use it will be treated as a '**benefit in kind**'. This is just the same as if the company gave you a company car. Every year you will have to file a tax return declaring benefits in kind and pay UK tax on the sums involved – for some people at 40 per cent. If you have used the property for, say, six weeks in the year, the Inland Revenue is likely to treat the benefit as the rental value of the property for those weeks. So, for example, if your property would rent out for £600 a week you will have received a benefit of, say, £3,600 and you will pay tax (probably at 40 per cent) on that amount. This would be £1,440. Ouch! If you used the property for the majority of the year, then the Inland Revenue would probably treat your use of the property more favourably, as a long-term renter, which is generally at a lower weekly rate. Unfortunately, although the weekly rate is lower, the number of weeks for which you have occupied the property will mean that the taxable benefit will still be substantial. On the other hand, if you are not careful the value of your benefit might even be assessed as the rental value of the property for the period *during which you were entitled to occupy it* – not the period during which you actually *did* occupy it. If it is available for your use all year round, this could be a lot of money. If you do not declare this benefit and get caught there are substantial penalties.

There are ways in which this tax can be reduced. If you are buying a property primarily as an investment, to be let to the full extent possible except that you stay there for just a week or two a year, then the problem can be reduced substantially or, in some cases, eliminated entirely.

Detailed examination of which type of company to use and the means of setting up those companies is beyond the scope of this book. This issue requires careful consideration with your legal advisers.

Purchase through a UK Company

It is rare for a purchase through a UK company to make sense for a holiday home or single investment property. This is despite the fact that the ability to pay for the property with the company's money without drawing it out of the company and paying UK tax on the dividend is attractive. Once again you need expert advice from someone familiar with the law of both countries.

Purchase through an Offshore (Tax Haven) Company

This has most of the same advantages and disadvantages as ownership by other types of company, but with additional expenses and drawbacks. For someone tax resident in the UK and using legitimate UK tax-paid money it is likely to be of little interest. A 93-year-old buying a £10 million property, or someone who wishes to be discreet about the ownership of the property, might think the price is a small price to pay for the avoidance of inheritance tax or for privacy. Someone who is not tax resident in the UK and who has offshore funds might think about buying in this way. Needless to say, anyone thinking of buying through an offshore company should take detailed advice from a lawyer familiar with the law of both countries.

Trusts

As a vehicle for owning a property, trusts are of little direct use. In Turkish law the concept of the trust is much more restricted than either in the UK or other European countries. However, some people will want to take the opportunity of restructuring their affairs generally. Such an arrangement can prove very beneficial for asset-protection and tax-reduction. Trusts are usually expensive to set up and so only of interest to people buying higher-value properties or where they have substantial savings and investments – say, as a rough guide, over £350,000 – and particularly useful if you are thinking of living overseas. The trust will usually own the property through the medium of a limited company.

Which Is Right for You?

Choosing the right way to finance your purchase of property abroad is of fundamental importance. If you get it wrong you will pay massively more tax – often many thousands of pounds – than you need to, both during your lifetime and on your death. The tax consequences arise not only in Turkey but also in your own country.

One of the options set out above will suit each buyer perfectly; another might just about make sense; the rest would be an expensive waste of money. The trouble is, it is not obvious which is the right choice! Take advice *in every case*. If your case is simple, so will be the advice. If it is complex, the time and money spent will be repaid many times over.

Introduction to Turkish Property Law

As you would expect, buying a property in Turkey is complicated. A basic textbook on Turkish property law might extend to 500 pages. There are certain basic principles, however, that it is helpful to understand.

The main legal provisions relating to property law are found in the Civil Code, which was introduced in 1926 but has been modified since. The Code was virtually a translation of the Swiss Civil Code and based legal relationships on the same footing as that of contemporary Europe in the 1920s. The law of procedure and bankruptcy is similarly Swiss-inspired. Subsequent modifications of Turkish law have reflected changes in Turkish society in parallel with those in Europe. Turkish law is, therefore, based on the same principles as European civil law.

Although Turkish law has maintained certain discriminations between Turkish nationals and foreigners, recent legislative amendments have removed virtually all of these. In the central field of property ownership, foreigners are now treated on a par with Turkish nationals.

Turkey is moving rapidly to introduce laws that are consistent with the requirements of the European Union. This will have far-reaching effects as more changes are brought in every year. Furthermore, in December 2004 the EU decided to open up the negotiations process for Turkish membership, and, although the political side of things seems to be moving slowly owing to the internal politicals of some member countries, Turkey continues to bring its laws up to date in line with EU regulations and requirements. This is likely to lead, for example, to the eventual removal of the requirement for EU nationals to obtain the military permission needed by foreigners wishing to buy property in Turkey (*see* pp.140–41). It should simplify and speed up the procedure – and encourage yet more foreigners to consider buying in Turkey.

For more detailed information about Turkish law, *see* **About Turkey**, 'Property Law', pp.24–5.

Two Classes of Property

Turkish law divides property into two classes – **movable property** (*taş ınabilir*) and **immovable property** (*gayrimenkul*). The whole basis of ownership and transfer of ownership depends on which classification the property belongs to. The distinction is similar to the English concept of real and personal property but it is not exactly the same. Immovable property includes land and buildings, but not the shares in a company that owns land and buildings. The sale of immovable property located in Turkey must always be governed by Turkish law.

Ownership of Land

The form of ownership of land used to be absolute ownership, which is similar to what we would call freehold ownership. There has been a move in recent years to limit this absolute form of ownership in favour of the public interest. Purchases of land from the government, therefore, tend to be on the basis only of a lease of 60 years, after which time the property reverts to the state.

It is possible to own the buildings – or even parts of a building – on a piece of land separately from the land itself. This is of particular relevance in the case of apartments.

Where two or more people own a piece of land or other property together, they will generally own it in undivided shares (*iştirak halinde mülkiyet*). That is to say, the piece of land is not physically divided between them. Each owner may mortgage or sell their share only with the consent of the others. Beware that some properties are offered for sale on this basis, which is usually dangerous, as the debts of one owner can be registered and claimed against a property that belongs to several other (innocent and debt-free) individuals.

Where a building or piece of land is physically divided between a number of units, a **condominium** (***site***) is created. The land is divided into privately owned parts – such as an individual flat – plus communally owned areas. The management of the communally held areas is up to the owners of the privately held area, but can be delegated to someone else.

In the case of a sale of land, certain people may have a right of pre-emption. One is the co-owner mentioned above. Others are (only in certain circumstances) the municipality or a sitting tenant and certain statutory bodies.

Transfer of Ownership

The transfer of ownership of immovable property (*gayrimenkul mal*) is usually made by simple agreement. This need not be in writing, but usually is. That agreement binds both the parties to it but is not effective as far as the rest of the world is concerned, who are entitled to rely on the content of the **land registry**. Thus, between buyer and seller, ownership of land can be transferred, for example, by signing a **sale contract** (*satış sözleşmesi*) even if the seller remains in possession and some of the price remains unpaid. But that transfer would not alter or damage the interests of someone other than the buyer or seller, such as someone owed money by the seller, who would be entitled to take action against the person named as owner in the land register. Ownership can also be acquired by possession, in certain circumstances, usually after a minimum of 10 or 20 years' undisputed occupancy.

Other Rights over Land, and Land Registries

Other rights – short of ownership – can exist over land. These include rights of way, tenancies, life interests, mortgages and option contracts. Most require some sort of formality in order to make them valid against third parties, but they are always binding between the people who made the agreements.

There are two **land registries**. Each municipality maintains a registry (***kadastro***). In this all the land in the district is divided into plots and assessed for tax purposes. The second registry is the deed and mortgage registry (***tapu sicili*** or ***tapu kaydı***). Not all land is registered here. The entries (size, boundaries and so on) usually correspond in the two registries – but not always. Be careful.

The Process of Buying a Property in Turkey

General Procedure

The general procedure when buying a property in Turkey seems, at first glance, similar to the purchase of a property in England and very familiar to anyone who has bought a property in continental Europe: sign a contract; do some checks; sign a deed of title. This is deceptive. The procedure in Turkey is very different, and even the use of the familiar English vocabulary to describe the very dissimilar steps in Turkey can produce an undesirable sense of familiarity with the procedure. This can lead to assumptions that things that have not been discussed will be the same as they would in England. This would be a wrong and dangerous assumption.

In most cases, the basic procedure is this:

- You sign a **reservation contract.** This takes the property off the market for a limited period – say 30 days. You will usually pay a holding deposit of, say, £2,000.
- You decide whether to have a **survey** done if the property is a resale or completed new property (*see* pp.127–8).
- Your lawyer makes enquiries about the property. These will include a **title search** to ensure that the person trying to sell the property to you actually owns it, and a **planning search** to ensure it has planning permission. Depending on the nature of your case, other searches may be needed.
- Your lawyer reports his or her findings.
- If all is well, you sign a **preliminary contract** of purchase. This commits you to the purchase and you pay over a deposit, typically of 30 per cent of the price of the property.
- If building work is involved, such as in a new property, **stage payments** are made. At the end of the building work a **habitation certificate** is issued, certifying that the property is fit to be lived in and complies with the terms of the building licence.
- A **final purchase contract** is signed and your title is registered at the land registry.

Along the way there are, of course, other steps to be taken. Normally a power of attorney will be needed and military permission to buy is required. In some cases a company will have to be set up. Taxes must be paid. But these are the main steps. The steps will be different if you are buying a resale property or if you are buying either a new or a resale property via a Turkish limited company.

Choosing a Lawyer

The Notary Public

The notary public (*noter*) is a special type of lawyer. He or she is in part a public official but is also in business, making his or her living from the fees he or she charges for his or her services. Notaries also exist in England but they are seldom used in day-to-day transactions.

Unlike in many European countries, however, the notary is not an essential figure in the Turkish conveyancing system. His or her prime importance is in the attestation and registration of contracts and documents other than the title deed itself.

Turkish Lawyers

Most Turkish people buying a home in Turkey will not use the services of a lawyer (*avukat*); they are more likely to rely on the estate agent (who essentially represents the seller) unless there is something unusual or contentious about the transaction.

Turkish lawyers are 'lightly' regulated. There is little practical redress if they make a mistake. They do not generally have designated client accounts (protecting clients' funds in their possession) or, until recently, professional indemnity insurance (protecting clients in the case of negligence on their part); however, professional indemnity insurance has now been introduced by the Bar Union and we highly recommend you use only a law firm that is covered by this insurance up to a satisfactory amount. Few have any real experience of property transactions, which in Turkey are not really seen as part of a lawyer's work. Lawyers in Turkey see themselves much more as court lawyers or lawyers dealing with commercial contracts. Nonetheless, there are good Turkish lawyers who can offer assistance when buying a property. Get recommendations from people who have already used their services, and be aware that few Turkish lawyers speak or write fluent English.

UK Lawyers

British people will often require advice about inheritance issues, the UK tax implications of their purchase, how to save taxes, surveys, mortgages, currency exchange and so on which is outside the scope of the service of the notary. They should retain the services of a specialist UK lawyer familiar with dealing with these issues.

The buyer's usual solicitor is unlikely to be able to help, as there are only a handful of UK law firms with the necessary expertise.

Agreeing the Price

This can be freely agreed between the parties. Depending on the economic climate there may be either ample or very little room for negotiating a reduction in the asking price.

The present explosion of property prices in Turkey has given rise to the opportunity for all sorts of shenanigans as far as prices are concerned. This is commonplace in emerging markets and will, no doubt, settle down over the next few years. Reputable agents, lawyers and developers will not get involved with them, but others will. Be careful that the price you pay is the price the seller receives. If the price is to be paid by stage payments, these must be clearly stipulated. Pay particular attention to agreeing the bank account into which they should be paid.

How Much Should be Declared in the Reservation Contract?

You must declare the full price that you are paying.

How Much Should be Declared in the Preliminary Contract of Sale?

Generally, you should declare the full price that you are paying. It is dangerous for the seller to declare any other price as the buyer might then try to make a contract at the lower price. Equally, the seller may be unwilling to declare the full price as you can then use that as a lever when insisting that the full price is declared in the final title document (*see* below). Such are the problems generated by the culture of under-declaration (*see* below).

How Much Should be Declared in the Official Contract of Sale?

There is still a tradition in Turkey of **under-declaring** the price actually paid for a property when signing the title deed (*tapu*). This is because the taxes and fees due are calculated on the basis of the price declared. A lower price means lower property transfer taxes for the buyer and less capital gains tax for the seller. Often the price declared is only 25 per cent of the price actually paid!

There are drawbacks to this. It is illegal – and it is likely to give rise to a much higher tax bill when you sell the property – both in England and in Turkey.

Under-declaration can be an advantage to your seller, whose share of the stamp duty will be reduced a little bit. Much more importantly, if the seller is liable to Turkish capital gains tax, the capital gains will be reduced substantially. If the seller is a company, then the reduced 'official' income will reduce its profit and therefore the company tax it has to pay. Furthermore, many Turkish people are very private and simply do not think that it is any business of the taxman how much they get for their property – they prefer to keep their money where they want without its existence coming to the attention of the authorities.

The under-declaration is generally much less of an advantage for the buyer, though it saves some property transfer tax (3 per cent of the value of the property, of which half is generally paid by the buyer and half by the seller). This is a modest saving. To set against it is the potential and substantial increase in capital gains tax to be paid when the property is sold.

This additional capital gains tax liability arises in two ways. First, there is Turkish tax. In Turkey tax is paid on the profit made when a person sells land, even if the seller is a foreigner. (After five years any sale is tax-free.) Unless you can find somebody who will also declare a lower value for the property when they buy it from you, you will generate an artificially high capital gain. Also, although at the moment there are few problems associated with under-declaring the price, this is likely to change in the near future. This is all part and parcel of Turkey's moving towards membership of the European Union. That, in turn, will impose the obligation to be more thorough and 'Western' in their approach to the collection of taxes.

Case Study: The Disappearing £20,000

John and Mary were buying an apartment in Bodrum. They had agreed to pay £70,000 for a large two-bedroom apartment with spectacular sea views. 'When the paperwork arrived we were slightly surprised,' says John, 'to see that the price was only £50,000. At first we thought that this was because the developer was not going to declare the true value of the property for tax purposes. This is a common (but illegal) practice in Turkey. However, closer enquiries revealed that £50,000 was the true price to be received by the developer and that the other £20,000 had simply been added to the price by the estate agent – who was clearly not satisfied by the mere 10 per cent commission that he was otherwise going to receive.'

Fortunately, there was a happy ending. John and Mary were able to buy their house directly from the developer, cutting the agent out of his illegal £20,000.

This sort of behaviour by the agent arises because the agents in Turkey are largely unregulated and because the rapidly rising prices in the marketplace give the unscrupulous the opportunity of making a quick – and illegal – buck.

Always get your lawyer to check the position carefully.

The pattern can be seen clearly in Spain. Twenty years ago it was commonplace to declare 25 per cent of the value of a property when buying or selling. Now it would usually be 80 per cent or 90 per cent. That change has come about as a result of government policy, largely influenced by the same need to bring Spain's policies into line with the European Union. In the writer's view, the same pattern will occur in Turkey – probably over a shorter time-frame. So, particularly if you think you might sell the property within five years, you are better declaring as high a value as you can negotiate with the seller. Even if you think you might keep the property for more than five years, there is no guarantee that the current five-year exemption from capital gains tax will continue in force. The cost of the extra tax will generally be hugely higher than the saving made by not declaring the property for property transfer tax.

The second tax liability arises in the case of people who are resident for tax purposes in the UK. They will have to pay British capital gains tax on their worldwide gains, including any gains generated in Turkey. When calculating that tax, at the starting point will be the gain generated when deducting the purchase price (as declared in the official contract) from the sales price (as declared in the official contract). So if you have to declare something like the full value when you sell but only declared 25 per cent of the true value when you bought, then once again there will be a large artificial capital gain. For many people, that will be taxed at 40 per cent. You will be allowed to deduct from the tax payable in the UK any tax that you have already paid on the same gain in Turkey, but this will still leave a substantial tax bill.

So, generally, saving a little bit of tax now creates a large potential tax burden in the future. The under-declaration is also illegal. So why do people not declare the full price? Generally, because the sellers will simply not sell to you if you insist on declaring the full value. This is true not only in the case of private individuals but in the case of some major construction and development companies. Fortunately, some of the sellers will be prepared to allow you to declare the full price provided *you* pay the extra tax due. Amazingly, they sometimes think only of the extra property transfer tax and forget completely about the extra tax liability on their profits (in the case of a company seller) or capital gains (in the case of a private seller) generated by showing the extra income.

Why Are There *Three* Contracts?

There are several reasons. First, the **reservation contract** is issued simply to justify the seller's taking the property off the market for a limited period during which you can check that everything is in order. It is little more than a gesture of good faith on your part. You pay a small sum to show you mean business.

The second, **preliminary contract** is generally only needed either by a private individual buyer (who needs to get military permission to buy before he or she can sign a full contract, *see* pp.140–41; or by a private individual buyer or a company buyer buying a new property still in the course of construction. If this is the case, you will not be able to sign the full contract at this stage because the property will not have been finished and it may not yet have any independent title. For a company buying a resale property, the preliminary contract can often be dispensed with. Sometimes, however, even in this case you will need the preliminary contract to record the true price of the property.

The third, **full contract** is in many respects the equivalent of our conveyance or property transfer form. It is this contract that is recorded at the land registry office to show your official ownership of the property. This is explained in more detail below.

Where Must the Money be Paid?

The price, together with the taxes and fees payable, is usually paid by the buyer to the seller in front of the land registrar, although this is not compulsory. It is also possible to make the payment from a bank in the UK to the account of the seller in Turkey, subject to a condition that the paying bank in Turkey sees a copy of the title deed registered in the name of the new owner. There are a number of other ways in which you can agree that the price should be paid. You can, in fact, agree to pay in whatever way and wherever you please.

Be aware that, in Turkey, payment by cheque, bankers' cheque or bankers' draft – common in Britain and other countries – is almost unheard of. In fact, amazingly, the most popular means of paying for a house in Turkey is still cash. This is even if the price is expressed in pounds sterling, US dollars or euros. It involves a visit to a bank and coming away with carrier bags full of cash. This clearly poses a significant security risk.

Times are changing and more purchases are paid for by bank transfer, but payment by bank transfer is no good if the person wants to conceal the money.

Agreeing the Description of the Property

Ideally, the full title description of the property should be included in the contract. If it is not, this can give rise to difficulties later in identifying precisely what you have agreed to buy.

Layman's description of the property – e.g. '3-bedroom 2-bathroom apartment known as G2, Seaside, Fethiye, Muğla, Turkey'
Address:
Village:
Town:
City:
District:
(*These details fully describe the address of your property.*)

Land Registry:
Zone:
Plot:
Parcel:
Boundaries :
Land Classification:
Record No.:
Book No.:
Page No.:
(*These details describe to the authorities the official location of the property.*)

Date Registered:
Value on Deed:
(*This is the current owners' date of registration and officially declared value.*)

Plot Classification:
Plot Allocation:
Block No.:
Floor No.:
Independent Plot No.:
(*This section identifies the location of the easement and its status.*)

Acquisition Details:
Present Owner:

Unfortunately, these full details seldom appear in draft contracts.

We recommend in all cases that, unless you and everyone else are absolutely sure of your boundaries, you have a registered surveyor conduct a survey and peg out the physical extent of your property. This will typically cost around £500, and you will receive a summarised translation of the report.

Property Inspection

Whatever property you are thinking of buying, you should think about having it inspected before you commit yourself to the purchase. It can cost nearly as much and cause just as much disruption to repair property in Turkey as in the UK, so you don't want any surprises. Very few buyers of property in Turkey do this.

A new property will be covered by a short guarantee running from the date of handover and covering minor but not trivial defects in a new property. The property will also benefit from a guarantee covering major structural defects that will last for five years. As a subsequent purchaser you assume the benefit of these guarantees. For property more than five years old (and, arguably, for younger property too) you should consider having a survey done. There are several options open to you.

Do it Yourself

There are several things that you can do yourself, and they will help you decide when to instruct a surveyor to do a proper survey and help direct him or her to any specific points of interest. *See* the checklist on pp.267–73.

Estate Agent's Valuation and 'Survey'

It may be possible to arrange for another local estate agent to give the property a quick 'once-over' to comment on the price asked and any obvious problem areas. This is far short of a survey. It is likely to cost about £200.

Mortgage Lender's Survey

This is no substitute for a proper survey. Many lenders do not ask for one and, where they do, it is normally fairly peremptory, limited to a check on whether the property is imminently about to fall over and whether it is worth the money the bank is lending you.

Turkish Builders

If you are going to do a virtual demolition and rebuild, then it might make more sense to get a builder to make a report on the property. A reputable and experienced builder will also be able to comment on whether the price is reasonable for the property in its existing state. Make sure you ask for a written quotation for any building work proposed. As in any country, it is as well to get several quotes, though this can be tricky. There is a lot of work for builders.

Turkish Surveyors

Your lawyer can put you in touch with appropriate Turkish surveyors, but in most rural areas there will be limited choice. The cost of a survey is typically £500–1,500 and most surveys can be carried out in 7 to 10 days.

You will find that the report is different from the sort of report you would get from an English surveyor. Many people find it a little 'thin', with too much focus on issues that are not their primary concern. The report will usually be in Turkish so you will need to have it translated unless you speak very good Turkish and have access to a technical dictionary. Translation costs amount to about £60–100 per thousand words, depending on where you are and the complexity of the document. Incidentally, always use an English person to translate documents from Turkish into English. An alternative to translation of the full report would be to ask your lawyer to summarise the report in a letter to you and to have any areas of particular concern translated.

It is unusual for contracts to be issued 'subject to survey' in Turkey. Legally there is nothing to stop a Turkish preliminary contract containing a get-out clause stating that the sale is conditional on a satisfactory survey being obtained. It is unlikely to meet the approval of the seller or his agent unless the transaction is unusual. In an ordinary case the seller is likely to tell you to do your survey and then sign a contract.

General Points

Whichever type of inspection report you opt for, its quality will depend in part on your input. Agree clearly and in writing the things you expect to be covered in the report. If you don't speak Turkish (and the surveyor doesn't speak good English) you may have to ask someone to write on your behalf – your UK lawyer would probably be the best bet. Some checks may cost extra: ask what will be covered as part of the standard fee and get an estimate for the extras.

These are some of the things you may ask your surveyor to check:

- **The electrics.**
- **The drains, back to where they join the mains sewers or septic tank.**
- **The septic tank.**
- **For rot.**
- **In a property constructed of cement, the quality of the cement.**
- **Under-floor areas, where access cannot easily be obtained.**
- **Heating and air-conditioning.**
- **If there is a pool, all pool-related equipment and heating.**
- **For wood-boring insects.**
- **Where the physical boundaries of the property are.**

General Enquiries and Special Enquiries

Certain enquiries are made routinely in the course of the purchase of a property. These include, in appropriate cases, a check on the planning situation of the property (*yapı ruhsatı*), which will reveal the position of the property itself. It does not, at least directly, tell you about its neighbours nor reveal general plans for the area. If you want to know whether the authorities are going to put a

Case Study: The Hotel

Ali and Maxine were buying an apartment in Turkey from a major developer. They had agreed to pay £80,000 for a large two-bedroom apartment with spectacular sea views. They had already paid a reservation deposit of €3,000. The seller suggested that they should ask the seller's representative to sign all the paperwork on the buyer's behalf and that using a lawyer was unnecessary.

When the searches were undertaken it turned out that the property was subject to debt and that it was being built on land that was zoned as a hotel using planning permission for the construction of holiday accommodation, not for permanent residence.

The seller was unable to grant individual titles to the individual buyers as there was one title for the whole hotel complex. This would have meant that the buyers would be exposed to the risk that if any other buyers on site suffered any claims, the whole of the site could be charged with those claims. This was unsatisfactory.

The sellers stated that they were intending to change the use of the land but they had no indication of whether they would be able to do so or when it was likely to happen. The buyers decided to cancel their contract and to buy in another location where the position was more secure.

Always get your lawyer to check the position carefully.

prison in the village or run a new power line through your back garden (both, presumably, bad things) or build a motorway access point or railway station 3km away (both, presumably, good things) you will need to ask. There are various organisations you can approach but, just as in England, there is no single point of contact for such enquiries. If you are concerned about what might happen in the area you will need to discuss the position with your lawyer at an early stage. There may be a considerable amount of work (and cost) involved in making full enquiries, the results of which can never be guaranteed.

Normal enquiries include a check that the seller is the registered owner of the property and that it is sold (if this has been agreed) free of mortgages or other charges. Depending on the type of property you are buying, where it is located and whether it is new or old, there will probably be other enquiries to make.

The Land Registry Search

The land registry search reveals the registered ownership of property and certain debts or charges registered against it. It will also show whether the property enjoys full title or a more limited type of title known as *kat irtifakı*.

As already mentioned, property ownership in Turkey, whether the property be an apartment or a villa, is generally the equivalent of what we would call freehold. This is normally recorded in a full 'absolute' document of title called *kat mülkiyetı*.

For property under construction, a **promissory deed of easements** (*kat irtifakı*) title is a document by which the owner of land promises to transfer full title once the project is completed and a habitation certificate has been granted. Until that time, even though the *kat irtifakı* has been signed in your favour, the seller can still mortgage or, in some circumstances, sell the property to another person. This document is, therefore, of little practical use as a guarantee of your rights unless those rights are also protected by your taking a formal charge over the property. These titles are inevitable when buying a new property, but proceed with caution.

The land registry will also show whether there are any mortgages, debts or charges registered against the property.

Technical Services (Planning and Building Consent) Search

This search shows the current planning status of the property – for example, whether permission to build has been granted and whether it is still current, or whether a habitation licence has been granted. In Turkey a property must now have a certificate stating that it is fit for habitation before it can be occupied or connected (officially) to the water and electricity supplies. Generally, property built before 1965 does not need a certificate and many other older properties built after 1965 do not have a certificate. In the case of such older properties the lack of a certificate may not, in practice, pose a problem.

In new or fairly new properties you should insist on a certificate because, technically, a property cannot be connected to the water, electricity or other services without it, although sometimes in fact it can.

Remember that, even if you do not think the certificate important, the person to whom you want to sell in a few years' time may want the certificate and not buy without it. Obtaining a certificate where none exists can be time-consuming and expensive, although it is not always so.

In the case of new properties still in the course of construction the builder often proposes completion before the certificate is granted, and such arrangements often work well. Be aware, however, that if for any reason the certificate is not issued by the authorities, you will be faced with the inconvenience and cost of sorting the problem out. In the worst case, you may have to do this from a property without water or electricity. We would always therefore recommend that, where possible, completion be deferred until the certificate is available, but this is often not acceptable to the builder.

Land Use Registry Search

The land use registry search (*kadastro*) shows the official plan of the plot, maximum build density (subject to suitable planning permission), projected new roads in the area and so on.

Museums and Antiquities Search

The museums and antiquities search shows whether the land or building is listed or is of archaeological importance. If the land is controlled, there are severe restrictions on what you can do on it. A lot of land in Turkey is of archaeological importance. If a building is listed there will be controls over it. These will vary with the status of the listing. In extreme cases they can result in your not being able to do any work at all on land or may severely restrict what you can do.

Environmental Search

An environmental search (*çevre ve bayındırlık*) shows nature reserves, areas liable to flooding and so on. It is not an environmental search in the Western European sense of showing toxic waste tips and other environmental hazards.

Military Status Search

The military status search (*askeri bölge*) is intended to reveal whether the property lies in a militarily sensitive area and, as a result, cannot be purchased by foreigners. This information will be disclosed when your application to buy land is processed. It takes about three months. In certain cases it may be important to know this without waiting for the result of that application. The information may then be available, but it is not available in all areas and will not be provided in writing. Sometimes the title deed register will disclose part of the position.

Local Taxes Search

The local taxes search (*emlak vergisı ve çop vergisi*) shows how many local taxes are payable and, with a bit of luck, whether there are any outstanding taxes that could attach to the property. That information is theoretically confidential but can sometimes be discovered. This search is only available in certain areas.

On new properties there won't be any local property taxes yet payable. The property will be assessed later for tax purposes and a demand will be issued.

The seller of an existing property will have to produce proof of payment of the local taxes when transferring title to you. Often the seller will try to shift the burden of payment of any unpaid taxes on to the buyer! The sums are generally small.

Enquiries about Neighbouring Land

As in England, the process of local enquiries (which, in Turkey, are much less formal than in England and are made in person) is likely only to reveal entries relating directly to the land you are buying. It will almost certainly *not* reveal any development plans relating, for example, to your neighbours' land or the area generally. If you have reason to suspect that any such developments may be afoot, let your lawyer know. He or she can then carry out such further investigations as are agreed between you.

Other Enquiries

There is no equivalent to the local search (an investigation into the entries relating to the property in the local land charges register and general enquiries at the town hall) for transactions in Turkey.

Equally, it is not the custom in Turkey to make the extensive written enquiries of the seller which are a key part of English conveyancing. Any attempt to make such enquiries is usually ignored as the seller simply cannot relate to them. If there are any points of particular concern to you, please speak to your lawyer to discuss how best to deal with them.

In order to advise you what special enquiries might be appropriate, your lawyer will need to be told your proposals for the property. Do you intend to let it? If so, will it be commercially? Do you intend to use it for business purposes? Do you want to extend or modify the exterior of the property? Do you intend to make interior structural alterations?

Agree in advance the additional enquiries you would like to make and get an estimate of the cost of those enquiries.

Your Civil Status and Other Personal Details

This is something you will have given no thought to. For most of the time it is a matter of unimportance in England but it is something the Turkish can get very worked up about.

When preparing documents in Turkey you will be asked to specify your civil status (*medeni hal*). This comprises a full set of information about you. You will be asked for your full name and address, occupation, nationality, passport number, tax office and number, maiden name and sometimes the names of your parents, date and place of birth, date and place of marriage and, most importantly, matrimonial regime.

The Matrimonial Regime

The matrimonial regime is something we do not have in England. However, if you marry in Turkey or adopt Turkish nationality, Turkish law and its matrimonial regime can apply to you.

In Turkey, when you marry you will specify the system of property ownership that is to apply to property acquired by the parties during the course of the marriage. There are essentially four types of matrimonial property ownership in Turkish law:

- **Separation of property** (*mal ayrılığı*): each party to the marriage retains ownership and administration of present and future property. The party owning the property also has the right to dispose of capital income and income relating to the asset freely; each party remains liable for their own personal debts during the marriage.
- **Joint property** (*mal birliği*): all property acquired during the marriage – other than that specifically excluded by any agreement between them – belongs jointly to both parties; the parties do not lose individual title to any asset owned by them, but they agree to the joint use of that property.
- **Common property** (*mal ortaklığı*): the property of each party is regarded as family property owned in common; each party loses the right of individual ownership over specific assets, which are then governed by the laws of co-ownership.
- **Participatory regime** (*edinilmiş mallara katılma rejimi*): a new category applying to marriages only after 2002: the parties to the marriage retain personal ownership of assets acquired before the marriage; assets acquired after marriage are regarded as joint assets.

Where the parties do not state a preference for which regime they prefer at the time of the marriage (after 2002), the participatory regime applies.

If you are not a Turkish citizen and you marry outside Turkey, as foreigners you will be governed by your own law and not the Turkish law. The above rules will not apply to you. Like UK law, Turkish law permits dual citizenship and, provided you meet certain conditions, you may apply for Turkish citizenship. In case of dual citizenship, Turkish law will regulate your civil status and rights. If in doubt about whether Turkish or UK law applies to matrimonial property, consult a lawyer.

Tax Numbers

To own a property in Turkey you will need to obtain a tax number – a tax identification number valid for Turks and foreigners alike. This is obtained from the local tax department through a relatively simple procedure; the number is issued on production of proof of identity. Alternatively, your lawyer can obtain this for you, using a power of attorney granted for the purpose.

Initial Contracts

In Turkey most sales start with some form of preliminary contract. The type of contract will depend on whether you are buying a finished or an unfinished property. Signing any of these documents has far-reaching legal consequences, which are sometimes different from the consequences of signing a similar document in England. Whichever type of contract you are asked to sign, always seek legal advice before signing.

Generally the preliminary contract is prepared by the estate agent or by the developer in the case of new property, and these contracts are often based on a pre-printed document or word-processed document in a standard format.

Many contracts coming from estate agents are legally muddled and are not properly thought through. They can blur or mix different types of contractual obligation, often referring to mutually exclusive concepts in the same document – for example, referring to it as a contract of sale and an option contract. Sometimes the contracts are extremely one sided, giving their client – the seller – all of the rights and taking away all of the rights of the buyer.

It is very important not to accept these contracts as final. In every case they will need to be modified, sometimes extensively. In fact, in many cases, when acting for the buyer, lawyers end up preparing the preliminary contract and seeking the agreement of the seller. This is because the document submitted by the seller is so defective that it is easier and cheaper to start from scratch.

Contracts on Finished Properties

If you are buying a finished property, you will be invited to sign one of four different documents. Each has different features and different legal consequences. Each is appropriate in certain circumstances and not in others.

Offer to Buy

This is, technically, not a contract at all. It is a formal written offer from the potential buyer to the potential seller. It will state that you wish to buy the stated property for a stated price and that you will complete the transaction within a stated period. The offer will normally be accompanied by the payment of a deposit to the estate agent or seller. The deposit is not fixed but will usually range from 10 per cent to 20 per cent of the price offered.

This document binds you. It is not a mere enquiry as to whether the seller might be interested in selling. If the seller accepts the offer from you in writing, then you both become legally bound to proceed with the transaction.

Generally offers are best avoided. It is a better idea to make a verbal enquiry about whether the seller would accept a certain price and, once the seller says yes, to sign a binding bilateral contract of sale (*satış sözleşmesi*).

Reservation or Option Contract

This is a written document in which the seller offers to take a stated property off the market for a fixed period and to sell it at a stated price to a stated person at any time within a stated period.

The seller will usually require that any person taking up the offer pay a deposit. This is a usually a relatively modest sum such as £2,000 or £3,000. Once the seller has received this deposit, he or she must reserve the property for you until the end of the period specified in the contract, commonly 30 days.

You will see that this is similar to an English 'option contract'. If you want to go ahead and buy the property you can, but you are not obliged to do so. If you do not go ahead, you lose your deposit.

The contract could contain special 'get-out clauses' stipulating the circumstances in which the buyer will be entitled to the refund of the deposit if he or she decides not to go ahead (such as after a bad survey). The drafting of these clauses is of vital importance. See your lawyer.

If you do want to go ahead, you can exercise the option at any point up to the end of the agreed period. If the seller then refuses to go ahead, the buyer is entitled to claim compensation.

Because the sum paid over on signing the reservation contract is modest and the whole purpose of the contract is to secure the property for a period and so to allow your lawyer to carry out the necessary enquiries, most people sign a reservation contract and pay over the money without making any prior enquiries. There is nothing wrong with this, but it is a good idea to have your lawyer look at the contract you are proposing to sign to make sure that it is, indeed, only a reservation contract (and not a full purchase contract) and that it doesn't contain any unfair terms.

Note that the mere fact that it says 'reservation contract' at the top of the document does not mean that it is truly only a reservation contract. The Turkish version of the document may differ, sometimes significantly, from the English version if one is supplied. Generally, the Turkish version is the binding version. For this reason, too, it is worth having the document checked briefly before you sign it.

Preliminary Contract

In most parts of Turkey the preliminary contract is the most common type of document. It is an agreement that commits both parties. The seller must sell a stated property at a stated price to a stated person on the terms set out in the contract. The buyer must buy.

This is the most far-reaching of the three documents and so it is particularly important that you are satisfied that it contains all of the terms necessary to protect your position. Take legal advice.

The contract will contain a variety of 'routine' clauses:

- **The seller and buyer should both be stated fully.**
- **The property should be described fully, both in an everyday sense and by reference to its land registry details (*see* p.126).**
- **A statement will be made as to when possession will take place – normally on the date of signing the title.**
- **The price is fixed.**
- **A receipt for any deposit is given.**

- **The property should be sold with vacant possession.**
- **The property should be sold free of any charges, debts or burdens and all bills should be paid up to date before signing the *tapu*, which transfers the ownership of the property.**
- **The contract will provide for who is to pay the costs of the purchase.**
- **It may confirm the details of any agent involved and who is to pay his commission.**
- **It will set out what is to happen if one or both parties breaks the contract.**
- **It will establish the law to cover the contract and the address of the parties for legal purposes.**
- **If the buyer or seller drops out of the contract or otherwise breaks it, various arrangements may be made.**

A special **deposit** (*depozito*) might be payable by the buyer. The buyer will lose the deposit if he or she fails to complete. If the seller fails to complete, he or she will have to return the deposit paid. Alternatively the contract may provide for a deposit to be paid as a simple part of the price of the property. The contract can provide for all or part of this deposit – and any other sums paid up to the relevant moment – to be lost if the buyer does not proceed.

If the parties fail to comply with their obligations there is the ultimate remedy of seeking a court order. As in any country this is very much a last resort, as it is costly, time-consuming and there is no guarantee of the outcome. If a court order is made in your favour this order can be registered at the land registry and/or enforced by its enforcement offices.

The preliminary contract can be a purely private contract, simply signed by the parties, or it can be a contract signed in front of a notary. Signing in front of a notary increases the cost of the purchase but does give additional protection in that the contract can then be enforced, in most cases, not only as a private right against the individual who signed it but also against the land to which it relates. In other words, signing in front of a notary can give the buyer the possibility of making a direct claim against the land if the seller does not comply with his obligations. This is a slightly complicated topic and one which you should discuss with your lawyer to see whether the additional expenditure is going to be justified in your case.

Even if the contract is to be signed as a purely private document, it is important to obtain proof of the identity of the seller and, if the seller is signing on behalf of a company or person, proof of their authorisation to do so. If the seller is a company, the document you should ask to check is called the signature circular (*imza sirkuleri*), in order to verify the signatory's authority to sign the contract on behalf of the company.

This contract should, if possible, either be in a two-column format (in English and Turkish) or should be supplied with a translation. You should be aware that the translations are not always accurate.

Full Contract

This is the final stage of buying a property in Turkey. Occasionally, there is no other stage! The final contract contains many of the same provisions you would expect to find in the preliminary contract and it will be in Turkish.

The full contract is signed in front of the local land registry officer. The land registry officer may well insist on an official translator being present at the time of the signing if you do not speak adequate Turkish or are not represented by someone holding a power of attorney who does speak Turkish.

Contracts on Unfinished Properties

Reservation Contract

Usually there is a reservation contract (*see* above) on unfinished properties, which allows you to reserve a plot when you see it and gives you time to sign one of the other types of contract when you have made the necessary enquiries.

Preliminary or Full Contract

There are three possible types of full contract on unfinished properties: contracts for the immediate sale of land, contracts 'off-plan', and contracts to buy once the property has been built.

- **Contract for immediate sale of the land.**

The buyer signs a contract agreeing to sign a title deed for the land – and anything the seller has so far built on it – now. This involves paying for the land and work so far undertaken in full at this stage. At the same time, the seller enters into a contract to build your house on the land. As the building continues it automatically becomes the property of the buyer. The buyer has the obligation to pay the agreed price, usually by instalments dependent on the progress of the building work.

This has the great advantage of securing the money you pay to the builder. If the builder goes bust you own the land and everything built on it. However, it only really works for property built on its own plot rather than, say, apartments. It can be tax- and cost-inefficient. The disadvantage is that (unless you bought in the name of a limited company) you would have to wait two to four months for the military permission that is a prerequisite for any foreigner purchasing property in Turkey to be granted (*see* pp.140–41). Until that time, the title deed cannot be transferred into your name.

- **Contract 'off-plan'.**

You agree to buy a property once it has been built and agree to make **payments in stages** as the construction progresses. Sometimes the payments are dependent on the progress of the building works; sometimes they are due on set dates. The latter are now the more common, though less attractive to the buyer. Once the property has been built, you will sign the deed of sale and pay the balance of the price. It is only then that you become the owner of the property and register your title. Until then, if the builder goes bust you are simply one of many creditors.

One potential solution to that risk is for the purchaser to obtain some form of security from the seller. A **bank letter of guarantee**, while being the most suitable from a purchaser's point of view, is usually unsatisfactory for the seller and is almost never available because, under Turkish law, banks are required to collateralise in full the amount of such a guarantee. A seller is unlikely to be able to freeze many of his assets in this way. As a substitute, the seller is most likely to offer a **promissory note** (*senet*) to the buyer by way of security. This is much less favourable from the point of view of the purchaser. The *senet* is only as good as the provider – you will be taking the seller's personal risk. A *senet* only gives a right of court action to recover the amount of the debt from the seller's personal assets should the seller default; it gives no direct rights against the land. A *senet* should only be considered if you know the seller well, trust him or her as a very reliable business person and are sure that he or she has more than ample personal assets to cover the money you are investing.

Turkish law has attempted to give some protection to the purchaser in such a situation by the device of the **deferred sale contract** (*vadeli satış sözleşmesi*). Under this device, the parties sign a contract detailing the specifications of the building to be constructed, the construction timetable and the schedule of payments by the purchaser. This contract is signed in front of the notary public, notarised and inscribed on the land registry entry for the property. This then constitutes notice to third parties of the purchaser's interest in the property. In the event of default by the seller, the purchaser will rank as a preferential creditor with a claim on the property against monies given to the seller.

This is an attractive way of proceeding but, unfortunately, there are differences of opinion about whether such a contract can be registered in the name of a foreigner *before* that foreigner obtains the necessary military permission required to buy property in Turkey. The better view is that it probably cannot be registered. At best, this diminishes the protection offered by such a contract.

Of course, the requirement for foreigners to get military permission can be eliminated by buying the property via a **Turkish limited company** wholly owned and controlled by the foreigner. This is because such a company is not considered to be a foreign entity. There are, however, considerable tax and practical implications to making that decision.

Alternatively, the seller can grant a **mortgage** over the land in favour of the buyer. The mortgage would be for the amount of money paid and it can be registered by the buyer. The buyer would, therefore, enjoy priority over most other people who could make any claim against the land, and the existence of the mortgage would act as a deterrent to the seller fraudulently selling the land to a third party or to that third party buying the land.

The question of security is obviously important. However, many sellers or developers in Turkey will expect you to part with your cash on the strength of their word alone. This is a traditional method but one that should be avoided by foreigners whenever possible. Always ask yourself: what am I getting in return for my money? If the answer is nothing except the promise of a beautiful villa in six months' time, you had best forget it. Remember that big companies and honourable men go bust: Rolls-Royce, Barings Bank, Enron. It is worth discussing the question of what protection you will have when buying the property in some detail with your lawyer. The chances of something going wrong are relatively small but the cost to you if it does can be significant.

- **Contract to buy once the property has been built.**

You agree to buy a plot of land and building and to pay once it has been built. Simple! You take title and pay the money at the same time. This is really the same as buying a resale property. This type of contract is little used. Although such a contract is wonderful for the buyer, who pays nothing during the construction period but enjoys all the capital growth on the property during that period, it is pretty dreadful for the seller, who will receive no cash flow from which to build the property.

Other Documentation

Make sure you have all the other documentation relevant to the purchase of your property, and pay particular attention to the specification. It is not unknown for the show flat to have marble floors and high-quality wooden kitchens but for the specification to show concrete tiles and MDF. You should be given a full specification for the property. Check also:

- **Does the property have planning permission or a building licence?**
- **Is the property built in an area for individual private housing?**
- **What guarantees will be supplied on completion?**

Also ask for a copy of the community rules (*see* pp.146–7) or management plan and the constitution if the property shares common facilities, and a copy of any agreements you have entered into about ongoing management or letting.

Key Points – a Checklist

Here is a checklist of points to check before signing a contract for a property. Note that most points apply whether you are buying a property in the course of construction or an existing property.

All Properties

Are you clear about what you are buying?
Have you taken legal advice about who should be the owner of the property?
Have you taken legal advice about inheritance issues?
Are you clear about boundaries?
Are you clear about access?
Have you seen the seller's title (*tapu*)?

Have you seen an up-to-date land registry extract?
Have you made all necessary checks or arranged for them to be made?
Have you included 'get-out clauses' for all important checks not yet made?
Is your mortgage finance arranged?
Is the seller clearly described?
If the seller is not signing in person, have you seen a power of attorney or mandate to authorise the sale?
Are you fully described?
Is the property fully described? Identification? Land registry details?
Is the price correct?
Are any possible circumstances in which it can be increased or extras described fully?
Is the date for signing the *tapu* agreed?
Does the contract provide for the sale to be free of charges and debts?
Does the contract provide for vacant possession?
Is the estate agent's commission dealt with?
What happens if there is a breach of contract?
Are all the necessary special 'get-out' clauses included?

Existing Properties

Are you sure you can change the property as you want?
Are you sure you can use the property for what you want?
Are you connected to water, electricity, gas, etc.?
Have you had a survey done?
Does the contract say when possession will be given?
Is there a receipt for the deposit paid?
In what capacity is the deposit paid?
Does the property have a habitation licence?

Properties in the Course of Construction

Are the stage payments fully described?
Are arrangements for stage payments satisfactory?
Is the date for completion of the work agreed?
Does the property have planning permission or licence to build?

Steps Between Signing the Contract and Signing the *Tapu*

Obtaining Military Permission

Any foreign individual buying a property in Turkey must have the permission of the military authorities there. Generally, obtaining such permission is not a problem, but there are exceptions to this.

The application for permission is made once you have signed the preliminary contract, and a copy of the contract is attached to it. The application is generally made by the seller (who is applying for permission for his property to be transferred into the name of a foreigner) rather than by the foreigner.

The permission has several components and is not exactly what its name suggests. First, obtaining military permission involves the authorities in Turkey confirming that you are 'a good person'. Problems in your past, such as being arrested for being drunk and disorderly when you were a student 40 years ago, convictions for shoplifting and the like are not likely to pose an obstacle. If, on the other hand, you have convictions for murder, drug-dealing or other serious criminal offences, the position might be more complicated.

The second component relates to the location of the property. Property that is militarily significant will probably not be authorised for transfer into the name of a foreigner. The Turkish concept of what property is militarily significant may seem rather strange. Much property on the coast is considered significant. Sometimes permission will be granted for the sale of a small plot of land but not for the sale of a larger plot. So an application made for, say, 10,000 square metres for development could fail where the application to buy the individual 500 square metre plots carved out of that development land might well succeed. There is a limit to the total land that can be purchased by a foreigner, which is currently 2.5 hectares, with the possibility of extending to 30ha by special permission from the Council of Ministers.

The process of obtaining military permission typically takes about two to four months and may be longer. (It is getting slower as more foreigners buy property in Turkey, which puts greater pressure on the staff who process the applications.)

There are persistent rumours that the need for military permission will be removed, at least for citizens of the European Union. This would be a logical step and in line with the many changes in the law being introduced by Turkey in preparation for its hoped-for acceptance as a member of the Union. Until then, you will need to apply.

Buying through a Turkish Limited Company

The only exception to the need to obtain military permission when buying property in Turkey is if you intend to buy the property through the vehicle of a Turkish limited company. (There is no exception if you are buying through a non-Turkish or offshore company.) No permission is needed for those buying through Turkish companies, as these companies are Turkish and thus not considered to be foreign.

There are a number of different types of Turkish company and various formalities and costs involved in creating and running each type of company. You cannot set up a Turkish limited company alone, as the minimum number of shareholders is two, or five for a joint stock company.

Take advice about the options before deciding whether to use a company and which type to use. *See* pp.115–16.

Powers of Attorney

Very often it will not be convenient for you to have to go to Turkey to sign the *tapu* in person. Sometimes there may be other things that, in the normal course of events, would require your personal intervention but where it would be inconvenient for you to have to deal with them yourself; sometimes you won't know whether you will be available to sign in person. Completion dates on Turkish property are notoriously fluid and so you could plan to be there but suffer a last-minute delay to the signing that makes it impossible.

The solution to this problem is the power of attorney (*vekaletname*). This document authorises the person appointed (the *vekil*) to do whatever the document authorises on behalf of the person granting the power (the *vekalet veren*).

The most sensible type of power to use will be the Turkish style of power that is appropriate to the situation. This will be signed in front of a notary, either in the UK or in Turkey. (If it is signed in front of a UK notary it has to be ratified by the Foreign and Commonwealth Office for use overseas.) This sounds very grand but is actually quick and simple.

The type of Turkish power of attorney that you will need depends on what you want to use it for – discuss your requirements with your specialist English lawyer, who will prepare the necessary document. Alternatively you can deal directly with the Turkish notary who will ultimately need the power.

There are notary firms in the UK with in-house Turkish legal expertise, and their documents are very acceptable and enforceable in Turkey.

Even if you intend to go to Turkey to take delivery of the property and to sign the *tapu*, it is sensible to think about granting a power of attorney 'just in case'. Also, if you have one you can delegate some of the boring and time-consuming tasks to the person who holds the power, so freeing your time to deal with the more interesting or exciting tasks such as buying the furniture or having a celebratory lunch. An additional advantage of appointing somebody under a power of attorney is that, if they accompany you at the signing of the title, the land registry officer will not require an official translator to be present if you do not speak Turkish. This will save you some money.

Granting a power of attorney is not something that can be done at the last moment. From making the decision to getting the document to Turkey will take at least 10 and more likely 14 days. If you are able to go, the power will not be used.

Even if you have granted a power of attorney, if you get the opportunity to go to Turkey at the time of the signing it is worth doing so. It is quite interesting but, more importantly, you will be able to check the house to make sure that everything is in order before the *tapu* is signed.

Getting the Money to Turkey

There are a number of ways of getting money to Turkey.

Electronic Transfer

The most practical is to have it sent electronically by Swift transfer from a UK bank directly to the recipient's bank in Turkey. This costs about £20–35 depending on your bank. It is safer to allow two or three days for the money to arrive in a rural bank, despite everyone's protestations that it will be there the same day. You can send the money from your own bank, via your lawyers or via a specialist currency dealer.

In February 2004 banks worldwide introduced **unique account numbers** for all bank accounts. These incorporate a code for the identity of the bank and branch involved as well as the account number of the individual customer, and are known as Iban numbers. They should be quoted, if possible, on all international currency transfers. Doing so seems both to speed the transfer process and reduce its cost.

For the sums you are likely to be sending you should receive an **exchange rate** that is much better than the 'tourist rate' you see in the press. There is no such thing as a fixed exchange rate in these transactions. The bank's official inter-bank rate changes by the second and the job of the bank's currency dealers is to make a profit by selling to you at the lowest rate they can get away with! Thus if you do a lot of business with a bank and they know you are 'on the ball' you are likely to be offered a better rate than a one-off customer. For this reason it is often better to send the money via your specialist UK lawyers, who will be dealing with large numbers of such transactions. This also has the advantage that your lawyer's bank, which deals with international payments all the time, is less likely to make a mistake causing delay to the payment than your bank, for which such a payment might be a rarity.

You or your lawyers might use a **specialist currency dealer** to make the transfer of funds instead of a main UK bank. Such dealers often give a better exchange rate than an ordinary bank. Sometimes the difference can be significant, especially compared with your local branch of a high street bank.

Although these dealers use major banks actually to transfer the funds, make sure that the dealer is reputable. Your money is paid to them, not to the major bank, so could be at risk if the dealer is not bonded or otherwise protected.

However you make the payment, make sure you understand whether you or the recipient is going to pick up the receiving bank's charges. If you need a clear amount in Turkey you will have to make allowances for it, either by sending a bit extra or by asking your UK bank to pay all the charges. Make sure you have got the details of the recipient bank, its customer's name, the account codes and the recipient's reference precisely right. Any error and the payment is likely to come back to you as undeliverable – and may involve you in bearing the cost of it being converted back into pounds sterling.

The bank in Turkey will make a charge – which can be substantial – for receiving your money into your account. See also 'Saving Money on Your Euro or Turkish New Lira Repayments', pp.111–12.

Banker's Drafts

You can arrange for your UK bank to issue you with a banker's draft (bank certified cheque), which you can take to Turkey and pay into your bank account. Make sure that the bank knows that the draft is to be used overseas and issues you with an international draft.

Generally this is not a good way to transfer the money. It can take a considerable time – sometimes weeks – for the funds deposited in Turkey to be made available for your use. The recipient bank's charges can be surprisingly high. The exchange rate offered against a pound sterling draft may also be uncompetitive as you are a captive customer.

Cash

This is not recommended. You will need to declare the money on departure from the UK – by law you must do this if the sum involved is over €8,000 and you are well advised to do so for smaller amounts. Even then, if you declare £200,000 or so, customs staff will think you are a terrorist or drugs dealer! That suspicion can have far-reaching consequences in terms of listings in police files, and even lead to surveillance. To add insult to injury the exchange rate you will be offered for cash (whether you take pounds sterling and convert in Turkey or buy the foreign currency in the UK) is usually very uncompetitive.

Don't do it.

Exchange Control and Other Restrictions on Moving Money

For EU nationals there is no longer any exchange control when taking money to or from Turkey. Some statistical records are kept showing the flow of funds and the purpose of the transfers. When you sell your property in Turkey you will be able to bring the money back to England if you wish to do so.

Final Checks about the Property

All of the points outstanding must be resolved to your satisfaction, as must any other points of importance to you.

Fixing the Completion Date

The date stated in the contract for signing the *tapu* could, most charitably, be described as flexible or aspirational. Often it will move, if only by a day or so. Sometimes it will move by weeks or months. For this reason it is not sensible to book your travel to Turkey until you are almost sure that matters will proceed on a certain day.

Equally, don't agree to let out your property until well after the suggested completion date and *never* plan to move from the UK to Turkey on the basis that your furniture will arrive on the day scheduled for completion.

Steps before Completion – a Checklist

Here is a checklist of points to follow before signing a *tapu*. Most apply whether you are buying a property in the course of construction or an existing property.

All Properties

Prepare power of attorney
Check what documents must be produced on signing the *tapu*
Confirm all outstanding issues have been complied with
Confirm all other important enquiries are clear
Confirm arrangements (date, time, place) for completion with your lender if you have a mortgage
Confirm arrangements (date, time, place) for completion with land registrar
Confirm arrangements (date, time, place) for completion with seller
Send necessary funds to Turkey
Receive rules of community or management plan
Any necessary final searches?
Insurance cover arranged?

Existing Properties

Proof of payment of community fees
Proof of payment of other bills

Properties in the Course of Construction

Sign off work or list defects

The Cost of Buying a Property in Turkey

There are various taxes and other charges payable when you buy property in Turkey; make sure you have budgeted for them all.

- **Property transfer tax**: charged on properties bought from private individuals at a rate of 3 per cent, usually split equally between the buyer and the seller, each party paying 1.5 per cent.
- **Value added tax** (*KDV* or *katma değer vergisi*): does not apply to property transactions.
- **Stamp duty** (*pul vergisi*): not payable for most purchases in Turkey; when payable it is 0.75 per cent of the value of the property.
- **Land registration fees**: not likely to exceed £100 for an ordinary property.
- **Estate agent's charges** (if payable by the buyer): if an estate agent has sold the property the seller and purchaser usually split the fees equally; this can be varied by agreement.
- **Miscellaneous other charges**: architect's fees, surveyor's fees, Turkish legal fees, UK legal fees (typically 1 per cent), connection to water, electricity, etc;

most, except the English lawyer's fees, are subject to Turkish KDV at 18 per cent; English lawyer's fees are usually outside the scope of English VAT.

Ongoing Expenses

There will, inevitably, be other expenses involved with owning property, including routine repairs, maintenance and so on. As a very general guide the basic annual cost of owning a holiday home in Turkey is about 2 per cent of the value of the property for self-contained properties and about 3 per cent of the value of properties in a community sharing common facilities. This basic cost includes routine repairs and maintenance, insurance, local taxes, standing charges for water and electricity. It does not include major repairs or renovations, consumables such as electricity and water or your personal taxation on income derived from the property.

Expenses will be higher if an individual property has its own pool or if a communal property has extensive facilities (*see* below).

The Community of Owners or Management Plan

The community of owners (*site*) or management plan (*yönetim planı*) is a device familiar in continental Europe but most unusual in England. The basic idea is than when a number of people own land or buildings in such a way that they have exclusive use of part of the property but shared use of the rest then a *site* is created. Houses on their own plots with no shared facilities will not be a member of a *site*.

In a *site* the buyer of a house or an apartment owns his own house or apartment outright – and shares the use of the remaining areas as part of a community of owners. The closest English term is 'commonhold', which has become more common in the UK after the Leasehold Reform Act. It is not only the shared pool that is jointly owned but (in an apartment) the lift shafts, corridors, roof, foundations, entrance areas, parking zones and so on. The members of the *site* are each responsible for their own home. They agree collectively on the works needed in common areas and a budget for those works. They then become responsible for paying their share of those common expenses, as stipulated in their title.

The community is managed by an elected committee with appointed officials who are residents in the community. Day-to-day management is usually delegated to an administrator, who need not be a resident in the community.

The charges of the *site* are divided in the proportions stipulated in the document creating the *site*. You pay the same *site* fees whether you use the place all year round or only for two weeks' holiday. Charges are usually billed monthly or quarterly. Of course, your personal bills (water, electricity and so on) will vary with usage.

The *site* should provide not only for routine work but, through its fees, set aside money for periodic major repairs. If it does not – or if the amount set aside is inadequate – the general meeting can authorise a supplemental levy to raise the sums needed.

The rules set by the *site* are intended to improve the quality of life of residents. They could, for example deal with concerns over noise (no radios by the pool), prohibit the use of the pool after 10pm or ban the hanging of washing on balconies. More importantly they could ban pets or any commercial activity in the building. These *sözleşme kuralları* (conditions of contract) are an important document. Every buyer of a property in a *site* should insist on a copy of the rules. If you do not speak Turkish, have them translated or, at least, summarised in English.

Key Points to Check for Different Types of Property

Key Points: Property Under Construction

There are several issues that arise in the case of new properties. The first is the risk that if the developer goes bust before delivering the property to you, you can lose your money. In some countries there is a system of bank guarantees to guard against this, but these do not generally exist in Turkey.

If the developer is substantial and/or the house is far advanced in construction, the risk is minor but not non-existent. If the developer is small and/or the house has not yet been started the risk is, obviously, much more substantial. When buying a new property:

- **Make sure you understand exactly what you are buying. How big is the property? What will it look like? How will it be finished? What appliances are included? What facilities will it enjoy?**
- **Think about who should own the property so as to minimise tax and inheritance problems.**
- **Don't assume that the title and planning permission will be in order.**
- **Make sure the contract has all the necessary clauses required to protect your position.**
- **Will there be any form of guarantee if you are buying 'off-plan'?**
- **Be clear about the timetable for making payments.**
- **Think about whether to forward-buy currency.**

When you take delivery of the property, consider carefully whether it is worth incurring the expense of an independent survey to confirm that all is in order with the construction and to help draft any 'snagging list'.

Key Points: Resale Properties

When buying a resale property:

- **Make sure you understand exactly what you are buying. Are the boundaries clear? What furniture or fittings are included?**
- **Think about whether to have the property surveyed, especially if it is nearly 10 years old and your statutory guarantee will soon be expiring.**
- **Think about who should own the property so as to minimise tax and inheritance problems.**
- **Make sure the contract has all of the necessary clauses required to protect your position.**
- **Think about whether to forward-buy currency.**
- **When you take delivery of the property, make sure that everything agreed is present.**

Special Points: Old Properties

When buying an old property – built more than, say, 50 years ago:

- **Are you having a survey? Not to do so can be an expensive mistake.**
- **Are you clear about any restoration costs to be incurred? Do you have estimates for those charges?**
- **Are there any planning problems associated with any alterations or improvements you want to make to the property?**
- **When you take delivery of the property, make sure that everything agreed is present.**

Special Points: Rural Properties

Rural properties have often acquired a number of rights and obligations over the years. If you are buying one:

- **If you have any plans to change the property or to use it for other purposes, will this be permitted?**
- **Are you clear about any obligations you might be taking on?**
- **You are probably buying for peace, quiet and the rural idyll. Are you sure that nothing is happening in the vicinity of your property that will be detrimental?**
- **If you intend to build on the site, be very clear about minimum permitted plot sizes – which can vary by up to 25,000 square metres – and other planning limitations. For example, foreigners are only allowed to own up to 2.5 hectares of land. Amounts in excess of this, up to a maximum of 30 hectares, require government approval and are only granted in exceptional circumstances.**

Special Points: City Properties

If you are buying a city property:

- **Unless you are used to living in a city – and, in particular, a continental city – do not underestimate the noise that will be generated nearby. If you are in a busy area (and you are likely to be) this will go on until late at night. How good is the sound insulation?**
- **Are you above a bar?**
- **Are your neighbouring properties occupied by full-time residents, are they weekday only '*pied à terres*' or are they holiday homes? Think about security issues.**
- **If you intend to use a car, where will you park?**

City properties are usually apartments (*see* below).

Special Points: Apartments and Houses Sharing Facilities

If you are buying an apartment or intend to share a house:

- **Have you thought about a survey of the property? Will it include the common parts? This can be expensive.**
- **Make sure you understand the rules of the community – *see* below.**
- **Make sure you understand the charges that will be raised by the community.**
- **Make contact with its administrator. Ask about any issues affecting the community. Are there any major works approved but not yet carried out? Make sure that the contract is clear about who is responsible for paying for these.**
- **Make contact with owners. Are they happy with the community and the way it is run? Remember that no one is ever fully happy!**
- **Understand how the community is run. Once you are an owner, try to attend the general meetings of the community.**

Immediately After the Purchase

Don't forget to:

- **Insure the property and its contents.**
- **Make a full photographic record of the property. This is useful in the event of an insurance claim and for your scrapbook.**
- **Make arrangements for your bank to pay your local property tax (*emlak vergisi*), local environmental tax (*çevre vergisi*) and utilities bills.**

- **Make a will covering your assets in Turkey. There are a number of ways of doing this. Discuss them with your lawyer as, depending on your personal circumstances, some will be much better for you than others. For most people the most important factors will be to ensure that English (rather than Turkish) law determines what happens to their property on their death and to minimise inheritance and other taxes in Turkey and in the UK.** ***See*** **pp.113–18, and Settling In, 'Death and Making a Will', pp.187–8.**
- **Appoint a fiscal or tax representative as your point of contact with the Turkish tax office. He will also usually complete and file your annual tax return. Your lawyer may provide this service or should be able to suggest a suitable person.**

Coming Back to the UK

You are, of course, free to return to the UK at any stage. Few people do.

Many people wonder whether they should preserve an escape route by, for example, keeping their old house and renting it out until they are sure of their intentions. This is unlikely to be a good idea. The house will be a worry and a distraction. How do you manage it? Are the tenants ruining your lovely home? The house will, in any case, probably not be ideal for investment purposes and may generate less than you could get by putting the value in an investment elsewhere. It may not be in an area with good capital growth. The income (and capital value in local terms) will be at the mercy of exchange rate fluctuations. The house might not even suit your requirements if you do return to England. It also encourages you to look backwards instead of forwards. You are usually better selling up and investing the proceeds elsewhere.

Financial Implications

06

Introduction to Tax Affairs

All tax systems are complicated and the Turkish system is no exception. Fortunately, most people will only have limited contact with the more intricate parts of it. Many owners of holiday homes in Turkey only have minimal contact with the system.

It is helpful to have some sort of understanding about the way in which the system works and the taxes that you might face. Be warned: getting even a basic understanding will make your head hurt. You also need to be particularly careful about words and concepts that seem familiar to you but which have a fundamentally different meaning in Turkey than they do in England. Just to confuse you, the rules change every year.

Books (and long ones at that) have been written about Turkish taxation. It is beyond the scope of this guide to give more than a general introduction; we do little more than scratch the surface of an immensely complex subject. We aim to give you enough information to have a sensible discussion with your professional advisers and, perhaps, to help you work out the questions to ask them. **It is not intended as a substitute for proper professional advice.**

Your situation when you have a foot in two countries – and, in particular, when you are moving permanently from one country to another – involves the consideration of the tax systems in both countries with a view to minimising your tax obligations in both. It is not just a question of paying the lowest amount of tax in, say, Turkey. The best choice in Turkey could be very damaging to your position in England. Similarly, the most tax-efficient way of dealing with your affairs in England could be problematic in Turkey. The task of international advisers and their clients is to find a path of compromise that allows clients to enjoy the major advantages available in both countries without incurring any of the worst drawbacks. There is no perfect solution to most tax questions. That is not to say that there are not a great many bad solutions into which you can all too easily stumble.

What should guide you when making a decision about which course to pursue? Each individual will have a different set of priorities. Some are keen to screw the last ha'penny of advantage out of their situation. Others recognise that they will have to pay some tax but simply wish to moderate their tax bill. For many, the main concern is a simple structure that they understand and can continue to manage without further assistance in the years ahead. Just as different clients have different requirements, so different advisers have differing views about the function of the adviser when dealing with a client's tax affairs. One of your first tasks when speaking to your financial adviser should be to discuss your basic philosophy about the payment of tax and management of your affairs, to make sure that you are both operating with the same objective in mind and that you are comfortable with your adviser's approach to solving your problem.

Are You Resident or Non-resident for Tax Purposes?

The biggest single factor in determining how you will be treated by the tax authorities in any country is whether you are resident in that country for tax purposes. This concept of tax residence causes a great deal of confusion and can have different meanings in different countries.

Let us first look at what it does *not* mean. It is nothing to do with whether you have registered as a resident in a country or whether you have obtained a residence permit or residence card (though a person who has a card will often be tax resident). Nor does it have anything to do with whether you have a home (residence) in that country – although a person who is tax resident will normally have a home there. Nor is it much to do with your intentions.

Tax residence is a question of *fact*. The law lays down certain tests that will be used to decide whether you are tax resident or not. If you fall into the categories stipulated in the tests, then you will be considered tax resident whether you want to be or not, and whether it was your intention to be tax resident or not.

It is your responsibility to make your tax declarations each year. The decision as to whether you fall into the category of resident is, in the first instance, made by the tax office. If you disagree, you can appeal through the courts.

Because people normally change their tax residence when they move from one country to another, the basis on which decisions are made tends to be regulated by international law and to be reasonably, but not totally, consistent from country to country.

You will have to consider two different questions concerning tax residence:

- **whether you will be treated as tax resident in England.**
- **whether you will be treated as tax resident in Turkey.**

Tax Residence in the UK

There are some basic points of UK taxation law that you should understand in order for an explanation of Turkish taxation to make any sense.

In the UK there are two tests that will help determine where you pay tax. They assess your domicile and your residence.

Domicile

Your domicile is the place that is your real home, the place where you have your roots. For most people it is the place where they were born. You can change your domicile but it is often not easy to do so. Changes in domicile can have far-reaching tax consequences and can be a useful tax reduction tool.

Residence

Residence falls into two categories. There is a test of simple residence – actually living here rather than staying temporarily – and of ordinary residence.

People are generally treated as **resident** in the UK if they spend 183 or more days a year in the UK. Visitors are also treated as resident if they come to the UK regularly and spend significant time here. If they spend, on average over a period of four or more years, more than three months here per year they will be treated as tax resident. People can continue to be **ordinarily resident** in the UK even after they have stopped actually being resident here. A person is ordinarily resident in the UK if their presence is a little more settled. The residence is an important part of their life. It will normally have gone on for some time.

From our point of view, the most important thing to understand is that, once you have been ordinarily resident in this country, the simple fact of going overseas will not automatically bring that residence to an end. If you leave this country in order to take up permanent residence elsewhere then, by concession, the Inland Revenue will treat you as ceasing to be resident on the day following your departure; but it will not treat you as ceasing to be ordinarily resident if, after leaving, you spend an average of 91 or more days a year in this country over any four-year period. In other words, it doesn't want you to escape too easily!

Until 1993 you were also classified as ordinarily resident in the UK if you had accommodation available for your use in the UK even though you may have spent 364 days of the year living abroad. This very unfair rule was cancelled, but many people still worry about it. It is not necessary to do so provided you limit your visits to the UK to fewer than the 91 days referred to above.

Tax Residence in Turkey

Tax residence in Turkey is determined largely by one rule – if you spend more than six months a year in Turkey, you are regarded as being resident there for tax purposes.

Tax Residence in More than One Country

Remember that you can be tax resident in more than one country under the respective rules of those countries. For example, you might spend 230 days in the year in Turkey and 135 days in England. In this case you could end up, under the rules of each country, being responsible for paying the same tax in two or more countries. This would be unfair, so many countries have signed reciprocal **double taxation treaties**, and the UK and Turkey have such a treaty. It contains 'tie breakers' and other provisions to decide, where there is the possibility of being required to pay tax twice, in which country any particular category of tax should be paid. *See* p.163.

Decisions to Make about Residency

The most basic decisions that you will have to make when planning your tax affairs are:

- **whether to cease to be resident in the UK.**
- **whether to cease to be ordinarily resident in the UK.**
- **whether to change your domicile to another country.**

Each of these decisions has many consequences, many of which are not obvious. You must also decide when in the tax year to make these changes. Once again, that decision has many consequences.

For many ordinary people getting these decisions wrong can lead to unnecessary extra taxation and a great deal of aggravation and inconvenience. It is vital that you seek proper professional advice from specialist lawyers, accountants or financial advisers, all of whom should be able to help you.

See also **About Turkey**, 'Turkish Law', pp.14–30.

Taxes Payable in the UK

The significance of these residence rules is that you will continue to be liable for some British taxes for as long as you are either ordinarily resident or domiciled in the UK. Put far too simply, once you have left the UK to live in Turkey:

- **You will continue to have to pay tax in the UK on any capital gains you make anywhere in the world for as long as you are ordinarily resident and domiciled in the UK.**
- **You will continue to be liable for UK inheritance tax on all of your assets located anywhere in the world for as long as you remain domiciled in the UK. This will be subject to double taxation relief (*see* 'The Double Taxation Treaty between Turkey and the UK', p.163). Other, more complex rules apply in certain circumstances.**
- **You will always pay UK income tax (Schedule A) on income arising from land and buildings in the UK, wherever your domicile, residence or ordinary residence.**
- **You will pay UK income tax (Schedule D) as follows:**
  - **income from 'self-employed' work carried out in the UK (Cases I and II) – normally taxed in the UK in all cases if income arises there.**
  - **income from interest, annuities or other annual payments from the UK (Case III) – normally taxed in the UK if income arises there and you are ordinarily resident in the UK.**
  - **income from investments and businesses outside the UK (Cases IV and V) – normally only taxed in the UK if you are UK-domiciled and -resident or ordinarily resident in the UK.**
  - **income from government pensions (fire, police, army, civil servant, etc.) – taxed in the UK in all cases.**

- **sundry profits not otherwise taxable (Case VI) arising out of land or building in the UK – always taxed in the UK.**

- **You will pay income tax on any income earned from salaried employment in the UK (Schedule E) only in respect of earnings from duties performed in the UK unless you are resident and ordinarily resident in the UK – in which case you will usually pay tax in the UK on your worldwide earnings.**

If you are only buying a holiday home and will remain primarily resident in the UK, your tax position in the UK will not change very much. You will have to declare any income you make from your Turkish property as part of your UK tax declaration. The calculation of tax due on that income will be made in accordance with UK rules, which will result in a different taxable sum than is used by the Turkish authorities. The UK Revenue and Customs will give you full credit for the taxes already paid in Turkey.

On the disposal of the property, you must disclose the profit made to the Revenue and Customs, which again will give full credit for Turkish tax paid. Similarly, on your death the assets in Turkey must be disclosed on the UK probate tax declaration but, once again, you will be given full credit for sums paid in Turkey.

Taxes Payable in Turkey

Introduction

A lot of people who live in Turkey and who are legally obliged to pay tax there simply do not do so. A lot of people who do not live in Turkey but who are obliged to pay tax to the Turkish government because they have, for example, let out their home in Turkey also do not pay tax to the government in Turkey. If they do not pay taxes in Turkey, they usually also fail to pay the taxes they owe in Britain or wherever else they live.

They do not think of this as being wrong (although it is illegal). It is just that there has, in the past, been a culture of not paying taxes. This is particularly true of people working for themselves or who receive income from property rental.

So the first decision you will have to make, when dealing with Turkey, is to decide whether you are going to abide by the law or whether you are going to follow the old-fashioned local 'customs'.

The author believes that the time has come when it will be necessary to comply with your obligations. The changes that came about in Spain, Portugal and Italy after their accession to the European Union will inevitably occur in Turkey, and this will dramatically reduce the scope and possibility of tax evasion. It will also – over time – change people's attitudes so that evading tax liabilities will be much less acceptable than it is now – and more heavily punished.

Tax Numbers

To own a property in Turkey you will need to obtain a tax number – a tax identification number valid for Turks and foreigners alike. This is obtained from the local tax department through a relatively simple procedure; the number is issued on production of proof of identity. Alternatively, your lawyer can obtain this for you, using a power of attorney granted for the purpose.

That does not mean that if you don't make a full tax declaration you will be in immediate danger of detection or punishment by the Turkish authorities – that is likely to be a year or two away. But if you have not laid the foundations of payment of tax then the time is likely to come when someone will ask you questions. If it is not the Turkish authorities it could well be the English authorities. This is because one of the features of recent international relationships is the extensive exchange of information between countries, using the threat of terrorism, drugs and money-laundering to justify the unprecedented disclosure of confidential information between governments.

Most people will sleep easier in their beds if they pay their taxes that are due. That does not mean that you have to pay a lot of money. Under the Turkish tax system there are so many opportunities for successful tax planning and the significant reduction of the taxes that would otherwise be payable that you can stay well on the right side of the law and still have a minimal tax bill.

It comes down to the choice between two different types of tax reduction. Some 'tax planning' is what we call 'hide and seek' tax planning. You try to hide the money and let the government try to find it. This will, inevitably, sometimes work. Sometimes it will fail. If it does fail you will face substantial penalties including, potentially, jail sentences for tax evasion. The second type of tax planning is what we call 'kiss and tell'. Kiss-and-tell tax planning is when you make your arrangements to reduce your tax liabilities and then tell the tax office about them on the basis that they are perfectly lawful. If they want to challenge them they can do so but they cannot suggest that you have tried to hide the truth from them. This is also called 'tax avoidance'.

If you prefer the second option, get advice before you become involved in owning property in Turkey, working in Turkey or doing business in Turkey – there are many more tax reduction opportunities available if they are implemented correctly at the outset. They will include the choice of different legal vehicles for your project and different financial structures. If, for example, you buy the property through a Turkish limited company you will have the opportunity to offset the running costs against the profit from, say, letting. However, there are many other aspects you should consider before buying the property through a Turkish limited company. Take advice.

Under Turkish law it is your responsibility to fill in a tax return for each year where you have any taxable income. The tax office (*vergi dairesi*) provides a lot of help and advice – including tax forms and guidance notes – over the Internet. It is almost all in Turkish. Tax offices are organised by municipality.

Local Taxes

Both residents and non-residents pay these taxes. The taxes payable fall into various categories.

Property Tax

Property tax (*emlak vergisi*) is paid if you own a residential property and use it yourself (or have it available for your use). It is paid by the person who owned or occupied the property on 1 January in any year. It is not usually apportioned if they later move. The tax is raised and spent by the town hall (*belediye*) of the area where you live.

The tax is calculated on the basis of the notional value (*nominal değer*) of your property. You can appeal against the valuation decision, but the sums involved are usually so small it is not worthwhile. The amount charged is the nominal value of the property multiplied by the tax rate fixed in your locality.

Environment Tax

Environment tax (*çevre vergisi*) is the tax imposed by each municipality for collecting your rubbish.

Other Local Taxes

Town halls can also raise taxes for other projects and to cover shortfalls.

Payment of Local Taxes

No demand for payment of local taxes is sent in Turkey. It is the taxpayer's responsibility to learn the amount and the latest payment date due for them. This information is available from the local elected city official (*muhtar*) for each ward found in every locality or ward of a city.

The combined total of these taxes is low, representing between 0.1 per cent and 0.3 per cent of the declared value of the property – perhaps £50 for a small cottage or £200 for a larger house.

Other Taxes Payable in Turkey by Non-residents

In general, a person who is non-resident for tax purposes has few contacts with the Turkish tax system and they are fairly painless.

Income Tax

As stressed above, the Turkish tax system is complex: this is only a brief summary of the position.

Non-residents generally only pay income tax (*gelir vergisi*) on:

- **income generated from land and buildings located in Turkey; if you own a building in Turkey and let it out, the Turkish government collects the first wedge of tax from you.**
- **income from Turkish securities and capital invested in Turkey; there are certain exemptions and the rules change frequently.**
- **income from business activities in Turkey.**
- **earned income if you are employed or self-employed in Turkey.**

Income tax is calculated on these amounts at various band rates going from 15 per cent to 37 per cent. If you are letting out your property you will usually have to pay tax on every penny earned, without deductions or allowances. However where you let a property out for accommodation purposes, for the year 2007 the first YTL2,300 of rental income is exempt from tax. For some people it can therefore be more sensible to set the rental up as a business and claim the normal business reliefs and allowances.

Tax on your income for the year 1 January 2007 to 31 December 2007 is declared and paid in 2008.

Taxes on employment are, generally, deducted at source by your employer.

Corporation Tax

A foreign company will pay tax on the profits it makes from activities in Turkey but not its activities elsewhere. The tests of company residence and these taxes are not considered further here.

Wealth Tax

There is no Turkish wealth tax (*varlık vergisi*) on your assets in Turkey.

Capital Gains Tax

You will pay tax on any capital gain you make on the sale of real estate in Turkey. However, if the gain is a result of the sale of a residential property that was purchased more than five years previously, the gain will not be taxed. If the property was residential and purchased within the previous five years then the gain will be taxed, not under capital gains tax but as income tax under the rates prescribed. Currently, capital gains tax is around 20 per cent.

Inheritance Tax

Inheritance tax is paid in Turkey on the value of any assets in Turkey as at the date of your death. The tax is an inheritance tax rather than, as in the UK, an estate tax. That is, the tax is calculated by reference to each individual's inheritance rather than on the basis of the estate as a whole. Thus two people each inheriting part of the estate will each pay their own tax; even if they each inherit the same share, the amount of tax they pay may be different, depending on their personal circumstances.

All of the assets will have to be declared for the purposes of UK taxation. Again, double taxation relief will apply so you will not pay the same tax twice. UK tax is not further considered in this book.

The overall value of the part of the estate you inherit is calculated in accordance with guidelines laid down by the tax authorities. Any debts, including a mortgage or overdraft, are deducted from the asset's value, as are medical bills and funeral costs. Real estate, for example, is valued at fair market value and an exemption is allowed for the first part of the inheritance. There are discounts for inheritance by sons, daughters and spouses. In the case of a spouse and children (including legal adoptees) inheriting the property, YTL89,623 is deducted from the tax base of each person. If the spouse is the only heir, the deduction from the tax base is YTL179,352. In case of successions without reciprocity (gifts), the amount of deduction is YTL 2,068 from 1 January 2007.

Inheritance tax base brackets in 2007 are as shown in the table below (exchange rate at time of printing: £1 = YTL2.48; YTL1 = £0.40).

Inheritance Tax Rates in 2007

Tax base bracket (based on value of inherited asset)	Inheritance tax rate (%)	Succession tax rate (%) (where no reciprocity exists)
First YTL140,000	1	10
Next YTL300,000	3	15
Next YTL640,000	5	20
Next YTL129,000	7	25
Amount above YTL2,370,000	10	30

Other Taxes Payable in Turkey by Residents

Income Tax

Again this is a brief summary of the very complicated laws relating to Turkish income tax (*gelir vergisi*). The detail is immensely complicated and made worse because it is so different from the UK system.

Taxes are paid to the national government. Turkish tax returns are filed in the February and March following the year to which they relate.

If your total income is subject to any of the permitted exemptions, you need not file a tax return unless you are running a business or self-employed.

Types of Income Tax

As a tax resident you will generally pay tax in Turkey on your worldwide income. Remember that taken overall, not just in relation to income tax, Turkey is a high tax society, although the levels of tax collection remain low by EU standards. Whether for this reason or out of an independence of spirit, many people (probably 30 per cent of Turkish people and just as many foreign residents) significantly under-declare their income. As mentioned above, this is dangerous. The penalties are severe. There are, however, quite legitimate tax-saving devices that you can use to reduce your liabilities. These issues are best addressed before you move to Turkey as there are then many more possibilities open to you.

The amount of an employee's share of the monthly social security premium plus a fixed monthly special allowance are exempt from income tax.

Tax Credits and Deductions

Currently, employees are eligible to claim a tax credit against the following year's tax liability on their salaried earnings. This tax credit relates to tax paid in the current tax year for one-third of documented rent, food, clothing, and health and education expenses in Turkey. The amount of this tax credit cannot exceed 35 per cent of the income tax base for the year.

Private insurance premiums are deductible against the tax base for the year.

Tax Rates

Until recently, income tax payable was different for employment income and for non-employment income, and there were two elements to the tax that was payable. However, from 1 January 2006, a single tariff for employment and other individual income was adopted.

Tax is not just calculated according to what rate band your income is in, but income in a certain band is subject to a percentage tax plus a fixed-figure tax. Thus employment income of YTL7,500–YTL19,000 is not only taxed at 20 per cent but is also liable to a fixed-figure tax of YTL1,125.

Examples of the tax rates and fixed-rate taxes for income tax payable in 2007 are shown in the two tables below.

Income Tax Rates in 2007

Employment Income	Rate (%)
YTL0–7,500	15
YTL7,500–19,000	20
YTL19,000–43,000	27
More than YTL43,001	37

Fixed Figure Tax in 2007

Employment Income	Tax
YTL0–7,500	–
YTL7,501–19,000	YTL1,125
YTL19,001–43,000	YTL3,425 plus the previous slice
More than YTL43,001	YTL9,905 plus the previous slice

Capital Gains Tax

Capital gains are generally only taxed when the gain is crystallised, such as on the sale of the asset. You will pay tax on the capital gain you make on the sale of real estate in Turkey. However, if the gain is a result of the sale of a residential property that was purchased more than five years previously, the gain will not be taxed. If the property was residential and was purchased within the previous five years then the gain will be taxed, not under capital gains tax but as income tax under the rates prescribed. Currently, capital gains tax is around 20 per cent.

Inheritance Tax and Gift Tax

Property acquired as a gift or through inheritance is subject to taxes of between 1 and 30 per cent of the valuation. Tax paid in another country on inherited property is deducted from the taxable value of the asset. Inheritance tax is payable over a period of three years, in two instalments per year.

The taxes are similar to the taxes paid by non-residents (*see* pp.159–60).

VAT

VAT is a major generator of tax for the Turkish. Detailed consideration of VAT is beyond the scope of this book.

Other Taxes

There is a miscellany of other taxes and levies on various aspects of life in Turkey. Some are national and others local. Individually they are usually not a great burden. They are beyond the scope of this book.

Taxes Payable by New Residents

New residents are liable to tax on their worldwide income and gains from the date they arrive in Turkey. Until that day they will only have to pay Turkish tax on their income if it is derived from assets in Turkey. The most important thing to understand about taking up residence in Turkey (and abandoning UK tax residence) is that it gives you superb opportunities for tax planning and, in particular, for restructuring your affairs. To do this you need good advice at an early stage – preferably several months before you intend to move.

The Double Taxation Treaty between Turkey and the UK

The detailed effect of double taxation treaties depends on the two countries involved – though they may be similar in concept, they differ in detail. This section covers only the double taxation treaty between Turkey and the UK.

The main points of relevance to residents are as follows:

- **Any income from letting property in the UK will normally be outside the scope of Turkish taxation and instead be taxed in the UK.**
- **Pensions received from the UK – except for government pensions – will be taxed in Turkey but not in the UK.**
- **Government pensions will continue to be taxed in the UK but are not taxed in Turkey, nor do they count when assessing the level of your income when calculating the rate of tax payable on your income.**
- **You will normally not be required to pay UK capital gains tax on gains made after you settle in Turkey except in relation to real estate located in the UK.**
- **If you are taxed on a gift made outside Turkey then the tax paid will usually be offset against the gift tax due in Turkey.**
- **If you pay tax on an inheritance outside Turkey, the same will apply.**

Double taxation treaties are detailed and need to be read in the light of your personal circumstances.

Tax Planning Generally

Do it, and do it as soon as possible. Every day you delay will make it more difficult to get the results you are looking for. There are many possibilities for tax planning for someone moving to Turkey.

Some points worth considering are:

- **Time your departure from the UK to get the best out of the UK tax system.**
- **Think, in particular, about when to make any capital gain if you are selling your business or other assets in the UK.**
- **Arrange your affairs so that there is a gap between leaving the UK (for tax purposes) and becoming resident in Turkey. That gap can be used to make all sorts of beneficial changes to the structure of your finances.**
- **Think about giving away some of your assets. You won't have to pay UK wealth tax on the value given away and the recipients will generally not have to pay either gift or inheritance tax on the gift if the amount is below the correct limits.**

Investments

The Need to Do Something

Most of us don't like making investment decisions. They make our heads hurt. They make us face up to unpleasant things – like taxes and death. We don't really understand what we are doing, what the options are or what is best. We don't know who we should trust to give us advice. We know we ought to do something, but it will wait until next week – or maybe the week after. Until then our present arrangements will have to do. But if you are moving to live overseas you *must* review your investments. Your current arrangements are likely to be financially disastrous – and may even be illegal.

What Are You Worth?

Most of us are, in financial terms, worth more than we think. When we come to move abroad and have to think about these things it can come as a shock.

Take a pencil and list your actual and potential assets in the table opposite.

This will give you an idea of the amount you are worth now and, just as importantly, what you are likely to be worth in the future. Your investment plans should take into account both figures.

Who Should Look After Your Investments?

You may already have an investment adviser and be very happy with their quality and the service you have received, but they are unlikely to be able to help you once you have gone to live in Turkey. Moreover, they will almost certainly not have the knowledge to do so. They will not know about the Turkish investments that might be of interest to you nor, probably, about many of the offshore products that could appeal to someone no longer resident in the UK. Even if they have some knowledge of these things, your investment adviser in the UK is likely to be thousands of miles from where you will be living.

Nor is it a simple question of selecting a new local (Turkish) adviser once you have moved. They will usually know little about the UK aspects of your case or about the UK tax and inheritance rules that could still have some importance for you. We recommend you use a UK-based law firm with Turkish expertise which will have the ability to cover both jurisdictions and where you can seek advice before you move.

Choosing an investment adviser competent to deal with you once you are in Turkey is not easy. By all means seek guidance from your existing adviser and from others who have already made the move. Do some research. Meet the potential candidates. Are you comfortable with them? Do they share your approach to life? Do they have the necessary experience? Is their performance

Asset	Value – Local Currency	Value – £s
Current Assets		
Main home		
Holiday home		
Contents of main home		
Contents of holiday home		
Car		
Boat		
Bank accounts		
Other cash-type investments		
Bonds, etc.		
Stocks and shares		
PEPs, Tessas, ISAs		
Value of your business		
Other		
Future Assets		
Value of share options		
Personal/company pension – likely lump sum		
Potential inheritances or other accretions		
Value of endowment mortgages on maturity		
Other		
TOTAL		

record good? How are they regulated? What security, bonding and guarantees can they offer you? How will they be paid for their work: fees or commission? If commission, what will that formula mean they are making from you in 'real money' rather than percentages?

Above all be careful. There are lots of very dubious 'financial advisers' operating in the popular tourist areas of Turkey. Some are totally incompetent. Fortunately there are also some excellent and highly professional advisers with good track records. Make sure you choose one.

Where Should You Invest?

For British people the big issue is whether they should keep their sterling investments. Many will have investments that are largely sterling-based. Even if they have investments in, for example, a Far Eastern fund, these will probably be denominated in pounds sterling and they will pay out dividends in pounds.

You will be spending Turkish new liras (YTL). Because of the chronic inflation experienced in Turkey from the 1970s through to the 1990s, the old lira experienced severe depreciation in value. Turkey has had high inflation rates compared to developed countries but has never suffered hyperinflation. From an average of 9 lira per US dollar in the late 1960s, the currency came to trade at approximately 1.65 million lira per US dollar in late 2001. This represented an average inflation of about 38 per cent per year. Prime minister Recep Tayyip Erdoğan called this problem a 'national shame'. With the revaluation of the Turkish old lira the country's economy started to improve. In late December 2003, the Grand National Assembly of Turkey passed a law that allowed for the removal of six zeroes from the currency, and the creation of the new lira. It was introduced on 1 January 2005, replacing the previous lira (which remained valid in circulation until the end of 2005) at a rate of 1 new lira = 1,000,000 old lira.

However, it is still early stages, and, as the value of the Turkish new lira fluctuates against the pound sterling, the value of your investments will go up and down. That, of itself, isn't too important because the value won't crystallise unless you sell. What does matter is that the revenue you generate from those investments (rent, interest, dividends and so on) will be paid according to the fluctuations in value.

Take, for example, an investment that generated you £10,000 per annum. Rock steady. Then think of that income in spending power. In the last few years the Turkish lira has varied in value from £1 = YTL2.3 to £1 = YTL2.7. Sometimes, therefore, your income in Turkish liras would have been YTL23,000 a year and at others it would have been YTL27,000 a year. This is a huge difference in your standard of living if it is based solely on exchange rate variations. On the other hand, the exchange rate devaluation of the Turkish new lira is matched more or less by the domestic rate of Turkish price inflation. And the country's inflation ratio has been dropping enormously since the revaluation of the new lira.

Despite the recent problems caused by the crisis of 2001, the Turkish economy is on the road to recovery. Recent years have witnessed considerable foreign investment in Turkey in areas other than property such as banking, energy and telecommunications. These developments also seem to have had a stabilising effect on the Turkish currency; however, for the foreseeable future it might still be a better idea to keep your sterling investments.

Keeping Track of Your Investments

Whatever you decide to do about investments, always keep an up-to-date list of your assets and investments *and tell your family where to find it*. Make a file. By all means have a computer file but print off a good old-fashioned paper copy. Keep it in an obvious place known to your family. Keep it with your will and the deeds to your house. Also keep in it either the originals of bank account books, share certificates and so on or a note of where they are to be found.

It is very frustrating for lawyers – and expensive for clients – when children of parents who have recently died come in with a suitcase full of correspondence and old cheque books. They have to go through it all and write to all these old banks lest there should be £1 million lurking in a forgotten account. There never is, and it wastes a lot of time and money.

Conclusion

Buying a home in Turkey – whether to use as a holiday home, as an investment or to live in permanently – can be as safe as buying one in England. The rules may appear complicated. Our rules would if you were a Turkish person coming to this country. That apparent complexity is often no more than lack of familiarity.

There are many thousands of British people who have bought homes in Turkey. Most experienced no real problems and have enjoyed years of holidays there. Many have seen their property rise substantially in value and some are now thinking of retiring to Turkey.

Although many Britons have already bought properties in Turkey, the number is far fewer than those who have bought in other Mediterranean countries such as Spain or France. The result is that the road will, inevitably, be a little more rocky and the experience a little more problematic if buying in Turkey than if you were buying in a more well-trodden market. You have to accept this fact if you are going to be a pioneer. The benefit, of course, is that as a relative pioneer in the market you stand to benefit from various advantages: buying at a lower cost (and thus making a better capital gain), getting the best choice of locations, experiencing a true local culture before it is destroyed and the enjoyment of feeling that you're doing something a little unusual and adventurous. Some people value these things. Some people hate them. If you hate them you shouldn't be thinking about buying in Turkey at the present time. If you like them you will enjoy Turkey and, probably, find that your property has performed well as an investment.

For a relatively trouble-free time you simply need to keep your head and to seek advice from experts who can help you make the four basic decisions:

- **Who should own the property?**
- **What am I going to do about inheritance?**

- **What am I going to do about controlling my potential tax liabilities?**
- **If I am going to live in Turkey, what am I going to do about my investments?**

If you don't like lawyers, remember that they make far more money out of sorting out the problems you get into by not doing these things than by giving you this basic advice!

Settling In

07

With the paperwork and legal red tape sorted out, you can finally contemplate the pleasure of property-ownership. But whether you have bought your property as a second home or as somewhere to live, you still have quite a bit to sort out. This chapter looks at some of the practical matters of life in Turkey for a foreigner.

If you intend to stay permanently, both employment and retirement have their own complications – though things will certainly become easier if and when Turkey gets EU membership. If you have children, you will also need to consider aspects of schooling in Turkey, and how your child will take to it.

The Turkish language will cause many headaches, but a little really does go a long way; even if you're based in one of the growing numbers of expatriate communities, learning some Turkish will reap dividends – both in terms of avoiding everyday hassles and linguistic confusions, and in making contact with the Turkish people. The Turks truly appreciate foreigners speaking a little Turkish.

All these things might result in culture shock, but if you relish differences between countries you can take most of them in your stride. Turkish food for most people will be a voyage of discovery and one of the great pleasures, but other aspects of life – such as haggling while shopping – may seem daunting.

Ultimately whether it works or not is entirely down to you – your expectations, your determination, your planning and above all your willingness to take things as they come.

Moving to Turkey

Turkey is a very long drive from the UK, so it is likely that you will employ a removal company rather than hire your own van and move everything yourself. If you wish you can take your property out yourself, but you may be asked when you arrive for an inventory in Turkish and proof of ownership. Neither is easy to provide. If you do this it will be an advantage to be able to speak Turkish.

Removal Companies

Removal companies charge about £4,000 for taking the contents of a medium-sized house from the UK to the south of Turkey. On pp.248–9 we list details of a few removal companies that deal with UK–Turkey house moves, but you will find many more if you search on the Internet. However, the best way of finding a reliable company is through personal recommendation, because it is almost impossible to assess the quality of these firms through the information they themselves provide, and it is very important to find a company that sticks to what you have agreed with them about the time, price and other details.

Local Time

Time in Turkey is two hours ahead of that in the UK, with clocks going an hour forward in spring and an hour back in autumn, in parallel with British Summer Time. So if it is 10pm in the UK, it is midnight in Turkey.

Most of the tasks in connection with moving will be familiar to anyone who has moved house, but a few extra factors come into consideration if you are moving to Turkey. Property removal is generally charged by volume – per cubic metre. Usually you pay the same price until the bulk to be moved reaches 30 cubic metres – ask for information about this. Make sure you are adequately insured for the move (most removal companies offer their own insurance for loss or breakages; check the excess limit).

Before You Go

A month or more before you move:

- **Book flights and car hire.**
- **Get several quotes from removal companies, and book the one that gives the best deal (personal recommendation is always best).**
- **Contact tax authorities.**
- **Locate all your legal and medical records.**
- **Arrange healthcare or insurance.**
- **Contact banks, insurance companies and other financial institutions to sort out accounts, credit cards, and so on.**
- **Transfer UK accounts for electricity, gas, water, phone and council tax if you will be letting your UK property after you leave for Turkey.**
- **Take photos of any valuable items in case you have to make an insurance claim for loss in transit.**
- **Arrange property (contents and building) insurance.**
- **Acquire the boxes, tape and string needed for moving (the removal company may supply these).**
- **Inform gas, electric, water, cable, phone and rubbish removal services in Turkey that you are coming.**
- **Send out notifications of your change of address.**

The day before moving:

- **Get marker pens and label each box with the room in your Turkish property to which you want it delivered.**
- **Check the registry of the boxes by the company staff very carefully before you sign it.**

- **Pack personal items you will need during the move; these will include clothes, wash kit, medicine, maps, reading material, food and drink, plus games, toys or other activities if you have children.**

Never send your valuable documents together with the things that you are sending through removal companies.

Customs Regulations

Before you arrive in Turkey, bear in mind that possession of certain items may be prohibited or restricted. These include obvious items such as firearms, explosives and drugs.

You may wish to send your belongings to Turkey in advance. If you intend to become resident in Turkey you may import your belongings for a period of up to two months before your arrival. You will have to pay a deposit for customs duties, which will be repaid once you arrive in Turkey, and prove that you qualify for relief. You may also import your belongings up to six months *after* the date you move. In addition, your belongings may be taken out of Turkey two months before or six months after you leave.

You are recommended to employ a shipping agent experienced in removals to Turkey to handle all customs documentation. If you intend to visit Turkey for less than six months in any tax year, customs are relaxed and most of your personal belongings need not be formally declared as long as they exist in the exemption list published by the customs authority. Provided any car is formally declared to customs, it may be kept in Turkey for a period of up to six months each year. You may be granted an additional six months' extension if you apply to customs before the end of this period.

In order to remove your personal goods from customs without duties being charged, you need to submit your work and residence permits, a letter of guarantee from a bank, and a letter from your employer stating the duration of your stay and that you will take your goods back to your home country.

Keep in mind that if you wish to bring electronic goods, such as televisions, radios, videos, satellite receivers and so on, into Turkey these goods may be subject to a special fee.

Visas and Permits

All foreigners entering Turkey needs the appropriate paperwork to justify their stay in the country. What paperwork you require depends on what you are doing in Turkey.

Residence and Citizenship

Many clients confuse the issue of visas and residence permits with that of citizenship. Any foreign national is entitled to retain their nationality for as long as they like, even though they live in Turkey. Most British people who have settled in Turkey will, 40 years later, still have their British passport and British nationality. The granting of a residence permit of whatever type makes no difference whatsoever to your nationality. You will remain British but be recognised in Turkey as *officially resident* in Turkey. Nor does your residence status make any difference to your tax residence or tax status, which will be calculated in accordance with the separate rules on taxation: *see* **Financial Implications**, 'Taxes', pp.153–5.

Avoiding the Paperwork

Many foreigners went to live in Turkey years ago and never got round to applying for a residence permit. Sometimes this was in the belief that they would not have to pay taxes in Turkey if they never applied for a permit; at other times the paperwork seemed too much trouble. Many of these people have never been challenged and, indeed, have never paid any tax in Turkey. Some immigrants have not only lived in Turkey for many years but have also been working there, which is illegal. There are severe penalties for living or working in Turkey without a permit and also for non-payment of tax. It is not recommended. Times have changed greatly in the last 10 years, and with Turkey's expected accession to the European Union they will change even more in the next 10 years; the odds of being able to get away with any of this are narrowing all the time.

For a British person seeking a residence permit in Turkey the procedure is generally simple and the authorities are very helpful. It is simply not worth trying to cheat the system. If you wish to work in Turkey, it is a little more complicated, but not that difficult and certainly not impossible. Again, it is better to bite the bullet and get the proper permission.

Visas for Visiting Turkey

People of most nationalities, including the British, require a visa before entering Turkey. For EU nationals, the visa is not a visa in the normal sense of the word, but more an unsubtle means of collecting taxes. Visitors must apply for the visa at the airport. No checks are made and your passport is stamped in return for payment of £10. The visa is a multiple entry visa and remains valid for three months, at the end of which time you simply apply for another one the next time you arrive in the country.

If you wish to stay in Turkey for more than three months you can extend the visa by applying to the nearest Foreigners' Office of the Security Police (*Emniyet*

Müdürlügü, Yabancilar Şubesı). The extension is for a further period of three months. In theory, only one extension is permitted, and the process can take anything from 2–8 weeks.

The process of applying for the extension is a classic example of Turkish bureaucracy. It involves dealing with a number of different people in a number of different departments, commonly over several weeks. It is usually simpler just to leave the country (for example, by going to Greece or Cyprus), then return, as soon as the next day, and apply for a new tourist visa at the airport. The Turkish authorities seem quite happy for this to be repeated many times, although there is a danger that after a few such visits they will tell you at the airport that you are abusing the system and that the next time you should apply for a residence permit.

Longer-term Residence in Turkey

If you travel to Turkey intending to spend more than 90 days, apply for a residence permit at once. If you decide to stay permanently (or, at least, for longer than six months) once you have arrived in Turkey on a Turkish tourist visa, apply for your residence permit at the earliest opportunity and no later than the date on which your tourist visa expires.

If at the end of your three-month tourist visit you are uncertain about whether you intend to remain long-term, or whether you intend to spend only a little more time in Turkey, you can apply to extend your tourist visa (*see* above) and then, once you have decided to stay in Turkey, apply for a residence permit at any point during that extra three-month period. (This would generally be a waste of time because you would end up having to go through much the same paperwork twice at double the cost.)

Applying for a Residence Permit

You can apply for a residence permit either from your own country or from within Turkey.

Applications for residence permits from within Turkey are essentially the same as applications for an extended tourist permit from the Security Police. If you don't own a property or work in Turkey, you can get a 'tourist' residence permit, valid for 6–12 months; a six-month permit and associated paperwork costs £165. You will need to show proof of funds of at least US$1,800 to be considered. But if you have property, or work in the country, you can apply for a full residence permit valid for up to five years. To do this, apply to the local Foreigners' Office (*Emniyet Müdürlüğü, Yabancılar Şubesi*), with:

- **three typed application forms.**
- **six recent passport photographs.**
- **your passport.**

- **a notarised copy of the title deed or rental contract of your abode.**
- **the appropriate valid visa obtained from the Turkish embassy abroad.**
- **proof that you have sufficient funds to support yourself without working.**
- **the appropriate fee (currently £200 for one year; £960 for five years).**

The whole process can take from a few weeks to three months. If you do not speak good Turkish you would be well advised to have professional assistance, particularly if you live outside a main tourist area.

Those applying from outside Turkey must submit their application, together with their work permit and work visa (*see* pp.177–8), to the Ministry of Internal Affairs (*İçişleri Bakanlığı*) in Ankara. As a UK national who plans to stay in Turkey for more than three months, you must obtain the appropriate visa from a Turkish embassy or consulate before arrival. You can find more information on this on the Turkish consulate website (**www.turkishconsulate.org.uk**). The process is usually a little quicker than from within Turkey, but this is not guaranteed. Once your application has been processed you will be given what amounts to a provisional permit, which you can use to enter Turkey. You then have four weeks in which to present yourself to the Security Police and apply for the provisional permit to be converted to a full permit. This process can take several weeks and involves several visits to the Security Police office. The advantage of this approach is that the initial permit is likely to be obtained faster. The disadvantage is that there is more work and that it will, therefore, prove to be more expensive than if you dealt with the whole application in Turkey. In the end you should obtain a residence permit authorising you to live in Turkey for one year. When that expires you can apply for an extension in Turkey, and the process for this is faster than the initial application. The extension is normally for two years on the first application and five years thereafter. The precise arrangements can, however, vary from place to place and often day-to--day.

A residence permit is what it says – permission to live in the country. It does not authorise you to seek employment in the country or to work there in a self-employed capacity. If you wish to do either of those things you will need a different type of permit in addition to your residence permit.

The rules change, so it is worth checking on the Turkish embassy or consulate website (**www.turkishconsulate.org.uk**) – download the application form and look at the current regulations, which are reproduced in English.

You should, like all Turkish nationals, in any case carry your passport and/or residence permit with you at all times in Turkey. It is compulsory for everybody to produce an identity card on request.

British nationals resident in Turkey who are entitled to the protection of the UK authorities should contact the nearest British consulate to register their details, taking their passport with them. Failure to do so may, in an emergency, result in difficulty or delay in according assistance and protection.

Retiring to Turkey

By retirement we mean living without being employed or self-employed. To be retired you do not need to be over the state retirement age in the country where you come from or in the country where you are now living. People may well 'retire' at the age of 45 or 50. This does not mean that they do nothing – they may be active in managing their own investments or in activities in the community, but they cannot legally work in a paid capacity.

Someone who wishes to retire to Turkey only needs a residence permit, whether they intend to live there permanently or to make several visits to the country, each of more than three months. Many people spend a lot of the year in Turkey without a permit. Some do this lawfully simply by making, say, three two-month visits each year. Others do so illegally by spending more than three months at a time in the country without officially extending their visit.

Although obtaining the necessary paperwork can be a nuisance, it is definitely worth doing if you intend to spend time in Turkey regularly. Doing so will have implications that can go beyond the simple question of residence and there may be tax consequences. Depending on your personal circumstances these can work to your advantage or disadvantage. In any case, you should be taking the opportunity to restructure and review your affairs if you are going to live in Turkey. When you do that, you will generally find that the restructuring can be done in such a way as to reduce your tax liabilities in Turkey, often to well below what the equivalent liability would have been in the UK. This is a complicated matter about which you should take specialist legal advice before you move to Turkey. *See* **Financial Implications** for more details.

Setting up a Business in Turkey

Like most countries, Turkey draws a distinction between the self-employed and those who work as a salaried employee for somebody else. In general terms, it is easier to get a permit to be self-employed than it is to obtain a permit to be employed, particularly if your business is going to generate local employment.

Starting a business in any country is a complex procedure and beyond the scope of this book. Take expert advice as quickly as possible once you know what you want to do and before you spend a lot of time or money developing your plans. The business activity you have in mind may be illegal or almost impossible to implement successfully in Turkey because of various local conditions. Such advice is not expensive and can save you a fortune.

Working in Turkey as an Employee

A person who wishes to work in Turkey in a salaried or wage-earning capacity needs a work permit. This also applies to anyone who intends to set up a company and to work for that company. They need the work permit in addition to the residence permit referred to earlier in this chapter.

The rules are strict. The government is keen to protect its own people from an influx of foreign workers. Turkey is not constrained by the restrictions in the other EU countries where European law gives (with very few exceptions) all European Union citizens the right to work in any other European Union country. Some jobs can only, legally, be carried out by people of Turkish nationality. These are set out in the Code of Arts and Services, which dates back to 1932, and in various other bits of legislation. Some listed jobs are not surprising – judges, lawyers, pilots and so on – but there are some curiosities on the list: barber, photographer and driver, to name but three (*see* p.178)!

Applying for a Work Permit

Obtaining a work permit can be time-consuming and sometimes tricky, but it is seldom impossible with a certain amount of ingenuity and dedication. You must obtain the permit before you leave your own country, through your Turkish employer, though in some cases employers pass the burden of dealing with the paperwork to the applicant.

In order to obtain a permit you need to show that you have been offered employment in Turkey, that the skills you have to offer are not available within Turkey, and that there is, therefore, some special reason why you should be employed instead of a local person. This sounds (and is) a tough test. It is basically the same test as is applied in almost all countries. Despite the high standards required to obtain a permit it is quite common to get one, even for jobs where it is in reality difficult to show that the tests are met in full.

Work permits are issued either by the consulates of the Turkish Republic abroad or by the Ministry of Labour and Social Security (*Çalışma ve Sosyal Güvenlik Bakanlığı*) in Turkey (**www.csgb.gov.tr**). If you apply for a work permit you will need:

- **an application form from the Turkish consulate.**
- **a passport.**
- **personal information (e.g. birth certificate) certified by a notary public.**
- **several passport photos.**

Those who apply for a work permit from the Ministry of Labour and Social Security need additional documents and to complete a two-page form. The following personal information is required:

- **passport number.**
- **name and surname.**
- **name of father and mother.**
- **date and place of birth.**
- **marital status and nationality of wife/husband, if married.**

If you obtain a work permit and commence work legally you will pay taxes in Turkey and you and your employer will pay social security contributions. These entitle you to Turkish social security benefits (*see* 'Welfare Benefits', pp.182–4).

Many people simply do not bother to apply for a permit. Especially in the tourist areas and Istanbul there is a big market for people with certain management and practical skills who speak good English, and that market is not satisfied by the available English-speaking Turkish people. As a result, many foreigners work without any paperwork. They are technically tourists and are working illegally.

Surprisingly, some reputable organisations offer employment on this basis. These people leave the country every three months or so and return to obtain a new tourist visa. As with the case of retired people who have decided to stay in the country without a residence permit, they are sometimes stopped and told that next time they really must apply for the residence permit if they wish to be readmitted to Turkey. These people rarely pay taxes or social security payments. They risk being denounced by their enemies or competitors, being detained, fined or deported.

Work Visas

After obtaining a work permit you also need to obtain a work visa by applying to the Turkish embassy in the UK. Work visa requirements, instructions and application forms are available through the Embassy of the Republic of Turkey website (**www.turkishconsulate.org.uk**).

Working and Employment

Only Turkish citizens can work as state employees in Turkey, and as a foreigner you can only work in jobs that are not **prohibited to foreigners**. Most of the jobs in medicine, dentistry, nursing, pharmacy, law and working as a notary public are prohibited to foreigners (though foreign expert doctors may be granted permission to work in Turkey). Only Turkish citizens can work as itinerant salesmen, musicians, photographers, barbers, typesetters, clothing and shoe manufacturers, stockbrokers, sellers of state monopoly products, interpreters or tourist guides, transport workers, or in the construction, iron and wood industry. Foreigners are also prohibited from working on water, lighting and heating installations, either temporarily or permanently, and on loading and unloading sites. You cannot legally work as a driver, day labourer, watchman, janitor, waiter or household help, or as a singer or entertainer in bars, nor as a veterinarian.

Foreign Journalists

Foreign journalists who plan to cover news events in Turkey for less than three months should visit the press officers of the Turkish embassy in their own country before departing for Turkey. Interview requests from the relevant Turkish authorities or other professional demands can be arranged before travel. Members of the foreign media who are assigned to Turkey for more than three months and who have acquired a work visa are considered to be applicants for 'permanent' accreditation. You should renew accreditations annually at the beginning of the calendar year.

Jobs for Foreigners

After reading the long list of the prohibited jobs for foreigners in Turkey, and the complicated process of getting permits, you may wonder whether there any job prospects for foreigners at all... In fact there are many jobs. Many international companies and organisations with branches in Turkey look for foreign employees from time to time, and the bureaucratic difficulties are usually dealt with by the employers. The best way to look for jobs in Turkey is to search the job announcements in newspaper sections targeting foreigners, such as the Sunday editions of the two main daily newspapers, *Hürriyet* and *Sabah* (*see* 'The Media', pp.202–203).

Teaching English in Turkey

Many of the jobs for foreigners in Turkey are positions teaching English as a foreign language. People in cities are very keen to learn English, and they really want to learn it from a native speaker of the language. Many want to learn English for the tourism sector or to improve their English for professional reasons. It helps to have a teaching or English degree if you want to teach English, but it is not necessary as just about all schools provide a training period before you are actually put in front of a class.

There are numerous English schools in large cities such as Istanbul, İzmir and Ankara for adult students offering mainly weekend and evening classes. There are over 200 private language schools in Istanbul alone. It is easier to find a job in these schools than in regular state schools, which means that you will probably work evenings and weekends, but this leaves your day free to explore this diverse city. There are language schools in other cities, but Istanbul is the cultural, historical and social centre of the country.

Some of the schools require a university degree or a diploma in any subject, but most of the schools require a CELTA or TESOL teaching certificate. All schools prefer teachers to be aged between 20 and 40. However, there are many foreign teachers of over 40 who easily find jobs in private schools. Major language schools in the UK offer training: you can either take it as a one-month intensive course (extremely hard work) or spread it out part-time over two or three terms (preferable by far, if you have the time). Both TESOL and CELTA include theory and practice, with observations of other teachers, assessed classroom teaching and written assignments.

Courses cost £600 and more, and bear in mind that not everyone passes, though most get through. You often see adverts for courses that promise to get you some kind of teaching qualification within a few days. Don't bother with these: you need the full TESOL or CELTA certificate. Lesser courses may cost less and take less time and effort but they are a false economy.

You can sometimes find three-month summer contracts as well, but work contracts with private schools are usually for 9–12 months. Jobs are available all year round but there is always more need for teachers around September and October. A contribution towards work permits and flight ticket expenses is made on completion of contract. If the teacher leaves before completing the contract, four weeks' notice is usually required. The work permit usually has to be arranged before leaving the country where you are currently resident and involves a visit to the Turkish embassy there. However, the work permit can be obtained after arriving in Turkey. This involves a short trip to Cyprus or Greece and re-entering the country.

English teachers in private schools earn £350–550 per month depending on qualifications, experience and the cost of living in the city they work in. As the schools usually pay the teacher's rent, and the cost of living in Turkey is quite low, this is sufficient to live on and even save from. The schools usually provide rent-free accommodation, and each teacher has a private room but shares a living room, kitchen and bathroom with other English teachers. The teachers sharing the flats also share all utility bills. You shouldn't go to Turkey to teach English expecting to make a fortune out of this work; however, it's a reasonably secure and often very fulfilling job, with the bonus that you can easily make contacts with local people.

One teaching 'hour' is usually 50 minutes. The classes mostly consist of small adult classes of 8–12 students, aged 18+, but also occasionally junior classes. Most teachers on a nine-month contract usually work between 24 and 30 guaranteed teaching hours per week but have the opportunity to do overtime if they wish. Teachers are normally required to work evenings and/or weekends, as in any school for adults. Teachers are entitled to all Turkish national and religious holidays, and have at least one full day off per week.

There are two useful websites for anyone thinking of teaching English:

- **Dave's ESL café (www.daveseslcafe.com) – useful for finding jobs; besides featuring listings from all over the world, it gives useful tips and warnings about schools where other teachers have had bad experiences.**

- **TURKENG (www.angelfire.com/biz/turkeng) – a recruitment agency for teachers of English as a foreign language, with two branches, in Norwich (UK) and Antalya. TURKENG aims to find the best schools for teachers, and to prepare them for their stay in Turkey; the placement services to teachers are free of charge. TURKENG places English-language teachers at private language schools for adults, private universities and private high schools in Istanbul and other parts of Turkey.**

Running a Business in Turkey

Turkey is a country where it is very difficult to become self-employed without any connection with the local business community and without a good understanding of its cultural and social structure, let alone knowledge of the language. The best way for a foreigner to learn the complicated bureaucratic and cultural structure and to get used to the informal rules of the Turkish market would be to work for some time as an employee before starting a business or buying an existing one. Working with a Turkish partner would also be the best way to cope with the problems of being a foreigner. There are enough companies of all sizes that are eager for any kind of partnership with a European company or individual, for their know-how or connections in the West. Most of the owners or managers of these companies are fluent in English and have a modern education, which will facilitate understanding. You should still be ready to learn some Turkish for an active partnership.

As a potential property-buyer in Turkey you will probably already have enough experience of living in Turkey or knowledge of the country if you are thinking of starting a business there. However, if you wish to establish a business in Turkey, discuss it first with your close friends at home and in Turkey. Then consult a Turkish lawyer. Details of English-speaking lawyers for Ankara, Istanbul and İzmir are available at the website of the British embassy in Ankara (**www.britishembassy.org.tr**).

You will also have to:

- **go through the complicated process of obtaining work visas and residence permits (*see* 'Visas and Permits', pp.172–8).**
- **prove that your investment will provide employment for Turkish nationals and not have any adverse effect on local Turkish-run companies in the country in the same business sector or geographical area.**
- **prepare a business plan.**
- **have a certain amount of capital to finance the business.**

Useful Contacts

- **UK Trade & Investment Enquiry Service,** Tay House, 300 Bath Street, Glasgow, G2 4DX, **t** (020) 7215 8000, **www.uktradeinvest.gov.uk**.
- **Turkish Attorneys Paralegals Online (TAPO), www.tapo.co.uk**. Information on the legislative issues on working and employment.
- **General Directorate of Foreign Investment (GDFI),** T.C. Başbakanlık Hazine Müsteşarlığı: İnönü Bulvarı No.36, 06510 Emek, Ankara, **t** 90 (312) 204 60 00, **www.treasury.gov.tr**. The Turkish authority responsible for foreign investment in Turkey.
- **International Investors Association, www.yased.org.tr**.
- **Foreign Economic Relations Board, www.deik.org.tr**.
- **Prime Ministry, State Planning Organisation, www.dpt.gov.tr**.
- **Prime Ministry, Undersecretariat of Foreign Trade, www.dtm.gov.tr**.
- **Privatisation Administration, www.oib.gov.tr**.

Welfare Benefits

In Turkey people can qualify for welfare benefits in one of two ways:

- **under the rules of the country where they pay social security contributions.**
- **under the rules of the country where they live.**

Turkey is not part of the EU, but, if it joins (*see* pp.11–13), enforced reciprocal EU-EEA rules should eventually apply.

What Turkish Benefits Can You Claim?

The law is complex, so if you think you may have an entitlement to benefit seek specialist advice. Your entitlement will be determined by any social security payments you have made in Turkey. These will only apply if you have been living legally as a resident in Turkey and paying Turkish social security payments and taxes.

Unless you have worked in Turkey for some time you are not likely to benefit from a Turkish pension. You will continue to receive your UK pension.

What UK Benefits Can You Claim?

Welfare benefits in the UK are divided into 'contributory' and 'non-contributory' benefits. You are only entitled to the former if you have paid (or been credited with) sufficient National Insurance (NI) contributions to qualify you for payment. The latter do not depend on paying any NI contributions.

In the UK there are various classes of NI contributions. Not all rank equally for benefits purposes and some types of NI contributions cannot be used to qualify payments for certain benefits.

The categories are:

- **Class 1: paid by employees and their employers: a percentage of income up to a certain maximum.**
- **Class 2: a flat-rate payment made by self-employed people.**
- **Class 3: voluntary payments made by people no longer paying Class 1 or Class 2 contributions; these protect their right to a limited range of benefits.**
- **Class 4: compulsory 'profit-related' additional contributions paid by self-employed people.**

The different NI payments qualify you for differing types of benefit, as shown in the table below.

NI Contributions and Entitlement to UK Benefits

	Class 1	Class 2 or 4	Class 3
Maternity Allowances	Yes	Yes	No
Unemployment Benefit	Yes	No	No
Incapacity Benefit	Yes	Yes	No
Widow's Benefit	Yes	Yes	Yes
Basic Retirement Pension	Yes	Yes	Yes
Additional Retirement Pension	Yes	No	No

As well as the distinction between 'contributory' and 'non-contributory' benefits, benefits are also categorised into 'means-tested' and 'non-means-tested' benefits. The former are paid only if you qualify under the eligibility criteria for the benefit in question and are poor enough to qualify on financial grounds – taking income and savings into account. The latter are paid to anyone who meets the eligibility criteria, irrespective of their wealth. Means-tested UK benefits are likely to be of little interest to the resident in Turkey.

- **Sickness and maternity benefits**: *See* 'Health and Emergencies', pp.185–7.
- **Accidents at work**: Any benefits you presently receive from the UK benefits system as a result of an accident at work should remain payable to you despite the fact that you have moved to Turkey.
- **Occupational diseases**: Any benefits you receive from the UK benefits system as a result of an occupational disease should remain payable to you despite the fact that you have moved to Turkey.
- **Invalidity benefits**: Any National Insurance benefits you receive from the UK benefits system as a result of invalidity should remain payable to you despite the fact that you have moved to Turkey. Attendance allowance, severe

disablement allowance and disability living allowances, however, are not usually payable if you go to live abroad permanently.

- **Old-age pensions**: If you are already retired and you only ever paid National Insurance contributions in the UK, you will receive your UK retirement pension wherever you choose to live. You will be paid without deduction (except remittance charges) and your pension will be updated whenever the pensions in the UK are updated.

If you have not yet retired and move to Turkey (whether you intend to work in Turkey or not), your entitlement to your UK pension will be frozen and the pension to which you are entitled will be paid to you at UK retirement age. This freezing of your pension can be a disadvantage, especially if you are still relatively young when you move to Turkey. This is because you need to have made a minimum number of NI contributions in order to qualify for a full UK state pension. It may be worth making additional payments while you are resident overseas by continuing to make Class 2 or Class 3 contributions.

You may pay Class 2 contributions if:

- **you are working abroad.**
- **you have lived in the UK for a continuous period of at least three years during which you paid NI contributions and you have already paid a set minimum amount of NI contributions.**
- **you were normally employed or self-employed in the UK before going abroad.**

You may pay Class 3 contributions if:

- **you have at any time lived in the UK for a continuous period of at least three years.**
- **you have already paid a minimum amount of NI contributions in the UK.**

Class 2 contributions are more expensive but, potentially, cover you for maternity allowance and incapacity benefits. Class 3 contributions do not. In both cases you apply in the UK on form CF83.

The decision of whether to continue to make UK payments is an important one. Seek advice.

- **Widow's and other survivors' benefits**: Any benefits you receive from the UK benefits system as a result of being widowed should remain payable to you despite the fact that you have moved to Turkey.
- **Death grants**: The position here is complex. Seek advice.
- **Unemployment benefits**: These will not be payable once you have gone to live in Turkey.
- **Means-tested social security benefits**: These will not, generally, be payable once you have gone to live in Turkey.

Health and Emergencies

Costs and Insurance

Turkey currently has no reciprocal health agreement with the UK. Medical costs, although lower than in Europe and the United States, can be expensive in Turkey, and all foreigners have to pay for medical treatment. Medical insurance typically costs around £25 a week, and a policy should provide for flying you home if need be. Travel insurance will give you medical cover providing you are not actually residing in Turkey. Check the details of your policy for the maximum number of days it covers. If you are spending extended periods of more than 60 days at a time away from home or making frequent holiday visits of two or three weeks, it is almost certainly worth investing in an annual travel insurance policy, which is available from a wide range of insurers in the UK, typically for around £80 to £120 for two people.

To compare prices, visit **www.moneysupermarket.com/TravelInsurance**.

You can also get reciprocal private health plans from the UK, which give you access to private hospitals and healthcare. UK insurers such as **BUPA International** (**t** (01273) 208181, **www.bupa-intl.com**) have no age limit. If you are under 55 you can purchase a health insurance plan in Turkey.

Turkish Healthcare

Assuming you have insurance, it is best to use private healthcare when you need it. Hospitals are marked by blue street signs with a large white H (*hastahane* – hospital). Turkish state hospitals aren't always endowed with the sanitary standards that you might expect in the West. Although some have better equipment than their private counterparts, they are often very busy and understaffed, and queuing is a tedious reality.

There are English-speaking doctors in most towns and resorts, who are often advertised as such on their premises, or you can ask at the local tourist office where they can be found. You could also try consulting a pharmacy (*eczahane* or *eczane*); every town has one that stays open at night. The Turkish word for night pharmacy is *nöbetçi eczahane*.

There are also free health clinics which can give prescriptions and diagnoses.

Inoculations

Although no inoculations are actually mandatory for visitors to Turkey, it is sensible to be vaccinated against tetanus and typhoid, as well as getting a gamma globulin vaccination against hepatitis A. These are particularly impor-

Medical Emergencies

For medical emergencies telephone t 112. For a directory of hospitals in Turkey go to www.turkeycentral.com/Health_and_Medicine/index.php.

tant if you are venturing to the eastern part of the country. Malaria is a problem during April to July in southeast Turkey, but not in the main tourist areas further west. But mosquitoes can make life pretty miserable, especially at night; mosquito coils, available widely, burn with a joss-stick-like smell to get you through the night and keep the little perishers off in a way that virtually nothing else does.

Daily Hazards

Generally you are no more likely to experience health problems in Turkey than in any other European country. Tap water is mostly safe to clean your teeth with but don't rely on it for everything. It tends to be unpleasantly chlorinated and bacteria can breed in the pipes in hot conditions; in some areas it is best to drink filtered water or bottled water instead. You might suffer a mild form of diarrhoea, so consider carrying some anti-diarrhoea medicine (widely available in Turkey and the UK) with you. The standards of food hygiene are usually very high, but take the same precautions you would in any country – avoid unwashed and unpeeled fruit and vegetables, street stalls selling mussels and other seafood, and restaurants where food stands around for long periods. If you do get struck down with food poisoning, take plenty of rest and drink plenty of fluids. After your body has had some time to recover, eat bland foods such as rice and yoghurt; if you have not recovered after 48 hours, see a doctor, who may prescribe antibiotics. You should also be on guard against sunstroke and dehydration – in fact diarrhoea itself tends to dehydrate the body.

As elsewhere in the world, it is very prudent to take a high-factor sun lotion to guard against the harmful effects of sun and to wear a hat to avoid heatstroke.

There is a risk of getting rabies in Turkey, though this is fairly small. Be extra wary of poisonous snakes and scorpions, often found lurking beneath rocks.

Pensions

Your UK state pension will be paid in the way described in the section on welfare benefits (*see* pp.182–4).

If you have a company pension it will be paid wherever the pension scheme rules dictate. Some permit the administrators to pay the money into any bank anywhere; others, ostensibly for security reasons, insist on the money being paid into a UK bank account. If this is the case, you can simply ask the bank to send it on to you in Turkey. Bank transfer costs mean that it is probably best to do this only a few times a year. You can also make an annual arrangement with some currency dealers whereby they will send the money at an exchange rate that will apply for the whole year. This provides certainty of income. Whether you will do better or worse than you would have done by waiting is in the lap of the gods.

If you have a government pension (for instance from the army, civil service or police), your pension will still be taxed in the UK. Otherwise the pension should be paid gross (tax-free) and it will be taxed in Turkey. *See* **Financial Implications**, 'Taxes', pp.155–6, for more information.

Death and Making a Will

If you die in Turkey, your death should be reported to the local police station within 24 hours. It should also be recorded at the British consulate. Cremation is unheard of in Turkey; everyone is buried.

Turkey is a secular country and does not distinguish between religious beliefs. However, each religious affiliation is recognised at death – there are separate Muslim, Christian and Jewish cemeteries and separate undertaker services for each of the major faiths. Funerals can be as expensive in Turkey as they are in the UK. Having your body taken home to England is possible, but complex and more expensive.

Inheritance and Wills

The Turks cannot do just as they please with their property when they die. Inheritance rules apply. These rules for Turks are much more restrictive than the rules under English law; certain groups of people have (almost) automatic rights to inherit a part of your property. *See* 'Turkish Law', pp.23–4.

Fortunately, if you are not Turkish you can dispose of your property in whatever way your national law allows. For British people this is, essentially, as they please – but you *must* make a will to ensure that this happens.

It is always best to make a Turkish **will**. If you don't, your English one will be treated as valid in Turkey and be used to distribute your estate. This is a false economy, as the cost of implementing the English will is much higher than the cost of implementing a Turkish will and the disposal of your estate, as set out in your English will, is often a tax disaster in Turkey.

If you are not a resident in Turkey, your Turkish will should state that it only applies to immovable property in Turkey. The rest of your property – including movable property in Turkey – will be disposed of in accordance with English law and the provisions of your English will.

If you are resident in Turkey you should make a Turkish will disposing of all of your assets wherever they are. If you make a Turkish will covering immovable property in Turkey only, you should modify your English will so as to exclude any immovable property located in Turkey.

Always use a lawyer to advise as to the contents of your will and to draft it. Lawyers love people who make home-made wills. They make a fortune from dealing with their estates because the wills are often inadequately drafted and produce lots of expensive problems.

A person who dies without making a will of any kind dies intestate and this gets complicated. Will the UK rules about what happens in this event apply (because you are British) or will it be the Turkish rules? This gives rise to many happy hours of argument by lawyers and tax officials, all at your (or rather your heirs') expense. It is much cheaper to make a will.

Money, Prices and Banking

At the start of 2005 Turkey revamped its currency, introducing the Turkish new lira (YTL), which effectively simply knocked six cumbersome zeros off the old Turkish lira (TL) (*see* also p.166). This was done in the hope that Turkey's new-found currency stability – since around 2003 – would hold. The stability is in sharp contrast to its performance over the previous 20 years, when the currency regularly bombed against the world's principal currencies.

Because of the Turkish lira's historical volatility, property prices in Turkey have often been expressed in euros (EUR), US dollars (USD) or British pounds sterling (GBP). Prices in this book are generally given in Turkish new liras (YTL), with an approximate conversion into pounds sterling, which at the time of writing (September 2007) was GB £1 = YTL2.53. Check the latest exchange rates on **www.xe.com/ucc**.

Only Turkish new liras are used for daily shopping and transactions, and, although a few places in touristy resorts or large cities will accept foreign currency, you should change your money in advance. You can do it in a bank, but usually you have to pay a considerable amount of commission. It is much wiser to change money in an exchange bureau; nearly every street in large cities has a private exchange bureau (*döviz ofisi* or *döviz bürosu*) that does not charge commission.

The Cost of Living

The cost of living in Turkey is considerably below that of Britain and even southern Europe. Food in particular is great value, with freshly grown local produce a fraction of its cost in the UK, and even a meal in a smart restaurant coming in at no more than £15 per head. Most other consumables are often also appreciably cheaper, so it is largely only in the areas of transport and communication that prices are higher. A litre of unleaded petrol will cost around £1.10 –

about 15–20p more than in the UK and more than double that of the USA – which won't drive up the cost of motoring appreciably, but is something to consider if you do decide to run a car. Equally steep are the costs of international telephone calls and Internet connections; a fairly slow broadband connection will cost around £35 per month.

But in general prices in Turkey are such that you can live far more comfortably on a modest wage or a UK pension than you could in Britain. To get a feel for what is possible, consider that a manual worker in Turkey will earn around £40 per week; a schoolteacher about £140.

Bank Accounts

Anybody can open a bank account once they are over 18 and can provide the bank with proof of identity, age, address in Turkey and other details. In these days of international terrorism, anything to do with the movement of money from one country to another gives rise to enquiry.

The type of bank account that you will open will depend on whether you are resident on non-resident in Turkey. For most practical purposes there is little difference between the two types of account.

Which Bank Should You Use?

Banking needs vary dramatically from person to person. If you are retiring to Turkey or running a business there you may need a full and fairly sophisticated banking service. If you are a tourist with a holiday home your banking needs are likely to be simpler. Most British people fall into this category. For them there is virtually no difference between the service offered by any of the major Turkish banks. The two major considerations when choosing between Turkish banks will be the convenience factor – whether the bank is located near your property – and whether staff at the bank speak English. If you do not speak Turkish, you may prefer, at least initially, to deal with a bank where the staff speak your own language. In many small towns you will have no choice of bank.

It is advisable to deal with your local bank if possible so that you feel part of a local community and, more importantly, the local community feels that you want to be part of it. Who knows, your bank manager might even take you out for lunch! If you have the luxury of a choice between various convenient banks where the staff speak English, perhaps the most significant factor to take into account is the bank's charging structure for receiving money. Turkish banks charge for absolutely everything. Some charge a lot more than others for the simple task of receiving money that you sent from England.

If you choose to use HSBC or another bank with British branches, note that they are a separate Turkish entity and that you are likely to receive the same service as from any other Turkish bank.

Most Turkish banks offer excellent – and, for non-residents, very useful – Internet banking facilities.

Which Type of Account?

Most people operate a simple current account (*vadesiz*) and ask the bank to make payments of utilities bills by direct payment from that account. There are no cheque guarantee cards in Turkey, yet cheques are still widely – if reluctantly – accepted because of the severe penalties that result from abuse of a cheque (*see* above).

Turkish banks generally pay very little interest on current accounts – around 0.1 per cent, making it sensible also to have a deposit account. Most banks will arrange for the balance on the current account over a certain sum to be transferred automatically into an interest-bearing account. In Turkey interest rates on foreign currency accounts are generally higher than those in 'Euroland'.

If your needs are more sophisticated than this, study carefully the various types of account available. These, and the terms of conditions of use, differ substantially from the accounts you may be familiar with in England.

Your Existing UK Account

There is no reason why you should not retain an account in the UK when you move to Turkey. It will probably prove convenient to do so.

'Offshore' Accounts

Offshore accounts are the subject of considerable mystique. Many people resident in Turkey think that by having an offshore bank account they do not have to pay tax in Turkey. This is not true. They only do not pay the tax if they illegally hide the existence of the bank account from the Turkish taxman. As the owner of a holiday home in Turkey or as a person resident in Turkey you can have an offshore bank account, but you should only do so for good reason. If you are thinking of taking up residence in Turkey, take detailed financial advice on the location of bank accounts.

Key Points

Whichever bank you use and whichever account you open:

- **Learn to write the date in Turkish and use the Turkish 7 rather than the English 7 when writing cheques.**
- **Remember that in Turkey numbers are written differently: £5,500.00 is written £5.500,00.**
- **Make sure that you do not write cheques when there are insufficient funds in the account to cover those cheques.**

'Bad' Cheques

Do not even think about writing a cheque on your Turkish bank account if there are not sufficient funds in that account to cover the value of the cheque. This is a criminal offence. Bounced cheques also lead to substantial bank charges and later problems with your bank and others.

- **Keep a close eye on your bank statements and reconcile them to the payments you sent to Turkey and the items you paid out in Turkey.**

Property Insurance

Small earthquakes are a frequent occurrence in southern Turkey. Large ones are, mercifully, rare but can be devastating. Insurance against the risk of earthquake is compulsory, though the cover tends to be limited. Turkey is at risk of earthquakes, but the main earthquake zone is some distance from the area where most foreigners buy property.

It has only recently been possible to take out multi-risk household policies in Turkey. However, these policies are becoming more common, especially in the major cities and tourist areas. They cover the fabric of the building, its contents and any civil responsibility that falls on the owner of the property other than in certain specified circumstances, such as liability incurred in connection with the use of a motor car.

Premiums are comparatively cheap in rural areas, but more expensive in Istanbul and the tourist areas. There are some important points to bear in mind when choosing a suitable policy.

- **Make sure that the level of cover is adequate.**
- **Just as in the UK, if you under-insure the building and the worst happens, the company will not pay you out for the full extent of your loss.**
- **The amount for which you should be covered as far as civil liability is concerned should be a minimum of the equivalent of one million euros and preferably higher. Because the risk of a claim under this category is small, the premiums for this part of the insurance are fairly small and so high levels of cover can be provided at low cost.**
- **Take out cover for the full cost of reconstruction of the building. (If you own an apartment, the cost of the buildings insurance for the whole block of apartments should be included in your service charge. You will then only need contents and public liability insurance.)**
- **As far as contents are concerned, make a detailed estimate of the value of the furnishings and possessions likely to be in the property at any time. Remember to allow for items such as cameras that you may take with**

you on holiday. Pay particular attention to the details of this policy and study the small print about what you have to specify when taking out the insurance and any limitations on claims that can be made against it. If you have any items of high value, notice whether there is a requirement to stipulate them and have them photographed and valued. The insurance company might specify security measures that must be in place in your home – if you do not use them, you may find that you are not covered.

- **If you are using the property as holiday accommodation (or spend long periods away from home), you must specify a policy that is a holiday policy. If you do not, you are likely to find that one of the conditions of the policy is that cover will lapse if the property is empty for 30 or 60 days. Premiums will be higher for holiday homes because the risk is higher.**
- **You will have higher premiums if you intend to let your property. Notify the insurance company of your plans and comply with any of their requirements about the lettings, otherwise your cover could be void.**

There are some UK-based insurance companies who offer cover for properties in Turkey. The main advantages in dealing with a UK company are that the documentation is likely to be in English and that, if you have to make a claim, that claim will be processed in English. There are some Turkish companies that can deal with claims in English, which is a considerable bonus. Unless your Turkish is fluent you would otherwise have to employ somebody to deal with the claim on your behalf or to translate what you have said into Turkish.

There are usually time limits for making claims. If the claim involves theft or break-in you will usually have to report the matter to the police, normally

Case Study: Insure Your Property

Paul and his partner bought a two-bedroom apartment in the centre of Kuşadası on the ground floor of a five-storey building for £24,000. They bought furniture for the apartment and returned to England.

In the winter the couple returned to Kuşadası for a week's holiday, but when they arrived they could not open the door. 'The shop owner gave us the terrible news that our apartment was flooded after heavy rain, and the neighbours had had to open the door with the permission and help of police to save some of our furniture. Bless the neighbours, they did a good job and saved most of our furniture, got the place cleaned and put it all back. When I asked how much I owed for this the shop owner only charged me £20, and he said that was only what he paid to get the unit cleaned. We were very unhappy about what had happened but what [the] neighbours did for us made us feel very special.' Since then, whenever Paul is not in Kuşadası he has left his contact number in the UK with his Turkish neighbours in case something like this happens again. He has also found out that it costs £50 a year for full insurance for an apartment that had cost £24,000.

immediately after discovering the incident and in any case within 24 hours. Notify the insurance company without delay. Check the maximum period before claiming allowed in your policy – it could be as little as 48 hours. As with all important documents in Turkey, the claim should be notified by recorded delivery post.

Home Utilities and Services

Electricity

Electricity is supplied by the state electricity company, **TEDAŞ**. It is cheap by UK standards.

When you buy a new property it will need to be connected to the electricity supply and you will sign a contract with TEDAŞ. In some areas you will stipulate the amount of electricity you want (the peak wattage that you think that you will need) and the tariff you want to subscribe to. Do not underestimate the amount of power you may consume, particularly during the winter months. If you contract for too little power, then your supply will keep cutting out at times of high demand – which is often when you need it most. The extra cost of contracting for, for example, 15kW instead of 12kW is well worth spending. This would be enough to run to electric fires, a washing machine, an electric cooker and a few lights at the same time. It is adequate for most medium-sized homes. Some holiday homes have ridiculously limited wattage.

When you take over an existing property you will take over the electricity supply already connected to it. You will have to ask the electricity company to put the supply into your name, and you will need to produce all your usual documents (passport, details of civil status, proof of residence, bank account details and so on), complete an application form and pay a fee. In the main tourist areas this process is a well-trodden and painless path. If you feel that the supply connected to the property is not going to be adequate for your needs then you can ask for it to be upgraded at this stage, when there will be an additional fee to pay. Any 'old' bill will have to be paid off before you can take over the account.

You can ask your local electricity office to make a special reading of the meter when you take over the property. The office, in rural areas, may be located in the town hall.

If your house is not already connected to the electricity supply, make sure that you get a quotation for connecting electricity to the property *before* you commit yourself to the purchase. The cost can be considerable, particularly if the nearest supply is some distance away.

Paying the Bills

The different bills for the utilities are either sent to your address every month or issued by an authorised employee of a company (for example, TEDAŞ and BEDAŞ for electricity, İSKİ for water and İGDAŞ for natural gas in Istanbul; BEDAŞ for electricity, ASKİ for water and EGO for natural gas in Ankara) when he visits the house or apartment building and reads the meters. He prepares an invoice immediately and places it in your post box. Be aware of fraudsters who may come to your door introducing themselves as authorised personnel requesting immediate payment of an invoice. You should not be taken in: payments are never made in person to someone at your door.

You can make cash payments at certain banks or by directly going to the offices of the company in question, which is common for Turkish people. Keep in mind that payments at the banks are accepted until 3pm. You can also, however, avoid late payments by paying your bills from your account using automatic payment methods. It is best to open an account and supply the bank with a copy of your bill to ensure that they receive the correct information.

If you miss the final date, you will have to go in person to the local office of the supplier and pay in cash. There is a penalty if you pay more than 10 days after the date of issue of the bill. Note that the electricity company is quick to cut off non-payers.

Wiring and Voltage

Electrical wiring in Turkey is done differently from in England. Do not be tempted to have a friendly English electrician re-wire your property in Turkey. If the authorities find that this has been done and that the wiring does not comply with their standards, they can condemn it and disconnect the electricity supply. In any case, mixed or incompatible wiring is dangerous to you and to any workmen working in the premises.

Almost all property in Turkey is now connected at 220 volts.

Interruptions of Supply

These are surprisingly common, including in main cities and major tourist areas, though things are getting better. Cuts can vary from a second or two to many hours. Get a UPS (uninterruptible power supply) to protect computers and other vital equipment and a surge protector to guard sensitive devices. Both are cheap.

Gas

Apart from in major cities like Istanbul and Ankara, which do have natural piped gas supplied by **İGDAŞ** and **EGO**, properties generally use bottled gas.

Some apartments and other developments in urban areas buy bottled gas in huge quantities and store it in their own gas tanks. They then supply the gas to the units in the development by their own pipe system and charge by meter.

Water

Water supplies in Turkey are metered. If your house is not already connected to the mains water supply, make sure that you get a quotation for connecting the property before you commit yourself to the purchase. The cost of the work can be considerable, especially if the nearest water is some way away, though the fee of the contract is small.

All Turkish tap water is drinkable unless marked otherwise. Not all water from wells is drinkable. Not all of the water that is drinkable tastes nice!

Shortages

Despite huge engineering projects to bring water from the areas where there is plenty to the drier south, and the construction of desalination plants in some areas, some of the tourist parts of Turkey are still short of water. The explosion in tourist numbers – and ever increasing *per capita* consumption – means that the authorities are barely holding their own.

As a result there are restrictions on supply, particularly in summer months. In the past some properties were built with a separate **water tank** (*depo*), which could be filled by tanker. This system has been reinstated in some areas so that properties have an emergency supply.

Plumbing

Turkish plumbing is, expressed in the nicest possible way, different from English plumbing! Just as you wouldn't ask an English electrician to wire a Turkish home so you are ill-advised to use your English plumber to plumb pipes in a Turkish home.

Hot Water

There are many different types of water heater, including gas and electric varieties. Solar-powered heating is probably the most common, particularly in the south where it is excellent for summer use but of more limited use in the winter. There is a much greater variety in the marketplace for them than there is in England.

When choosing a heater, make sure that it is adequate to deal with the times when the property is fully occupied by people who take lots of showers. Many 'standard equipment' heaters and hot water tanks in older properties are far too small.

Case Study: Year-round Maintenance

'Having visited Turkey on holidays for the last eight years, we fell in love with the country, its excellent climate and friendly people,' says Adam, 'so we decided to look for a holiday home initially, somewhere to bring friends and family, as we also found house prices very favourable. We looked for a large home big enough to bring a large family, and one which was close to the sea. A swimming pool was considered to be a necessity for the children. We have found and purchased a large three-bedroom apartment in a complex so everyone in the family is very happy. In our complex we are paying £20 a month maintenance which covers all the garden, pool, cleaning, security and electricity costs of the complex. Electric and water expenses in the apartment cost about £200 a year if you live there permanently and use air-conditioning. All the paperwork was arranged by the English-speaking solicitor and cost us only 1 per cent of the total amount.'

As a result of his experience Adam thinks it is worth looking for property that needs renovation – although they paid about £60,000, the value of the house has gone up to £75,000, and labour is cheap in Turkey.

Wells

A well is a good thing! Even though you may not use it for drinking water, it will be an excellent and cheap way of watering your garden or filling your swimming pool. Some wells dry up in the summer. Some have gone to salt, so are useless. If your property has a well and you think that it is going to be important to you, make sure that your rights to the well and its water are protected in your contract of purchase.

If you want to use your well for drinking water, get it checked by the health department or by your local water company, who will issue a certificate confirming that it is fit for human consumption.

Septic Tanks

Most rural Turkish properties depend on a septic tank or something more simple for drainage. A septic tank is, essentially, a filter that treats sewage by breaking it down bacteriologically before discharging relatively harmless water into the ground.

There are two types of septic tank commonly found in Turkey. Older tanks dealt only with the waste from toilets, leaving the waste from sinks and baths to be deposited in a gravel soakaway and thus to be dispersed, without treatment, into the surrounding ground. More modern septic tanks deal with all the waste water from toilets and sinks. It is all treated and ultimately dispersed.

Septic tanks have a natural lifespan, which can be extended by careful treatment but not indefinitely. If you have to replace an old-fashioned tank you will have to do so with a new-style tank, for which you need planning permission.

If you are replacing the tank, make sure that the size is adequate for your requirements. It should be based on the maximum use of the house and the amount of water that would be generated by people used to having lots of baths or showers. If you install a tank that is too small you will simply have to empty it with monotonous frequency and at considerable cost. If you install a large tank, emptying it will be a rare event and, more importantly for maintenance and longevity, it will not just be a means of disposing of excess volumes of liquid.

If you are buying a house with a septic tank, have it checked by your surveyor.

Swimming Pools

Swimming pools are expensive. There is not just the capital cost of building the pool (typically about £10,000 for a modest pool, £20,000 for a larger one) but the annual cost of maintaining it. That can be several thousand pounds if you are often absent from the property and thus require a professional maintenance company to come in and treat it – often twice a week in the summer.

You need permission to put a pool into an existing property, which involves applying for planning permission (*ruhsat*) from your local town hall. The process is swifter if entrusted to a local builder or pool specialist.

Television

British TV sets don't work in Turkey because of different transmission systems. However, they can sometimes be modified to do so.

Digital television broadcasts, both cable and satellite, began in 2000, one of the main providers being Digiturk (**www.digiturk.com.tr**); the usual mix of sport, lifestyle, entertainment and documentary channels is on offer.

For more on television channels and programming, *see* 'The Media', pp.204–5.

Telephones

Fixed Phone (Land) Lines

Telephone connections are readily available in all areas, although connections in rural areas can be very poor. However non-resident foreigners may not (at present) have a land line, though they may of course have a mobile phone.

Once you have a residence permit, the method of connecting to the system and billing for calls is similar to that for electricity. To get a phone line installed, contact your nearest **Türk Telekom** office and present your passport. You will pay a connection fee. If your property already has a phone installed, check with Türk Telekom before using it that there are no outstanding bills on your predecessor's account. If there are and you fail to tell Türk Telekom, the line will be suspended, and you will only get incoming calls (as well as someone else's bill).

Pay Phones

The national network, PTT, has phone booths throughout Turkey. Purchase a phone card at any post office; they come in denominations of 30, 60 and 100 units. Occasionally you will find phones where you use a token (*jeton*), although these are rapidly disappearing.

Tokens

Pick up the receiver and place the appropriate token into the slot. Dial when you hear beeps and a red light goes off. When you are about to run out of time, the beeping cuts in again until you insert additional tokens. If you dial an emergency number from a phone that takes tokens, you need to insert a token, which is returned to you after the call.

Phone Cards

You can choose the language! Pick up the receiver and place the card into the slot. When a beeping sound is heard, dial the number. As with tokens, more beeping is a signal that you are about to be cut off, but then a 'change card' message appears on the display to remind you to put in a new card or else the call will end. Press 'change card' and change it when the machine says so. You do not need to insert a card to dial an emergency number.

Other Cards

Smart cards can be also used in pay phones and are sold in units of either 100 or 350. There are also different telephone cards for different telephone boxes, sold in units of 50, and a growing number of credit-card-operated phones in major cities. The Türk Telekom Global Card is valid for making domestic and international calls in Turkey and to call anywhere in the world. Both types of

Area Codes and the Operator

When making domestic calls to anywhere in Turkey with a different area code, dial 0, then the area code, then the 7-digit number. Istanbul, true to its position spanning two continents, has two different area codes: 212 for the European side and 216 for the Asian side. If you are calling from one side to the other, you need to prefix this code with 0. This is counted as a 'within the city' (s‚ehiriçi) call.

For international calls from Turkey: dial 00 + country code (44 for the UK) + area code (omit the initial 0) + number. For calls from the UK to Turkey: dial 00 + 90 + area code (omit the initial 0) + 7-digit number.

To be connected with an operator to give instructions about the number you wish to call, and if you need to reverse the charges, call 115 for international calls and 131 for domestic calls. Operators generally speak Turkish only.

Useful Telephone Numbers

110	Fire	170	Tourist information
112	Ambulance	183	Social Services
115	International operator	184	Health
118	Directory assistance	185	Water breakdown
131	Domestic operator	186	Electricity breakdown
154	Traffic	187	Gas breakdown
155	Police	189	Tax information

cards are sold at a range of places including Türk Telekom shops, small vendors and news-stands near phone booths, and Bakkal or Büfe convenience shops (look for signs in the shop windows).

For services and tariffs go to **www.turktelekom.com.tr**.

International Phone Cards

International calls from Turkey are expensive, but discount calling cards can cut costs immensely. Fierce competition between a multitude of companies makes getting an overview difficult, but one good option is usually the Superonline Hasret Karti (**www.hasretkarti.com**), which is sold all over the country. All calling cards can be used on all fixed lines. Call the toll-free customer line and dial the PIN shown on the back of your card followed by the phone number that you wish to connect to. An automated voice informs you how many minutes you can talk with that card, and then the call is connected.

Mobile Phones

Like virtually everywhere else, the use of mobiles in Turkey has gone up and up, with many people pretty much relying on them rather than using the often less trustworthy Turkish land lines. There's no problem buying a pay-as-you-go phone or topping up your account in most towns and cities, and coverage in all places apart from remote mountain areas is good. If you cannot get a good signal, remember that you may be able to alter your phone so that it works with a different network.

If you want a prepaid line subscription you need to have a copy of your passport (as well as presenting your original passport) and a signed subscription agreement in which you indicate which GSM operator you have selected. For an invoiced line subscription you will need to present your passport, residence permit and a surety document certified by a notary public or a letter of guarantee from a bank.

International Mobile Equipment Identity (IMEI)

Mobile phone theft has become rife in recent years, so it makes sense to make a note of your IMEI number and keep this on you – away from your phone of course. The way to find your IMEI is to dial *#06#. Your 15-digit IMEI number then appears. Should your phone go missing, you must call your service provider and give your IMEI number. The provider will automatically stop anyone using your phone number, even with a different SIM card.

SIM Cards and International Roaming

If you want to use your UK mobile in Turkey then, at least 14 days before leaving home, contact your phone company to arrange 'international roaming' access. Even incoming calls from abroad using this method will be expensive, though there are some hefty discount plans. To pick up voicemails while you're in Turkey you need to arrange for a new access number.

Check the charges for international roaming services with your UK network provider, and remember to take an electrical adaptor for the charger plug. Vouchers for topping up calling credit may not be obtainable in Turkey, so stock up before you go. International roaming charges can be exorbitant (you can be charged twice, once in Turkey and once overseas, to send text messages, for instance), and you may do better having your phone unlocked from its UK network and installing a Turkish SIM card, or buying or renting a phone in Turkey. You can buy prepaid SIM cards, or subscribe via any of a range of pay-as-you-go packages to Aria-Aycell, Telsim and Turkcell.

A GSM mobile from northern Europe, Australia or New Zealand should work fine in Turkey (it is cheaper if you purchase a SIM card in Turkey).

Your Turkish mobile phone number will be prefixed 05 and common prefixes are 0535, 0536, 0542, 0543 and 0555. Phoning mobiles is expensive, so be aware of these codes even if you are just using land lines.

The Internet

E-mail and Internet use has spread rapidly through much of the country. Internet cafés are easy enough to find in resorts, towns and cities and you can pick up your e-mail there; most UK ISPs have a website where you can pick up your mail by typing in your user name and password – or you can use a web-based e-mail address such as those provided by Yahoo! (**www.yahoo.com**) or Hotmail (**www.hotmail.com**). If you are thinking of taking your own laptop, be aware that UK cables won't work – you need North American standard cable.

You can get an Internet connection through Türk Telekom or any number of private companies. Connections are via phone or cable TV lines. For dial-up phone line connections, contact your local Türk Telekom office in your district to set up payment of a monthly or annual fee. You can buy CDs from any Türk Telekom centre to install the software and start immediately; do the same if you want to extend it. Cable TV connection (through various companies) is not universally available but gives a faster connection speed; you pay an instalment charge and a monthly fee. Broadband is widely available across the country, but is expensive, costing around £35 a month for the slowest speeds.

Major Turkish ISPs include E-kolay, Superonline and Turk.net.

Postal Services

Postal services can be slow, and you should allow four to five days for getting a letter to or from the UK. Use an **express postal service** if it is urgent, or send by a private **courier** firm or cargo company such as DHL or Aras Kargo. If sending a parcel overseas, you need to complete a form declaring its contents, and if the destination is outside the EU the parcel should be unsealed to allow inspection.

Stamps are available only from the PTT.

Note the different slots in **post boxes**: *yurtdışı* for overseas, *yurtiçi* for inland and *şehiriçi* for local.

You can spot a Turkish **post office** (*postahane*, literally post house, or – as it's usually used in its shorter, but wrongly spelled form – *postane*) by its sign with black PTT letters on a yellow background. Major post offices are open Monday to Saturday 8am–12 midnight, and Sunday 9–7. Small post offices are open Monday to Friday 8.30–12.30 and 1–5. PTT also runs telephone services and phone booths. Post offices provide all the things you would expect, including:

- **foreign currency exchange at international rates.**
- **international money orders.**
- **fax service.**

Useful Post Vocabulary

airmail ***uçakla***
domestic mail ***yurtiçi mektup***
express postal service ***Acele Posta Servisi (APS)***
global mail ***uluslarasi mektup***
inner-city mail ***ehiriçi mektup***
letter ***mektup***
registered mail ***taahhütlü mektup***
small package ***koli***
stamp ***pul*** **or** ***posta pulu***
telegraph ***telegraf*** **or** ***telgraf***
telephone card ***telefon kartı***
telephone token ***telefon jetonu*** **or just** ***jeton***

- **banking services.**
- **Internet services.**
- **PTT telephone cards and tokens.**
- **express postal services (Acele Posta Servisi or APS) for Turkey and abroad, for letters and small packages.**
- **collection of mail *poste restante* from a central post office (*Merkez Postahanesi* or *Postanesi*) in any town; mail should be marked as '*poste restante*'; you will need to show an identity card or passport to collect it.**

The Media

Although Turkey is not one of the most liberal countries in Europe, it has a very lively media world. Apart from the state-owned TV channels and radio stations, there are numerous private channels and stations that represent or aim at different political, economic, social, cultural and generational groups. There is also a lively and colourful press that plays an important role in political, social and economic life.

Today, there are more than 250 television channels and 1,000 radio channels in Turkey, 16 of which are national, 15 regional and 227 local. Furthermore, approximately 3,500 periodicals (newspapers and magazines) are published in Turkey.

The military, Atatürk and his legacy, minorities (notably Kurds) and political Islam are still sensitive subjects for Turkish journalists to write about, and writing critically about official attitudes to these subjects can lead to criminal prosecution. It is often reported by human rights organisations that journalists are imprisoned, or attacked by police during demonstrations. It is also common for radio and TV stations to have their broadcasts suspended for airing 'sensitive' material. Programmes in Kurdish and other minority languages, which had been banned for many years, were introduced by the state broadcasting authority in June 2004 as part of reforms intended to meet EU criteria on minorities.

Newspapers and Magazines

There are more than 30 daily newspapers in Turkey. The mass-circulation dailies are based in Istanbul and distributed nationally; more than a dozen dailies are published in Istanbul. Nine dailies are published in Ankara and three in İzmir. Almost every city has at least one local daily newspaper.

The main national newspapers are:

- ***Birgün*** **– a left-wing daily.**
- ***Cumhuriyet*** **– a republican, left-wing nationalist daily.**
- ***Evrensel*** **– a left-wing daily.**

- ***Hürriyet* – a mass-circulation, liberal-conservative daily.**
- ***Milliyet* – a mass-circulation liberal daily.**
- ***Posta* – a mass-circulation daily.**
- ***Radikal* – a liberal-left daily.**
- ***Sabah* – a mass-circulation liberal daily.**
- ***Turkish Daily News* – an English-language daily.**
- ***Ülkede Özgür Gündem* – a left-wing, pro-Kurdish daily.**
- ***Vakit* – a right-wing Islamist daily.**
- ***Yeni Şafak* – a conservative, liberal Islamist daily.**
- ***Zaman* – a conservative daily with an English-language web version.**

The total circulation of magazines (including news magazines), which are generally published weekly or monthly, is around 2.3 million.

News magazines, which carry interesting news stories and detailed information on current topics, underwent an important change in terms of context and form in recent decades. The majority of them are now printed and presented more aesthetically and have a more modern look.

Turkey also has a long tradition of publishing satirical and cartoon magazines and is one of the leading countries of the world in this regard.

English-language Press

The English-language *Turkish Daily News* is published in Ankara and is available in larger cities and resorts. There is an online version at **www.turkishdailynews.com**; reading it is a good way of really getting into Turkish current affairs and life. There is also an English-language web version of the right-wing Islamist daily *Zaman* (**www.zaman.com**).

Foreign newspapers and magazines are available in Istanbul and major resorts, but sometimes they are one or two days old.

Internet news sites can also sometimes be useful for following developments in Turkey, particularly **www.turkishpress.com**.

Radio

The state broadcaster **Turkish Radio and Television Corporation (Türkiye Radyo Televizyon Kurumu – TRT)** was established in 1964. Consequently the transmission power of radio stations and the number of licensed receivers greatly increased. Today, TRT also broadcasts television and radio programmes abroad in Turkish and in several foreign languages.

TRT has four national radio channels: *Radyo-1*, *Radyo-2* (*TRT-FM*), *Radyo-3* and *Radyo-4*. It has one local radio channel, which is the Hatay Provincial Radio (*TRT*

Hatay FM), and eight regional channels, including: *Trabzon Radyosu* in the Black Sea region, *Erzurum Radyosu* in the east Anatolia region, *GAP Radyosu* (Diyarbakır) in the southeast Anatolia region, *Çukurova Radyosu* in Mersin, and *Antalya Radyosu* in the Mediterranean region.

Radyo-1 is a national radio station that broadcasts 24 hours a day and deals with daily subjects and current events. ***Radyo-2*** (*TRT-FM*) has a big following and broadcasts popular music programmes; it has studios in Ankara, Istanbul and İzmir. ***Radyo-3*** appeals to music fans with its classical music, pop music, opera, ballet and jazz programmes. ***Radyo-4*** broadcasts Turkish classical music and Turkish folk music. The ***Türkiye'nin Sesi Radyosu*** ('Voice of Turkey Radio') and the ***Turizm Radyosu*** ('Tourism Radio') are other radio stations which broadcast under the TRT umbrella.

TRT had a constitutionally mandated monopoly on radio and television broadcasting before 1993. A dual structure appeared in Turkey with the establishment of **private radio stations** after a change in legislation that authorised private radio and television in tandem with public broadcasting. Today, more than 1,000 radio stations, around 35 of which are national, are active in the country.

These are some of the private radio stations:

- **www.acikradyo.com.tr** – commercial.
- **www.capitalradio.com.tr** – commercial, pop music.
- **www.showradyo.com.tr** – commercial.

Television

As mentioned above, the legislation to authorise private radio and television in tandem with public broadcasting was approved by parliament only in 1993. However, private stations had begun to broadcast programmes even before they were legalised. After the amendment, many national, regional and local radio stations and television channels applied to the Supreme Board of Radio and Television. Because of the advances in this field there was a huge expansion in the diversity and richness of TV channels between 1990 and 1998.

Nowadays, **TRT television** (**www.trt.net.tr**) broadcasts are made via seven different channels: *TRT-1*, *TRT-2*, *TRT-3*, *TRT-4*, *TRT-GAP*, *TRT-INT* and *TRT-TÜRK*. These channels provide news, relay information and entertain viewers of various ages and professions as well as different educational and cultural backgrounds. ***TRT-1*** is a general public broadcasting station; ***TRT-2***, which broadcasts non-stop for 24 hours, is a news channel. *TRT-3* and *TRT-GAP* share air time; ***TRT-3*** attracts sports fans with its sports programmes, and in addition functions under the name *TBMM-TV* on days when the Turkish Grand National Assembly (*Türkiye Büyük Millet Meclisi* – TBMM) is in session. ***TRT-GAP*** broadcasts programmes aimed at citizens living in east and southeast Anatolia. ***TRT-4*** is an educational channel that supports the national education policy. ***TRT-INT*** serves as a bridge for Turkish citizens living abroad. ***TRT-TÜRK*** is Turkey's voice in Central Asia and the Caucasus.

Apart from these channels there are over 15 private television channels in Turkey, broadcasting nationwide. ***ATV***, ***Kanal D***, ***Show TV***, ***Star TV***, the music channels ***Kral TV***, ***Number One TV*** and ***Best TV***, the economy channel ***CNBC-e*** and the news channels ***NTV*** and ***CNN-Türk*** are among the leading specialist private television channels. As with the printed media, there is also intensity in the visual media. These are some of the private TV channels with an indication of their political leanings:

- ***ATV*** **– a widely watched network, channel of the centrist Sabah Newspaper Group.**
- ***CNN-Türk*** **– the Turkish offshoot of the well-known news channel.**
- ***NTV*** **– a private news channel.**
- ***Kanal D*** **– a widely watched network, centre, belonging to the Doğan Group (which also owns *Hürriyet*, *Milliyet* and *Radikal* newspapers).**
- ***Show TV*** **– a widely watched network, centre.**
- ***Star TV*** **– the first station to break state TV's monopoly, centre-right.**
- ***TGRT*** **– conservative, right-wing network.**
- ***TV7*** **– conservative, right-wing network.**

Security, Crime and the Police

Turkey is as safe as most European countries for travellers. Nevertheless, street crime is on the up, and it is always prudent to exercise reasonable caution, especially in crowded places such as airports, railway stations and street markets, where valuables should be kept well out of sight, away from snatching hands and bag-slashers.

The big cities – Istanbul, İzmir and Ankara – are relative hotspots where you need to be particularly wary. Common ruses are pickpocketing – for instance someone tries to clean off something from your clothing while his accomplice relieves you of your valuables – and bag-slashing, achieved with a razor blade while you stand in a crowded place oblivious to what's happening. If you notice quickly enough that you've been robbed, don't run after the thief (who may be armed); you could shout '*kapkaççı!*' (pronounced cup-KATCH-chuh and meaning 'thief') – it might just save the situation.

Regular **police** (*polis*) wear blue uniforms and are generally helpful, though don't expect them to be fluent in English. The traffic police (*trafik polisi*) wear white caps and deal exclusively with road traffic. Some cities have their own tourist police. In remote country areas you will see a division of the armed forces known as the *jandarma*, sometimes armed with rifles. There are also military police, dressed in army uniform with the letters ASİZ, who keep order among the conscripts.

The phone number for the police is **t** 155.

Protecting Your House

Since your house or flat in Turkey may be left unattended for long periods if you do not intend to live there, it is particularly important to make it as burglar-proof as possible (if only for your own peace of mind), with good window locks, substantial door locks and maybe even a security camera or alarm system. Double glazing is good news as far as security goes, as it is hard to break through; but a burglar needs only one point of entry, and it is worth thinking how you yourself would get in if you lost your keys – that's the way the burglar would go.

The Terrorism Threat

Unfortunately, minor terrorist attacks are fairly commonplace in Turkey, though rarely have attacks been directed at foreigners. One notable exception to this was the 2003 al-Qaeda car bomb attack on the British Consulate, the HSBC Bank and two synagogues in Istanbul which killed numerous people and wounded hundreds. But more commonly terrorism in the country occurs largely as part of the separatist campaigns in the southeast of the country, part of a 25-year guerrilla war that has left 35,000 people dead. It was these Kurdish separatists who hit the headlines in the British media in August 2006, when bomb blasts in the resorts of Antalya and Marmaris injured 21 people including 10 Britons. This was part of an attempt to derail Turkey's burgeoning tourist industry – worth £10.5 million annually – and force government concessions.

While there is a possibility of further attacks, generally Turkey and particularly the resorts along its southern coast are no more likely to become terror targets than London. For the latest on the country's security situation, check the website of the British Embassy in Ankara (**www.britishembassy.gov.uk**) and look under 'Travel Advice'.

Women and Safety

Most foreign women visiting or living in Turkey encounter no major problems from either men or women, and if you are a woman you should not let the possibility of hassle deter you from travelling alone if that's what you want to do. It is extremely rare for women to be subjected to violent crime, but many Turks aren't used to seeing women travelling alone and, unfortunately, a few Turkish men assume all Western women are sexually available. As a result, you

Case Study: Roy and Angela

Roy and Angela have recently retired and are in their late 60s. They holidayed in Turkey after Greece became too expensive, and were attracted by the general tempo of things, the cost of living, the friendliness of the people and the low crime rate. 'Here,' says Roy, 'we can safely walk the town or city streets at any hour of the day or night.' In 2003 they bought a semi-detached three-bedroomed villa for £26,000 on a small complex at Caliş near Fethiye. They considered Bodrum too commercialised and Marmaris too rowdy.

The villa is a holiday home for themselves, family and friends, where Roy and Angela spend around four fortnights a year, including Christmas. 'Fethiye suits us as an elderly but active couple. It's not overcommercialised. We've found the Turks to be the friendliest and most honest people we have ever come across. We cannot think of any bad points worth mentioning, and may buy a second house this year to let as holiday accommodation.'

may suffer unwelcome attention – stares, groping, pinching, unwanted advances, comments and noises – but most Turkish men are emphatically not like that. If harassed, shout *ayıp!* (shame!) loudly – this might get the message across. In more extreme cases you could shout *utanmaz!* (you shameless!) and try to get the attention of others (especially women) around you – most of them would intervene and support you. By introducing yourself to other Turkish women you meet, you may be included in their group and be much less likely to suffer such problems.

Do as the Turkish do – act formal – avoid overt smiling at male strangers (which tends to indicate that you are being more than just friendly), and avoid being alone with a man you do not know at all, especially in a car. Be aware that men will have different experiences and expectations of women according to their social and cultural background or the region that they come from, and their standards of behaviour will vary accordingly.

Tips

Here are some obvious and not-so-obvious tips to help you avoid being the subject of crime, or to help you deal with it should you be unlucky:

- **Keep copies of everything – insurance, credit card and bank account details, driving licence and so on – securely in an obscure place at home (for example, inside a book). It is also a good idea to scan the first two pages of your passport into your computer, in case your passport disappears – if you have a scanned copy it will be much easier to obtain a replacement. If you e-mail your scanned passport to yourself whenever you go travelling, you will always have some kind of backup if disaster strikes.**
- **Avoid using cash machines in dodgy-looking (particularly quiet) areas.**

- **Carry handbags on the opposite side from the traffic in the street to avoid motorcycle muggers.**
- **Lock car doors if you're inside and don't leave valuables on the seat next to you (stow them under the seat instead).**
- **If you get robbed, cancel any cards you have lost immediately, and change your locks if your keys have been stolen. Don't try to chase after thieves – they might be armed.**
- **Do not take letters, parcels or other items from strangers for delivery either in or outside Turkey.**
- **Don't let paranoia about crime spoil your enjoyment of Turkey. On the whole it is a peaceful country, and violent crime such as robbery is very rare.**

Owning a Car in Turkey

Don't take your car from the UK. You will be much better off buying a car when you arrive in Turkey and it is much safer to drive a car with the steering wheel on the left-hand side. This is particularly the case if you will be driving in towns or country areas without the benefit of a passenger to help you check for oncoming vehicles when overtaking. You will also find that it is much easier to get spare parts for Turkish cars. Even if you think your present car is sold throughout Europe you will find that there are many parts that are different on the UK model because its steering wheel is on the right. It is also widely reported that a local car makes you less visible in the community and thus less likely to be burgled. Cars in Turkey are generally cheaper than in England and so selling your car in the UK and buying another one when you arrive could be financially advantageous.

If you insist on taking your British car you will be able to use it on Turkish roads only for a maximum of six months. You need an **international green card** from your insurers and a document showing proof of your ownership of the vehicle. A further six months' extension may be granted if you apply to the customs authorities before the expiry of the initial six-month period; apply to the **Turkish Touring and Automobile Club** (**Türkiye Turing ve Otomobil Kurumu**; **www.turing.org.tr/eng**) or to the **General Directorate of Customs** (**Gümrükler Genel Müdürlüğü**), Ulus Ankara, **t** 0312 310 38 80/18, **f** 0312 311 13 46.. The car can only lawfully be used on Turkish roads when it complies fully with the requirements necessary for use on English roads, including rules relating to testing and taxing it. Insurance will only be available from British insurance companies and you will have to disclose to the company that you are using the vehicle abroad.

If you intend to keep a British car in Turkey for more than six months you will need to insure and tax it in Turkey. Additionally you will have to obtain a Turkish visitor's plate, for which you require the following:

- **a work permit.**
- **a residence permit.**
- **a letter from your employer confirming your employment in Turkey.**
- **a letter of guarantee from a bank in Turkey.**
- **a valid driving licence.**

The minimum age for a class A licence is 18. For car hire insurance purposes the rules for other classes are as follows:

- **Classes B, D, E and F – age 22 and over, must have one year's valid national or international licence.**
- **Classes G and H – age 25 and over, must have 2 years' valid national or international licence.**
- **Classes L, X and M – age 27 years and over, must have 3 years' national or international licence.**

Speed limits are 120kph on highways, 90kph in the country and 50kph in built-up areas unless otherwise indicated.

Driving Licences

Whether you buy a car in Turkey or import your own car, you will have to decide what to do about your driving licence. UK driving licences are valid in Turkey, but you have the option of exchanging it for a Turkish one. This does not require you to take the Turkish driving test. Should you decide to keep your UK driving licence and stay in Turkey for an extended period, you will be obliged to have your licence translated into Turkish. This must be notarised either by a notary public or the UK consular authorities in Turkey.

Taking Your Pet

Rules about taking pets to and from Turkey have changed dramatically over the last few years. Get up-to-date information before making any plans by contacting your local vet or the Department for Environment, Food and Rural Affairs (DEFRA), especially if you want to take an exotic animal to Turkey. Animals other than ordinary pets would require a special importation certificate from the Turkish Ministry of Agriculture, which could have conditions attached to it.

You must decide whether you intend ever to bring the pet back to the UK. If so, you will have to comply with the British rules for the importation of pets into the UK, which are more stringent than the rules about the importation of pets into Turkey. At present Turkey is not part of the PETS travel scheme of Pet Passports that avoid the need for quarantine on return; for an up-to-date list of countries included in PETS, *see* **www.defra.gov.uk/animalh/quarantine/pets/territory.htm**.

If you know that you are not going to want to bring your pet back to the UK, all you need is an export certificate from the Department for Environment, Food and Rural Affairs and a health certificate issued within 15 days of your departure by an approved vet. Cats must be vaccinated against various ailments. Individuals are generally only allowed to take two animals into Turkey at any one time, but this doesn't prevent you from coming back and bringing more animals later.

Once you arrive, see a vet and find out what vaccinations are advisable.

Food and Drink

Turkey has one of the great cuisines of the world, which more than holds its own against the inevitable incursions of Western restaurant chains. It has many familiar elements: yoghurt ('yoghurt' is derived from the Turkish word *yoğurt*), salads, stuffed vine leaves (*yaprak sarma*), syrupy filo pastry desserts and fish in olive oil among them.

It is easy to eat interestingly, healthily and cheaply in Turkey. Fresh produce costs generally about half of what you pay in the UK, and often for better quality. There's a wonderful array of fruit and nuts on offer, including peaches, strawberries, bananas, almonds, chestnuts, hazelnuts, pistachios and cherries. Weekly markets in your neighbourhood (*semt pazarı*) are a great hunting ground, with the benefit that you can taste before you buy.

During the Ottoman Empire, laws were passed to ensure the freshness of food. The effect of this is still noticeable today: freshly baked bread, seasonal fruit and veg – including peaches in spring, figs in summer and quinces in autumn – and nuts and olives year-round.

Many Turkish foods have origins dating centuries back. Wine-growing in Anatolia, in the eastern part of the country, began with the Greeks, while the Persians were responsible for the introduction of sweets and rice, and yoghurt dates from Ottoman days. Nomadic tribes cooked up the first shish-kebabs and flatbreads, the latter baked on a griddle known as a *sac*. Some recipes were perfected by chefs working at Topkapı, the sultan's palace in Istanbul.

Turkey is almost unique in being self-sufficient in food production (although it doesn't manage to grow coffee), with endless supplies of fish and shellfish from the Black Sea, Marmara, Aegean and Mediterranean coasts, tea plantations in the north, and hot pepper and melon production in the south and southeast. Grapes producing wine and sultanas are ubiquitous, while lamb and chicken provide the bulk of the meat. There are also some excellent cheeses, made from cow's, sheep's and goat's milk. The regional differences provide boundless gastronomic possibilities, as well as culinary variations – there are for example at least 40 ways to prepare aubergine. The abundant supply of inexpensive but high-quality ingredients makes it easy to concoct some impressive Turkish dishes yourself. Classic tastes are provided by such seasonings as dill, mint, parsley, garlic, cinnamon, the lemony *sumac* and yoghurt. To pep things up, a handy condiment is Aleppo pepper flakes (*pul biber*), a semi-moist, hot, flaked red pepper used like black pepper. There's plenty of vegetarian choice, including tempting honeys, preserves, nut products and cheeses.

Eating Out

Prices for eating out are low compared with the UK, and even if you're on a tight budget it can be barely more expensive than cooking for yourself. As this is a Muslim country, pork and pork products are always off the menu, but there are plenty of other meat dishes, along with seafood and vegetables. English, Italian and Indian restaurants can also be found, especially in the more touristy places, though standards may not be high.

Eateries are called either *lokanta* or restaurant (usually pronounced and sometimes also spelled as *restoran*), with the latter generally being a more expensive establishment, although it is not that clear-cut.

In cheaper restaurants you usually find ready-cooked dishes on a steam table, with a choice of chicken and lamb dishes, kebabs, salads, aubergine (*patlıcan*), beans, pilaf rice and bulgur wheat: point to what you want, and choose several if you like. It is prudent to avoid food that looks as if it has been standing around for some time, as this can be a source of food poisoning. You won't pay more than £5 for a course in these places. *Esnaf lokantası* (shopkeepers' restaurants) or *çarşıs* can be found in the side streets of city centres and are usually simple but clean, and offer very delicious 'Turkish' meals for good prices.

In the more upmarket restaurant, usually a *restoran*, you will typically pay £10 or so, rising to £60 without drinks in top establishments. There will be glass cabinets with *mezes* – known in Turkish as *meze* (plural: *mezeler*). Either hot (*sıcak mezeler*) or cold (*soğuk mezeler*), these are Turkish specialities that show off the skill of the chef and provide very substantial starters. They might include pureed aubergine, seafood, miniature filled pasta (*mantı*), stuffed vine leaves, pickles, hot *mezeler* with cheese or meat stuffing (*börek*), or mackerel stuffed with pilaf. Additionally, soup comes in many forms, one of the most ubiquitous being *mercimek çorbaşı*, a red lentil soup with a dash of lemon. The *zeytinağlı* or olive oil course includes peppers or tomatoes steeped in olive oil and usually served at room temperature. Main courses feature barbecued chicken, steaks, mixed grills, roast lamb, lamb chops (*pirzola*), spiced lamb meatballs (*köfte*), and numerous forms of kebab (*kebap*) – the last of these include the familiar shish kebab (*şiş kebap*) and *döner kebap*, as well as items such as *kağıt kebap* (lamb and vegetables cooked in foil) and *iskender kebap* (a mixed platter covered in melted butter with a tomato-based sauce). As an accompaniment there are chips, pilaf, almost universally excellent bread, and salads featuring tomatoes, cucumber, hot peppers and onion. This is rounded off with a dessert, maybe made of filo pastry or flavoured with rosewater or saffron, or a fruit platter (including water-melon, plums, strawberries and cherries), followed by tea or coffee.

Among more specialist eateries, the Turkish pizza parlour (*pide salonu*) is another institution. Kebab salons are just that, while *işkembeci* focus on tripes, sweetmeats, brains and the like. For snacks, there are speciality pastry shops (*muhallebeci* or *pastahane*) offering extremely sweet nutty cakes (*baklava*), and Turkish delight (*lokum*).

In some areas, outdoor restaurants are sometimes set up with a few tables and chairs; you will find them in coastal areas and at some places out in the country. It is all rather cheerfully impromptu, with no signs or menu, and can be a great bargain, with delicious *mezes*, salads, fish and desserts. There's no shortage of street food, with vendors selling sandwiches, bread rings covered with sesame seeds, fruit, freshly squeezed fruit juice, kebabs and *köfte*.

Drinks

The one drink you can hardly avoid is **tea**, which is grown on the Black Sea coast and offered to guests as soon as they arrive anywhere. It is usually served in glasses (though comes in china cups in posher hotels and some cafés) and is served from a porcelain teapot, or occasionally from a samovar-style urn. Here and there you stumble across old-fashioned teahouses and tea gardens (*çay bahçesi*), and occasionally you still might find a *nargile*, or hubble-bubble water pipe, for smoking fruit-flavoured tobacco. If you're entertaining a Turk to tea, remember to make it from tea leaves, as tea bags are often frowned upon. Apple peel tea (*elma çayı*) is also popular with some people.

Turkish coffee is seriously strong, and served black in small espresso-sized porcelain cups (sometimes followed by fortune-telling of coffee grounds) – very sweet (*şekerli*), slightly sweet (*az şekerli*) or without sugar (*şekersiz*). **Coffee** is taken as a morning drink around 11am and after meals. Instant coffee does exist, and tends to be called Neskahve or *kahve* regardless of brand.

Soft drinks (*meşrubat*) feature the usual sweet fizzy stuff, as well as bottled or fresh fruit juice (such as sour cherry or apricot), and *ayran*, made of whipped yoghurt and water.

Turkey produces **wine** – red (*kırmızı*), white (*beyaz*) and rosé (*roze*) – and although little of it finds its way abroad it is inexpensive and often of reason-ably good quality; there's also a market for expensive imported wines. Thrace, the Euphrates Valley, Cappadocia and western Anatolia are among the main wine-producing areas. Look out for the red Buzbağ from eastern Turkey and for the white Turasan from the Cappadocia area.

Beer (*bira*) is much more popular: Turkish varieties include Efes Pilsen, sold Dark, Extra or Lite (the latter being low- alcohol). There are also imported beers such as Tuborg, Heineken, Becks and Budweiser.

Rakı, the national drink of Turkey, is a 50 per cent proof spirit made of raisins and aniseed, similar to Greek ouzo. Turkish **liqueurs** such as *acıbadem* (almond) sometimes appear at the end of the meal.

Protocol

It is not the done thing for household members to eat on their own, grazing from the fridge or on the go while others are at home. Turkish families eat together, sitting down for meals three times a day, starting with a breakfast (*kahvaltı*) of bread, feta cheese, jam, olives and tea. The evening meal is elaborate and lengthy, with *mezes*, olive-oil dishes, dessert, fruit and coffee. Turks also go in for serious picnics in the countryside, but then the concept of the host providing everything disappears – instead all members of the party agree in advance who will bring what.

Shopping

Shopping in Turkey is a unique experience for foreigners, not only for tourists but also for residents. There are a few things you may find helpful to know in advance so that you can shop more effectively and enjoyably.

When shopping for daily supplies of food and drink you can choose the 'modern' way of 'weekly shopping' in supermarkets, hypermarkets or shopping malls, which can be found in every large city, town or tourist resort. Supermarkets offer a very large variety of products, especially European ones, and, as in Western Europe, prices are cheaper in them.

However, for your daily needs you can always use a small grocery or corner shop (*bakkalliye*, or *bakkal* for short) near where you live or work. Some of them are nowadays called '*market*' or even '*süpermarket*', although they are very small, but the main difference is the fact that in the traditional *bakkal*s you usually don't have access to the shelves behind the counter and are served by the shopkeeper (*bakkal*) himself. You would find such traditional shops in small cities or in the neighbourhood (*mahhale* or *semt*) you live in.

Smaller shops or kiosks doing the same job are usually called *büfe* and sometimes there is no access into these shops – you buy things through a window. The smaller the shop is, the more expensive the prices, but usually the difference is not that great.

Very few of these *bakkal*s or *büfe*s sell things apart from packed food and drinks. For fruit and vegetables go to a *manav* (greengrocer), where you can always find fresh products in open boxes and, as in *bakkal*s, you will be served by the shopkeeper, though sometimes you may be allowed to select the products from the boxes. The butcher is called *kasap* and the fishmonger *balıkçı*. In all these small shops you will establish personal communication with the shopkeepers, who are usually very friendly – especially to any foreigners who can say a few Turkish words. It may be a good place to start practising your Turkish, as most of them will not know any English! Besides this, shopkeepers in your neighbourhood will know a lot about the district and can always provide a wealth of information and opinions about local matters. Some of them are even more effective than estate agents in finding a flat to rent or to buy.

The cheapest way to go to any place for shopping beyond your neighbourhood is by *belediye otobüsü* (public bus) or *dolmuş* (shared taxi/minibus). However, it can be very difficult to travel back home in a crowded bus if you are carrying bags. So *dolmuş* are a better choice, but even ordinary taxis are relatively cheap; going by *dolmuş* and coming back by taxi in comfort is often the best option.

The *Çarşı*

Apart from corner shops, you can go to the local *çarşı* (shopping district). Traditionally, a *çarşı* consists of several small streets on which you can find many small shops next to each other. Sometimes there are even some supermarkets or hypermarkets in a *çarşı*. They are usually very crowded and always very colourful, as most the shops exhibit their products outside the shop as well. In a *çarşı* you may find many shops dealing with products that you haven't even thought of before! Nowadays, the word *çarşı* is sometimes used for a shopping centre, which is more generally called an *alışveriş merkezi*, where again you can find small shops – not on the street, but inside the same shopping centre.

Supermarket Chains

Alternatives to *bakkal*s and *çarşıs* are the supermarket chains like Migros, Dia, Gima, BIM and Tansaş, the branches of which can be found in almost every town. The prices there are usually cheaper than in *bakkal*s and the fruit and vegetables can sometimes be even fresher. There are also some large supermarkets with only a few branches (like Kopuzlar in Istanbul), which offer more products than the other ones. However, in all of these supermarkets you would always miss the personal and friendly contact or even the potential 'friendship' that you will discover in a *bakkal*: a place where people know your name.

Markets

You may prefer a *haftalık semt pazarı* (weekly local market) for shopping, as they are good for cheaper and fresher fruit and vegetables. A *haftalık pazar* is an outdoor market (*pazar*) that takes place at the same place once a week (*haftalık*). Find out from your neighbours where and on which day the *haftalık pazar* in your neighbourhood is. It would be very good to shop there with a neighbour at the beginning to learn the manner and tactics of effective shopping. There are also some *sabit pazar*s (fixed markets) where you can find the same market every day. These are less common than the weekly ones and are usually in city centres.

Water

You can use tap water for brushing your teeth but it is advisable only to drink bottled water, as tap water may not taste very nice and is occasionally not for drinking. You can buy bottled water in different sizes from any small or big market, but the best way is to find a local water supplier (*su istasyonu* or *sucu*) who will bring water to where you live – 10-litre bottles of water can be delivered to your doorstep for a much lower price than you would pay in a shop or market. At the beginning you will have to pay a small deposit for the first bottle, but thereafter every time you order water you will not be charged for a new bottle – it will be swapped with your empty one.

Shopping Malls

There are also modern, very big shopping malls in the centre (for example Akmerkez and Galleria Alışveriş Merkezi in Istanbul) and periphery of the cities. These are usually more expensive than the modest shops in *çarşıs*. Carrefour and Metro, for example, are two hypermarkets that offer a wide variety of Turkish and European products. Bauhaus is an international DIY superstore.

Etiquette

Dress

As far as etiquette goes, casual wear is normally appropriate, and it's fine for a woman to wear either trousers or a skirt; however, topless sunbathing and wearing bikinis away from the beach or swimming pool is frowned upon. When visiting a mosque be respectful: don't wear shorts (whatever your sex) and take off your shoes on entering. If you are a woman, take a scarf for covering your head, though you may well be provided with one by the mosque.

For practical purposes, light clothing plus a cardigan or thin fleece for evenings will be fine for the Marmara, Aegean and Mediterranean coasts for most of the year, but you will need warm clothing in winter and in mountain regions. Sturdy trainers or walking boots are sensible for visiting archaeological sites, where the ground is often uneven.

Forms of Address

In all but the most formal situations Turkish people tend to use first names rather than surnames – a habit that goes back to Ottoman days. When addressing a woman, *Hanım* is added and for men *Bey* – so Joan Bloggs becomes Joan Hanım and Joe Bloggs becomes Joe Bey, or it becomes French-style Madame Joan and Monsieur Joe. In business meetings, however, people use *Sayın* followed by the surname, whether to a man or woman. An alternative way of addressing someone formally would be to use *Bay* (for men) and *Bayan* (for women) followed by the surname: Bay Bloggs for Joe Bloggs and Bayan Bloggs for Joan Bloggs. (The initials of both words must be in upper case.)

It is also normal to address people by their professions – *Avukat* for lawyer, *Doktor* for a male or female doctor, and *usta* for servicemen such as electricians and plumbers. Vendors often address young customers as *abla* or *ab*; middle-aged ones as *teyze* or *amca*; and older ones as *anne*, *baba*, *dede* or *nine*.

Body Language

You can get a surprisingly long way without speaking a word of Turkish. Bow your head forwards for 'yes', backwards for 'no'. A shoulder shrug with open arms will do for 'don't know'. Turkish people also go in for noises: *hı hı* for yes, and a *shk* noise for no. Join your fingers together and wave your hand up and down to show that you thought the meal was delicious. Kissing on greeting and leaving is *de rigueur*, but only with someone you have some familiarity with. Otherwise shake hands, or wait for the other person to make the first move. A touch on your shoulders means the person making contact trusts you. Flirty gestures of affection in public places should generally be avoided. Although it is getting rarer now, people in Turkey often kiss the hand of an elder, such as a teacher, as a mark of respect. Be careful, though: hand gestures have a nasty habit of being misconstrued if you're not sure of what you're doing. For example the Turkish equivalent of the V sign is clenching your fist and either putting your thumb between your middle and index fingers or raising your middle finger (imported from Europe?). An index finger softly knocking one's own head means 'Are you stupid?' Also, don't use the symbol with thumb and index finger making a circle – although in many cultures this denotes approval or complete satisfaction, to Turks it means homosexual.

Turkish Hospitality

To a Turk, a guest (*misafir*) is someone to be treated with almost overwhelming hospitality, and there's a genuine warmth towards others that shouldn't be mistaken for anything devious. It can become trying, as you're pressed to eat helping after helping.

If invited to dinner, flowers or a box of chocolates are safe bets as gifts for your hosts; wine might be OK, but remember Muslims are likely to be teetotal. You are usually expected to take off your shoes and put on a pair of guest slippers on entering someone's home, although some city-dwellers don't bother to do so nowadays.

Lots of people are keen to practise their English and want to hear English visitors say something nice about Turkey. In more out-of-the-way places such as eastern Anatolia there's still a refreshing curiosity about outsiders. If you're in Turkey with children, this is sure to be an ice-breaker pretty much wherever you go, as children are almost universally doted on.

Turkish Baths

To many, a visit to the *hamam*, or Turkish bath, is an essential part of the Turkish experience, and although they're fast receding from use in everyday life, a good number of such baths still survive, particularly in Istanbul and Bursa. The origins of the *hamam* can be traced back to Roman and Byzantine times, when it became a place not only to clean oneself but also to meet, talk business, gossip and socialise – and even to show off one's figure. In many ways, things have changed remarkably little over the centuries, and a lot of *hamami* date from Ottoman times.

Hamami are domed structures, lit naturally by bottle glass windows. You go first into a square court (*camekan*), which has a fountain and changing cubicles. Leave your valuables in a small locker and hold on to the key. Bring your own soap, shampoo and shaving mirror, as they are not always supplied. Beyond is the cooling-off room (*soğukluk*), where men shave their faces, which leads into the steamy marble baths (*hararet*). Here you will have a wash-down: each customer has one set of taps and a basin, and you mix the water to the right temperature and wash yourself using scoop dishes, taking care not to splash anyone else. Remember to clean your marble slab with water when you finish. In the centre of this room is a raised marble platform (*göbek taşı*) or navel stone, located over the wood or coal-powered furnaces. Here you lie down for a fairly fierce massage (*kese*), in which any dead skin is removed by the masseur or masseuse (*tellâk* or *keseci* – agree a fee first) with an abrasive cloth. Generally the *tellâk* will be the same sex as you, but in some tourist areas men massage women; if you feel uncomfortable about this, ask for a same-sex masseuse.

Bathing is strictly single sex – some baths are for men only or women only, while others have separate bathing schedules for men (*erkekler*) and women (*kadınlar*). If you're planning a trip it might be best to find a Turkish person to show you the ropes. It is not nude bathing, and you need to screen your nether regions even when washing them: men are supplied with a checked cloth known as a *peştamal* to be worn around the waist, while women usually have to ask for one or else go without, but keep their knickers on (in some places women wear bathing costumes). Footwear tends to be plastic flip-flops, although sometimes you get the traditional wooden clogs (*takunya*). After leaving the *hamam*, it's a good idea to rehydrate with a cold drink or glass of tea (extra charge payable), and you can relax on a couch in your changing cubicle. Tips are expected.

Apart from the so-called historic *hamami*, which you find in areas frequented by tourists, there are also *mahalle hamami* and *çarşi hamami*, which are visited mainly by the local people and are usually more authentic and certainly much cheaper than the historical *hamami*. The only problem is that you may not find many English-speaking people around.

Tipping

Generally, tipping (*bahşiş*) is the done thing and a tip of 10 to 15 per cent is normal in a **restaurant** (unless there's a service charge). *Garsoniye* refers to the service offered by the waiter ('*garson*') and on a receipt the *garsoniye* is the amount of the service that is included. The expression '*garsoniye dahil değildir*' (*garsoniye* is not included) or '*garsoniye hariçtir*' (*garsoniye* is excluded) means that this service is not included in the receipt and it is expected that the guests will pay it as a tip ('*bahbib*'). The expression '*garsoniye (fiyatlara) dahildir*' means that the tip is already added in the prices in the receipt so customers are not expected to give a tip. Sometimes you can even see that *garsoniye* is added to the total amount on the receipt by the waiters. In **taxis**, round up sums.

Smoking

Cigarette smoking is ubiquitous, but there is a smoking ban on most public transport and in banks and airports. Non-smoking areas in restaurants are rare.

Toilets

Western-style public toilets are prevalent in cities and resorts, but in country areas you will find the oriental-style squat toilet, with two platforms for your feet and a hole in between. Flush using the bucket, which you fill up from a nearby tap. It is worth carrying your own supply of toilet paper, plus a small bar of soap.

The Turkish Language

The main language in Turkey is Turkish, one of the Turkic languages, which is spoken by the vast majority of the population, if not always as their mother tongue. It was the official language of the Ottoman Empire from the 14th century until the First World War. Throughout that time many elements of vocabulary and grammar were adopted from Arabic and Persian, and Turkish was written in Arabic script until Atatürk introduced the Latin alphabet in 1928.

Turkish has roots closely related to Mongolian, Korean and other Ural-Altaic languages, and is far removed from European languages. So it probably won't roll off the tongue that easily – but fortunately in the main tourist areas English is quite widely spoken (though you can't rely on it), especially by younger people, and a knowledge of German and French can be useful too.

As with any country, learning a few basic words and phrases and getting to grips with the pronunciation will make life easier and more fun, and the Turks appreciate it when foreigners have a go.

Relatively few English people who live in Turkey or who own homes there have mastered Turkish to any significant degree, in large part because Turkish people often speak English. They are keen to practise their English and give you little chance to speak Turkish! And Turkish is not the easiest of languages to learn.

Methods of Learning

The best way to learn Turkish is one-to-one or in a small class with a good teacher. You will need frequent lessons (ideally at least twice a week at the beginning) and lots of them. Learning from a book and from tapes is a long way second best, as you don't get practice and feedback, but this method has the advantage that you can pick up your study at any time, and it is also a lot cheaper than having lessons. Good publications that include audio cassettes or CDs are *Teach Yourself Turkish* by Asuman Celen Pollard and David Pollard (Hodder Arnold/Teach Yourself, 2004), *Linguaphone PDQ Turkish* (Linguaphone, 2001) and *Colloquial Turkish* by Sinan Bayraktaroğlu et al (Taylor and Francis, 2000). Alternatively you could try one of many online language courses, such as **www.onlineturkish.com** or **www.tomer.ankara.edu.tr**.

A useful compact dictionary is Milet's *English–Turkish, Turkish–English Pocket Dictionary* (Milet, 2001).

In parallel with or after your training, read, listen and use the language at every opportunity. When speaking English with native Turkish speakers whose command of English is less than perfect, you can expect various blips to creep into their conversation. These can cause misunderstanding, so it helps if you are aware of some of the problems. For example the 'a' in 'back' often becomes like the 'e' in 'beck', and 'survive' becomes 'surwiwe'. The 'th' sound – either as in 'bath' or 'bathe' – does not exist in Turkish, and 'l', 'm' or 'n' at the end of a word tends to be scarcely voiced at all. Word order can get muddled and inverted question forms can go awry. In general, people in Turkey have great pronunciation problems in English, so that it may be very difficult to understand someone even when he or she knows English well. So, be patient at the beginning to get used to people's pronunciation; it won't take very long. Remember, when you try to speak Turkish, they will bear with you patiently as well.

Quirks about Turkish

These are some of the quirks of the language:

- **The structure is regular, unlike most European languages. It is based on suffixation, so that a complicated idea that might be a sentence in English ends up as one word full of suffixes. Plural forms are suffixes *-ler* or *-lar* added to words, so that the plural of *adam* (man) becomes *adamlar* (men).**
- **There are 29 letters in Turkish alphabet. These include the characters ç, ğ, ı, ö, ş and ü. The letters q, w and x do not exist in Turkish.**
- **There are an awful lot of synonyms, so learning vocabulary is tricky.**
- **Word order goes into reverse in certain situations, and verbs are at the end of sentences. There are no genders, so there is no distinction between 'he' and 'she'.**
- **Personal pronouns (its, their, and so on) are used less than in English.**
- **There are no verbs for 'to be' or 'to have' in one word.**
- **Plurals are used less than in English.**
- **Each letter always sounds the same whenever it appears, unlike some letters in English, for example 'c', which sounds different in the words 'car' and 'peace'.**
- **Every sound is represented by only one letter, whereas we have both 'k' (as in 'kite') and 'c' as in 'America' for the same sound in English, where also some sounds are represented by two letters (like 'ch').**

Quick Pronunciation Guide

Turkish syllables generally carry equal weight, and any stress usually falls at the end of the word. Try not to anglicise Turkish pronunciation by putting in English-style stress where there shouldn't be any, as people probably won't understand you at all.

Most consonants are pronounced as in English. Vowels are generally trickier, and vowel harmony is the source of much confusion among foreigners. There are two types of vowel – 'back' vowels (a, ı, o and u) and 'front' vowels (e, i, ö and ü). Usually words of pure Turkish origin have all of one type only – all back or all front vowels – while words that have foreign origins, such as *şoför* (chauffeur), may have a mixture of back and front vowels.

Letters to take special note of are:

a like the vowel in 'part'
e like the vowel in 'met'
ğ like a 'y' if between two vowels; otherwise silent and lengthens preceding vowel
ı/I unstressed vowel (known in phonetics as the 'schwa'), as in 'a' in 'local'
i/İ like the vowel in 'pit'
o like the vowel in 'wrote'
ö like the vowel in 'word'
u like the 'u' in 'sue'
ü like the vowel in 'few'
c like the 'j' in 'join'
ç like 'ch' as in 'chin'
g always hard, as in 'got'
j like the 's' in 'measure'
ş as in the 'sh' of 'sharp'
v midway between 'v' and 'w'
y always as in 'yet', never as in 'lazy'

â, **î**, **û** are usually a longer vowel sound but preceded by weak 'y' or 'h' if following the consonants 'g', 'k' or 'l'. The **â** and **î** letters are officially obsolete although you still come across them sometimes.

For some useful Turkish vocabulary, *see* **References**, pp.254–6.

Education

As in many other developing countries, education has always been one of the most important means for individuals to achieve upward social mobility in modern Turkey.

The formation of the contemporary Turkish education system started in the 19th century and was completed in 1924 when religious schools were closed, new secular schools were set up, and elementary school attendance was made compulsory by the new Republic. In order to cope with educating the youngest population in Europe, the educational system has been expanding in the last few decades. Compulsory basic education was extended from five to eight years in 1997. This has brought new problems. However, attempts have been made to reduce average classroom sizes from 50 to 30 students by increasing the number of classrooms and teachers. The teaching of foreign languages and computer skills are emphasised but under-funding has made it difficult for state schools to maintain high levels of staff professionalism and standards. Furthermore, there is neither strong student motivation nor parental and community involvement, so many private schools, universities and institutes of higher education have been established, claiming to offer better standards and facilities. Native speakers are commonly employed in these private schools to encourage the learning of foreign languages.

State Schools

Preschool Education

In Turkey preschool education is optional and includes the education of children aged three to five who are not old enough for obligatory primary education. Preschool education is provided by various ministries and institutions, and by the Ministry of National Education in kindergartens, preparatory classrooms, application classrooms, day nurseries, nursery schools, day-care centres and childcare centres.

Primary Education

Primary education includes the education and training of children in the 6–14 age group. It is compulsory for all citizens and free of charge. A primary school diploma is given to graduates.

Secondary Education

Secondary education includes all the general, vocational and technical institutions of education that offer at least three years of study. Every student who completes primary education and who has the right to enter a secondary school can benefit from the opportunities of secondary education.

There are two types of secondary education: general secondary education and vocational-technical secondary education.

General secondary education comprises those institutions that provide a three-year additional education opportunity to students between the ages of 15 and 17 after the completion of their primary education. Within the scope of general secondary education there are the general high schools, the Anatolian high schools, the science high schools, the Anatolian fine arts and teachers' high schools, the evening high schools and multi-programme high schools. All of these prepare students for higher education.

Vocational-technical institutions prepare students for professional life and also for higher education. These comprise institutions such as technical high schools for girls and boys, schools of commerce and tourism, and religious education schools.

Special Needs Education

Special needs education is provided in special schools established according to five disability groups: visual impairment, deafness, orthopaedic disability, mental retardation and long-term illness. Education for these groups is limited and under-resourced.

Private Schools

Private education is provided at every level and in many varieties, including private courses, specialised vocational classes, private driving courses and other private study centres, as well as private schools, colleges and universities. These institutions continue their activities under the supervision and surveillance of the Ministry of National Education.

Higher Education

In Turkey, higher education includes all educational institutions that provide at least two years of higher education after secondary education and educate students to diploma, bachelor, master or doctorate degree levels. Institutions of higher education consist of universities, faculties, institutes, schools of higher education, conservatories, vocational schools of higher education and application-research centres.

The faculties and higher education institutions of the universities accept students according to the results of one-stage examinations held once a year by the Centre for Student Selection and Placement (ÖSYM) of the Higher Education Council. A separate examination is held every year by ÖSYM for foreign students who want to study in Turkish universities. This examination is given in Turkish and English, so it is not necessary to know Turkish in order to take the examination. Students who pass it and acquire the right to enter higher education in Turkey, but whose knowledge of Turkish is inadequate, are granted a leave of one year after they have registered at the university to learn Turkish. The Turkish Education Centre (TÖMER, affiliated to Ankara University) and other private schools provide Turkish courses for foreigners. Universities in Istanbul and İzmir also offer Turkish courses for foreigners.

All universities and higher education institutions in Turkey are under the jurisdiction of the Higher Education Council (Yüksek Öğretim Kurumu or YÖK). YÖK is an autonomous organisation and operates within the framework of the duties and authorities denoted by the higher education law that regulates higher education and directs the activities of the higher education institutions. YÖK directs policy relating to higher education. It is responsible for plans to establish and develop higher education institutions and to educate the necessary teaching staff in Turkey or abroad, and monitors the way these activities are carried out. It also provides for co-operation and co-ordination among higher education institutions.

There have been efforts to enable YÖK to function as only an inter-university co-ordination institution and to provide full autonomy to university teaching staff members, research assistants and students so that they are represented in the administration of the university. However, this is an ongoing process.

Education for Foreigners

Private schools are probably the best place for the children of foreigners to be educated. There are several private schools that offer foreign-language-based education serving the international community in Turkey. They provide the compulsory eight-year centralised Turkish curriculum of the Ministry of National Education, and are supervised by that department's inspectors. However, usually, international staff teach the English-language curriculum in subjects such as mathematics, science, computer use, art and library education. Only Turkish grammar, literature and social studies lessons are in Turkish in these schools.

For Turkish students there is a general private school examination that determines entrance, but this is not applicable to foreigners, although a general exam to determine the level of foreign students is customary. Considering the limited number of spaces at schools with good reputations, you should register your child well before he or she is due to start school.

Check with each school for entrance conditions and fees and bear in mind that the fees these schools charge will not necessarily translate into teaching quality. Before choosing a private institution, inform yourself as fully as possible, then write to a few schools and make appointments with the principals. They usually speak English.

Normally, a student visa is required to register at a school or university as a student in Turkey. However, the legal dependants of someone in Turkey on a diplomatic visa or with a work visa will not need such a visa.

Religion

Turkey is a predominantly Muslim country (98 per cent of the Turkish population), with the rest composed of Jews (Greek, Armenian or Assyrian), Orthodox (Armenian or Assyrian), Catholics and Protestants. As this is a traditionally multi-religious and multi-ethnic country, in some Turkish cities one can still find Catholic, Orthodox, Protestant and Armenian churches alongside synagogues. Istanbul in particular used to be a city where people of different religions lived side by side, but in the course of the last century this changed considerably and nowadays only 1–2 per cent of the population is non-Muslim.

However, generalisations such as 'Muslim' are tricky in Turkey, as the practice varies widely among the population and there are many people who have little to do with the daily practice of Islam – like praying five times a day, going to the mosque regularly, participating in the pilgrimage to Mecca or fasting during the month of Ramadan. Nowadays, there are very broadly two distinct cultures in Turkey: a secular, élitist culture that defines what is 'progressive' and 'modern', and a mass culture that continues to espouse religious values, ranging from traditional to mystical, from modern to radical interpretations of Islam.

Most of the population is fairly tolerant and respectful of others' freedoms and creeds. This is attributable to the secularisation process that started in the 19th century and reached its peak with the foundation of the Republic in 1923. Today, in terms of its laws and political order, Turkey is a secular country. However, only the Sunni Muslim majority are represented by a state institution, known as the Directorate of Religious Affairs (*Diyanet İşleri Başkanlığı*), resembling a ministry, and non-Sunni Muslims and non-Muslims are not officially represented, although they generally are not subject to overt discrimination.

Although over the past 15 years there has been something of a religious revival and the emergence of political Islam, there is also a traditional Muslim group in Turkey that differs from the average Muslim image of the Western world. *Alevis* number up to 20 per cent of the Muslim population and do not practise the five tenets of Islam (such as worshipping in mosques and fasting during Ramadan). Furthermore, among Sunnis there are some sub-groups (*Hanbeli, Hanefi, Shafi* and *Nakshibendi*) and numerous orders (*tarikats*) that have some differences in interpretation of Islam in theory and practice.

It may take time for a foreigner to grasp the complexity of religious life in Turkey, but in general it is important to know that for a great number of the population religion is mainly a private affair and Turks live a comparatively modern life, especially in the main areas where property is sold to foreign buyers. However, it is courteous to be respectful, especially in small cities in non-touristy regions, and in some neighbourhoods in big cities that are dominated mainly by people who do not tolerate the open consumption of alcohol, and may disapprove of men and particularly women wearing revealing clothes. The best way to find out about these cities and neighbourhoods, and about religious life in Turkey in general, would be to take advice from Turkish friends.

See also **About Turkey**, pp.13–14.

Ramazan

It is important for foreigners living in Turkey to be aware of the religious fasting month of Ramadan (*Ramazan* in Turkish), which lasts for 30 days and which, because it follows the Islamic calendar, occurs at a slightly different time each year. During Ramadan those Muslims who choose to fast do not eat or drink between sunrise and sunset. Children, pregnant women and travellers don't have to fast, nor do those who have a medical condition. So you should not be surprised to find some restaurants closed during Ramadan, especially in small cities, nor to hear drums thundering at dawn. This is an old custom to wake up the faithful for the last meal before fasting begins for the day. Some drummers in your district may come to your door collecting money for their services during or immediately after Ramadan, but you are not obliged to pay.

Letting Your Property

08

A growing number of people who buy houses in Turkey let them. Many of those people let them out seriously; they try to make money through letting and do all they can to find the maximum number of tenants each year. Others let casually to family, friends and friends of friends. They are looking not so much to make a profit from renting but to defray some or all of the costs of ownership.

There are fundamental differences in the way these two groups should approach the task. Anyone in the first category, the 'serious letters', should put themselves in the head of the person they want to rent their property. Which part of the market are they trying to capture? You cannot please everybody. The single person or childless couple wanting to enjoy Turkish culture and cuisine will have very different requirements from the family wanting a cheap and quiet holiday in the countryside. Where would they like to rent? What type of property would they prefer? What features do they require? The person who wants to let property seriously should buy it, convert it and equip it solely with their prospective tenants in mind.

Those in the second category, the 'casual letters', should make few concessions to their tenants. After all, the property is first and foremost a holiday home for their own use. They will have to make some changes to accommodate visitors but they should be as few as possible. Perhaps slightly darker shades of upholstery, an area where they can lock away their valuables when not in residence, and more sets of bedding. Most importantly, they should provide a 'house book' and a visitor pack. The first gives visitors guidance about what tourist attractions are available in the area and emergency contact numbers for the inevitable time when someone is ill or the plumbing springs a leak. The second gives directions to the property, maps and other information useful before they set off on holiday. (These facilities should also be provided to guests who will rent from properties in the first category.)

This section relates mainly to the first group, the 'serious letters'. Some comments are directed specifically at the second group, and anyone in this category can choose from the other ideas, depending on how far they are prepared to compromise their wishes to increase letting income.

Some of the issues covered in detail in this chapter were briefly outlined in **Selecting a Property**, pp.76–7 and pp.91–3, which you should read first.

First Steps and Questions

It is essential to sit down and establish your financial objectives before starting to let your property, since many other decisions will depend on them – what kind of tenants to aim for, whether to use a management company, and so on. You should also work out what your outgoings are likely to be –

fitting out the house, general and garden maintenance and paying someone to clean the house and greet tenants may all take a chunk out of any rental income. You can employ an agent or management company to manage the lettings for you, but this will cut into the income you can expect to get from letting the property.

Questions to Ask Yourself before Starting to Let

- **What are your financial objectives?**
- **Do you plan just to cover your costs or do you want to maximise the income from your property?**
- **Do you want to use the property yourself – if so, when? If you'd like to use it at Easter and in the summer – that's exactly when other people will want to be there as well.**
- **Do you want to be there on set dates, or can you be flexible and only go on weeks with no bookings?**
- **What kind of people do you want to have in your house – are children OK? What about a hen party or a group of amateur sailors?**
- **What advantages does your property have – is there anything that makes it stand out? What amenities is it near?**
- **Will you have the time (or inclination) to manage the lettings yourself? This can entail a substantial amount of work.**

Choosing the Right Area

The choice of the area in which to buy your rental property is far and away the most important decision that you will make. There are many parts of Turkey where it is fairly easy to let your property frequently enough to make it a commercial proposition. There are other areas where this is almost impossible.

The factors to take into consideration when deciding on the area are slightly different from the factors relevant when you're thinking about buying a home for your own personal use. They will also vary depending on your target clientele and your preferred way of administering the property. Most are related to the tourist traffic of an area, its attractions and services, and also to the practical services it has available that you can call on to help manage the letting.

Letting Agencies and Target Markets

Strange as it may seem, deciding *how* to let your property is one of the first decisions that you are going to have to make, even before you actually buy it. This is because, if you decide to use a professional management or letting agency, it will alter your target market and therefore the area in which you ought to be buying. *See* pp.239–42. If you are going to let your property through a professional agency, it is worth contacting a few before you make a final choice of location, to see what they believe they can offer in the way of rental returns. They will also be able to advise you on what type of property in that area is likely to be most successful as rented property.

If, on the other hand, you expect to find tenants yourself, you need to decide on your primary market. Most British people who let their property themselves in Turkey do so mainly to other British people, because that is the market they are familiar with and where they have the most connections, and there is no language barrier. The rest of this section is targeted mainly at the person wishing to let to a British market.

Climate

Most people going on holiday hope for decent weather. Fortunately, not everybody has the same idea about what this means. The number of people taking summer holidays in Normandy in northern France shows that a higher than average annual rainfall is clearly not fatal! Despite this, you are likely to have more success if you are in an area that is known to be warm and dry.

It is particularly important that the area has decent weather during the prime British holiday season, normally July, August and September. Apart from this main holiday season, May, June and October offer reasonable letting prospects if you are in an area with a mild climate. There is also a relatively small (but growing) market for longer-term winter lets in areas with particularly mild climates or which are socially desirable. Study the climate charts in **References**, pp.265–6 and read pp.78–80. Information is also available from your tourist office, in travel publications and on the Internet.

Access

As important as climate and the charms of the locality is the ability of tenants to get to your property. This has two sides to it. The area where your flat or house is located must be reasonably accessible from the places where your prospective tenants live; and the property itself must be easy to find.

For most British and other foreign visitors, convenient access to the area means convenient access from a major local airport. (Convenient access is much more difficult to define if you are trying to attract Turkish visitors.)

It is worth repeating here the travel industry figures that show that 25 per cent of all potential visitors will not come if it involves travelling for more than an hour from a local airport at either end of their journey, and that if the travelling time rises to 1½ hours this will deter around 50 per cent of people. Of course, this does not mean that if your home is over an hour's drive from an airport you will never let it – with charming rural houses, for example, a different set of rules applies, and their very remoteness can be an attraction in itself. For more conventional homes, though, there is no doubt that finding interested tenants will be simpler if you are within the magic hour's distance of an airport.

Do not underestimate the importance of being able to find your property! Navigation in the depths of rural Turkey can be trying. There are few people to ask for directions (especially if you don't speak Turkish) and there are few signposts of much help when it comes to locating a rural cottage. The closer to the main road, the better. Providing decent maps and directions is also essential; and do erect a clear signpost to show they have arrived. Nothing is guaranteed to ruin the start of someone's holiday as much as cruising around for three hours to cover the last 500 yards of their journey.

Attractions

Governments are keen on tourist attractions because they attract tourists. The fact that they are prepared to invest billions of taxpayers' money in encouraging these attractions should persuade you that having one near to you is an asset when it comes to letting your property.

'Tourist attractions' is a term that covers a multitude of possibilities. Although Turkey is not as well developed in this respect as some other Mediterranean countries, the picture is changing. World-class golf courses are beginning to be established in the south of the country, and Turkey has now joined the club of the Formula One Grand Prix. In many areas, however, the 'formal' attractions are likely to be more modest. That doesn't matter. The point is that there must be something to bring people to your area so that they will need to use your accommodation. The mere fact that the house is located in the middle of the countryside or near the sea is not, of itself, enough to attract a significant number of tenants.

To find out what the tourist attractions are in the area you are thinking of buying, contact the Turkish tourist office and study tourist guides to Turkey.

It may be enough for an area to have one major attraction that brings many visitors, but there will probably be lots of competition to provide accommodation. It may be better to choose an area with several smaller attractions, or a mix of them. For instance, somewhere with an annual local festival, which is also near a recognised historic site, could attract a large number of tourists for a limited period but would also have a steady stream of visitors year-round.

Explore what is available. Remember that facilities such as golf or access to first-class beaches are themselves tourist attractions. Equally, local activities could bring in all the visitors you'll ever need (*see* 'Doing Deals', pp.238–9).

Other Facilities

Many people going on holiday want to eat out. Even those who will probably end up buying food in their local supermarket and cooking at home *think* they want to eat out. It will be much easier to let your property if it is within easy distance – preferably walking distance – of one or more restaurants. It should also be within walking distance or a short drive of shops and other facilities – so ideally would be near a village or a town.

Choosing the Right Property

Picking the right property is just behind choosing the right area in terms of letting potential. Not all properties let to the same extent – villas and flats that most potential clients find attractive let up to five times more frequently than others that do not stand out for any reason. New properties are generally cheaper to maintain than older ones; however, they are not likely to be as attractive to potential tenants. Most people going on holiday to a rural part of Turkey are looking for a character property (preferably with a pool), while most going to the coast are looking for proximity to facilities and the beach.

Can You Let the Property?

Make sure that there is no restriction on your ability to let your property. This will normally only be the case in a very small number of apartments or condominiums (*sites*).

To let legally, register your property with the tourist authorities. Many people ignore this rule.

Pick a Pretty Home and Keep it Attractive

Most people will decide whether to rent your property after they have seen only a brief description and a photograph. The photograph is by far the more important. Research that we carried out showed that 80 per cent of a group shown 32 potential rental properties picked the same three properties. The common factor in these properties was that they were all pretty. If the person was looking at properties in Normandy the pictures looked like a Norman cottage and not a modern semi-detached house. If they were looking for somewhere by the sea they looked like a seaside cottage, preferably with either sand or water in view. Brittany Ferries (which runs a property rental programme) has properties that are so pretty they can find tenants 50 weeks of the year, when most properties in Brittany have tenants for 16 weeks a year.

When buying a house for rental purposes, make sure above all that you buy one that will look good in a photograph.

Make sure the external decoration and garden and any pool area are kept in good order. These are what will show up in your photographs and will create the first impression when your guests arrive.

Equipping the Property

Having selected an area and a property, you will then have to fit out the villa or flat with all the features that tenants will expect. If you advertise the property well, you will get tenants. You will only get *repeat* tenants and recommendations from existing tenants if the property meets or exceeds their expectations in terms of the facilities it offers and its cleanliness.

The facilities required will depend on the target clientele you are trying to attract. Think about those potential customers and what you would want if you were one of them. For example, if you are trying to attract mountain walkers or sailors or windsurfers, they will appreciate somewhere to store their gear and dry their clothes quickly so that they can be ready to get wet again the following day. If you want to attract families with small children, a cot, high chair and selection of safe, durable toys will be appreciated. This will help attract people who are choosing between your property and that of your neighbour, and will bring repeat visitors.

The top general tips are as follows.

A Warm Welcome

It is much better if someone is present either at the property or in a nearby house to welcome your guests when they arrive. Someone greeting the visitors can sort out any minor problems or particular requirements of the guests straight away. If you are not using a letting/management agent, you may be able to find a local person to pay to do this – perhaps the same person you employ to clean the property between tenants.

Leave basic groceries such as bread, milk, coffee, sugar and a bowl of fruit in the house to welcome your guests. A bottle of wine goes down well too; Turkey produces some first-class wines.

Cleanliness

The property must be spotlessly clean. This applies in particular to the kitchen and bathroom. You will probably employ a local cleaner, to whom you may well need to give some training and/or a detailed schedule, as people's expectations when going into rented accommodation are often much higher than their expectations in an ordinary home.

Kitchen

This must be modern, even if traditional in style, and everything should (of course) work. The fridge should be as large as you can manage since, in hot weather, your tenants will need to keep a wide range of things chilled. The kitchen should have a microwave, and you should check regularly that there is sufficient cutlery and cooking equipment and that it is all in good condition. Providing a cookbook giving local recipes is a nice touch.

Bathroom

Or, these days, more usually bathrooms plural – an en-suite bathroom for each bedroom is the ideal. Make sure there is soap in the bathrooms, and guests will also much prefer it if you provide towels as part of the service.

Laundry

A washing machine and tumble-dryer are now standard.

Bedrooms

The number of bedrooms you choose is very important. Generally in cities you will get a better return on your investment on properties with fewer (one or two) bedrooms – which will be cheaper to buy – than on larger properties. In rural areas, or by the seaside, where the majority of your guests may well be families, a three-bedroom property is probably your best compromise.

Bedrooms should have adequate storage space and, most importantly, clean and comfortable beds. The only beds that last well in a frequently used property and where the people sleeping will be all sorts of different sizes and weights are expensive beds such as those used in the hotel industry. Nothing, except dirtiness, produces more complaints than uncomfortable beds.

Beds should be protected from obvious soiling by the use of removable mattress covers, which should be changed with each change of tenants. Clients will much prefer it if you supply bedding as part of your service rather than expecting them to take their own. After all, they are likely to be flying to Turkey, and an aeroplane baggage allowance does not leave much room for sheets and pillowcases.

Living Areas

Furniture and upholstery should be in good condition. The style is a matter of personal preference but a 'local' style often appeals most. The furniture must be comfortable and there should be adequate means of cleaning, including a vacuum cleaner.

Air-conditioning and Heating

Air-conditioning is probably best avoided except in the most expensive lettings. It is not yet considered compulsory and can be expensive to run and maintain. Heating is essential. It should be effective and cover the whole house.

Swimming Pool

If you are catering to the British market, a swimming pool is highly desirable. In a rural area it will significantly increase your potential number of tenants. A pool should be of reasonable size but need not be heated.

Documents

Make sure that all guests are sent a **pre-visit pack**. This should include notes about the area and local attractions (usually available free from your local tourist office), a map showing the immediate vicinity, notes explaining how to get to the property, emergency contact numbers and instructions as to what to do if they are delayed for any reason .

A **house book** should be available in the property. It should give much more information about local attractions, restaurants and so on, and a comprehensive list of contact numbers for use in the case of any conceivable emergency. The more personal recommendations you can give (best bakery, best café, etc.), the more people will appreciate it. The house book should include detailed instructions about how to work any equipment, switch on the heating and any idiosyncrasies of the house, and the whereabouts of manuals for the washing machine, cooker and dishwasher. It should also include an inventory of the equipment in the house.

Provide some space in it too, or in a separate book, for use as a **visitors' book**. As well as being a useful vehicle for obtaining feedback, this builds up positive feelings about your home, and can also be a means of making future direct contact with visitors who might have been supplied by an agency.

How Much Rental Income to Expect

See **Selecting a Property**, 'Paying the Right Price', pp.92–3, for important information about choosing a property at the outset with the intention of maximising rental potential.

You should be careful not to be over-optimistic about the number of weeks per year that you might be fairly certain of letting your property. In our experience a reasonably diligent person – doing their best to find tenants and not relying wholly on a management company but not totally obsessive about the property – can expect to produce roughly the results shown in the table overleaf. If you are willing to make the property available for rental through July, August and early September (particularly August) and also at Easter, and forgo using the property yourself during these peak periods, you will dramatically increase your rental income. '**Target weeks**' are the number of weeks you could expect to let an average property provided you did not use it for July or August. The '**percentage return**' is the amount you should expect to generate as a percentage of the value of the property, after payment of all agents' fees, water, electricity, cleaning and other outgoings related to the rental period but before taking into account your own personal tax liability. These are general guides only and will vary significantly from property to property, management company to management company and owner to owner.

If your property is well located, attractive and clean, you should expect about 30 per cent repeat visitors in most areas. Generally it takes four or five years for a rental property to reach its full potential.

Letting Your Property – Performance Targets

Area	Type of Property	Target Weeks	Return (%)
Istanbul	apartment	35	6
Alanya	small house or apartment	14	5
Fethiye or Bodrum	small house or apartment	14	5
Fethiye or Bodrum	larger house	12	4

Marketing the Property

Properties do not let themselves, and anyone wishing to let their Turkish home regularly will have to do some marketing. In the early years you will have to do more than later on, because you will have no existing client base.

As in any other business, the cheapest type of marketing is catching repeat clients, so a bit of money spent on making sure the property lives up to, or exceeds, expectations (and brings them or their friends back next year) is probably the best spend that you will make. Otherwise, there seems to be no correlation between the amount spent on marketing and the results achieved, and this is a field in which much money spent is often wasted.

Bear in mind that any form of marketing of a holiday property is only as good as the quality of the response you give to people making enquiries. Owners would often do better spending less money on advertising and paying more attention to following up leads they have already generated.

These are some key points to remember in relation to marketing any kind of short-term let:

- **Choose the method of marketing most appropriate to your property.**
- **Follow up all enquiries and leads immediately. Contact the people involved again after a couple of weeks to see whether or not they have made up their minds.**
- **Send any contacts your details again next year at about the same time, even if they have not stayed with you, as they may be planning another trip.**

In your marketing it is well worth stressing that your property is clean, modern and well equipped at the same time as showing the traditional outside appearance and pool. A good photograph is worth a thousand words.

The UK Market

Directories

If your property is pretty, you are likely to get good results from the various directories and magazines focusing on properties to let in Turkey. They are only a good idea if the cost of listing in them is low, because for a private owner with only one property to let you only have one opportunity of letting each week, so a directory that produces, say, 50 enquiries for the first week in September is not particularly helpful.

Advertising

The problem with traditional methods of advertising is their scattergun approach and, usually, their cost. As mentioned above, if you have just one property you only need a very small number of responses, and you cannot afford to pay a large amount in advertising fees for each week's let. For individual owners, better places to advertise are the small-ad pages in the travel sections of newspapers such as the *Sunday Times* and the overseas property press.

Some people have been successful advertising in apparently unconnected special interest magazines – such as literary or historical or sporting publications – where their ad did not get lost among 20 others. On the other hand, you can also get good results from a card on your local supermarket noticeboard.

Your Own Contacts

Your own contacts are, without doubt, the best opportunity you have for marketing your property in Turkey. Remember how few people you need if you want to let it out for, say, 25 weeks a year. Given that many people will take it for two weeks or more, you will probably only be looking for 10–15 lettings.

The people who find this easiest are those who work for large organisations. If you are lucky enough to work in a major hospital, company or a large factory you will almost certainly be able to find enough people to keep your property fully occupied, just from within your working environment. You will have the additional advantage of knowing the people who are going to rent the property, which reduces the risk that they will damage it or fail to pay you.

Even without people from work, most owners will be able to find enough friends, neighbours and relatives to rent a nice property in Turkey for 10 weeks a year. This will leave only a relatively small number of tenants to be found by advertising or other marketing means.

When renting to family and friends or indeed close working colleagues, you will have to learn how to raise the delicate issue of payment. Given that you are not going to be incurring any marketing costs and probably very little in the way of property management costs, you should be able to offer them an attractive price and still generate as much income as you would have done by letting through an agency. Make sure that you address the issue when you accept the booking, as doing so later can be very embarrassing.

Other Markets: The Internet

Most British people do not speak Turkish sufficiently well to be able to offer the product on the Turkish market, other than through a letting agency.

There are, however, significant English-speaking markets in Scandinavia, Germany, the United States and elsewhere. They are most successfully addressed via the Internet. The Internet offers tremendous opportunities for bringing a specialist niche product to the attention of a vast audience at very little cost. It also offers the possibility of showing lots of pictures and giving other information about your property and the area it is in. As such, it is ideal for the person wanting to let out property. It is worth having your own website designed especially for this purpose. Not only can it be your brochure, but it can also act as a way of taking bookings. It is much cheaper to have someone print off a copy of your brochure from their own computer than it is for you to send it by post. You may have the expertise to create your own website (if you don't, consider learning how to – it can be fun). Those without the time or inclination to create a website themselves can have a simple but very effective site put together for £250–£300.

As well as having your own website, consider listing your property on one of the many Turkish property websites you can find on the Internet. These listings are either free or inexpensive. You will soon find the ones that work and the ones that don't.

You will have to decide whether you want to use the site only as a brochure or whether you are prepared to take electronic bookings, and whether to price your product only in sterling, only in euros or perhaps in multiple currencies including US dollars and Turkish liras. You will have to decide how sophisticated an electronic booking system you want or whether you are happy just to use the Internet to make contacts. Your website will, of course, have your e-mail address on it. You will only be able to take payment by cheque, unless you are already a merchant with a credit card account, or are prepared to incur the expense of setting one up.

Even if you do not set up a website, anyone letting out property regularly really should have access to e-mail, which is increasingly becoming people's favourite means of communicating. Remember to check it at least once a day.

Doing Deals

There are two kinds of 'mutual aid' deals that can be helpful to independent owners, both of which work best in slightly out-of-the-way areas. If your property, for example, is in a rural area where there is somebody offering a very local tourist service, it can be a good idea to make contact with the people running that service and try to arrange for the clients taking their hikes, cultural tours, cookery classes or religious pilgrimages to stay over in your property. This can significantly increase your lettings, particularly at off-peak times. If you agree to pay the tour organisers a commission of around 20 per cent you will still be well ahead.

The second type of deal involves co-operating with other people in the area who let properties, assuming there are any. One of the frustrations of marketing your property is when you have four lots of people who all want to rent it for the same week. Getting together with others in a mutual assistance group will allow you to pass excess lettings to one other.

Letting and Management Agencies

On the whole, the people who are most successful over a period of time in letting their second homes are those who find their tenants themselves. This, however, requires a level of commitment that many people simply cannot afford. For non-resident owners who cannot dedicate much time to keeping track of their property, it is far simpler to use a local letting agency.

Letting and management agencies – or at least good agencies – will have the opportunity to capture clients from the domestic Turkish market as well as from various international markets. Management companies generally operate only in popular areas where there is enough demand to keep them in business. The agency can look after letting the property, deal with the cleaning and handovers, pay the bills, look after repairs and so on. They will typically charge about 15–20 per cent of rental income received as their fee; they will argue that the fee that you will pay them will be recovered by extra lettings that they make during the season. This may or may not be true.

If you do not use a managing agent you will still (usually) need to employ a cleaner and someone to deal with handovers. This could be the same person and, in rural areas, would probably be a neighbour.

In our experience it is seldom sufficient to rely on a management company if you want to let the property to its full potential. Owners, through family, friends, workmates and other contacts, are usually better at filling the off-season weeks than a management company is. This, however, assumes a level of commitment that many people simply cannot afford. It is certainly simpler to use a letting agency. And the management company will capture passing trade that you would not pick up and can redirect visitors from overbooked property to yours.

If you decide to use a letting agency, the choice of agency is critical. There are some excellent agencies in Turkey and some operating from Britain. There are also some crooks. The difference in performance between the two will make the

Case Study: Letting a Villa Yourself

George and Chris don't think it's wise to rely on rental income for their villa near Fethiye, but see rentals as a useful boost.

'We take any rental generated by our villa (the rental season in Turkey is only between May and October, but we are trying to promote winter lets too) as a bonus, but we are careful to vet any renters, and most come through recommendations from other guests. Often, things you don't plan for pop up and surprise you. So far we have had a flood, and the local authority installed a new sewer and we were ordered to pay several hundred pounds to be connected to it. Then the varnish on the window frames blistered and had to be redone, the solar panels froze last winter and burst, the air- conditioner failed and had to be replaced and we had a key jam in the safe and had to replace that as well. Having some income from rentals to help with these small emergencies makes them all easier to take in your stride.

'Our website is a great chance to tell people all they need to know. I have never done a website before but using web software it was really simple to create and keep up to date. Marketing a villa is really plain common sense: it does take a bit of work, but my wife has had great success with work colleagues. Try simple things like an advert in the local library or newsagents; once again, if you get locals to rent, they are more likely to look after the place. There are many websites that let you set up free links or place details of your property, as well as Internet forums where you can become active and not only gain advice but share rental enquiries.'

difference between making a profit and making a substantial loss. The temptation is clear. If somebody comes into their office on a Friday in August and wants to rent an apartment, yours may be available. Will the agent put the rent – perhaps £1,000 – in your bank account or into their own pocket? Will the agent rent your apartment or the apartment belonging to a 'special friend'? In the past, too many agents have thought that their client would never find out that they had let the property – because they were 1,000 miles away – and so have succumbed to temptation. It is important both to choose the right agency and to check up on it regularly.

Selecting an Agency

When selecting which letting agency to appoint, there are various checks that you should make. These people hold the success of your venture in their hands. If it is a Turkish agency, are the staff professionally qualified and experienced? Many such services are offered as an adjunct to estate agencies. Find out as much as you can in advance about any agency that you are considering.

- **Check the premises. Do they seem welcoming and efficient? Is there evidence of significant activity?**

• What marketing does the agency do? If it relies on passing trade then, except in the most exceptional areas, it will not get you good results.

• Ask to see a sample information pack the agency has sent to a potential client. You will be able to judge a lot from this. Is it the image you want to give of your property?

• Inspect two or three properties that the agency is presently managing. If they are dirty or ill cared for then so will yours be. Then it will not let.

• Ask for references and take them up. Ideally they should be from other overseas clients. Try to speak to the people on the telephone – ask whether there are happy with the agency's performance and whether the financial projections given to them have been met.

• What kind of contract is the agency offering you? Unless you are familiar with Turkish law, it is sensible to get this checked before you sign it, as some contracts give you far more rights than others. Make sure that the contract gives you an entitlement to full reports showing when the property was let and for what rate. Do not accept an analysis by period; insist on a breakdown week by week and on a full breakdown of all expenses incurred in connection with the property. Make sure the contract gives you the right to dismiss the agency at fairly short notice.

• How many weeks' rental does the agency think you will be able to obtain in this area? What do the staff think it will generate for you after deduction of all expenses including the charges?

• What type of property do the agency staff think would be the best for letting purposes in this area? Does it match with yours?

Controlling the Agency

Once you have appointed a letting agency, you must control it.

• Check the report you receive from the agency and that the money you receive corresponds to the amounts shown in the reports.

• Let the agency staff know, in the nicest possible way, that you and all your friends in the area check each other's properties every time you are there and compare notes about which are occupied and the performance of your letting agencies. If they believe you, this will deter them from making unauthorised lettings.

• Telephone the property every week. If someone answers the phone, make a note and make sure that there is income shown for the week of the call.

• From time to time, have a friend pose as a prospective customer and send for an enquiry pack.

- **If you get the opportunity, call to see the property without warning, to see what state it is in.**

All this may sound like hard work. It is not. It will significantly increase the income you receive from your rental property.

Furnished or Unfurnished?

From the point of view of the landlord, the safest type of letting is a short holiday letting of furnished property. To be classified as furnished the property must be properly or fully furnished – it must have all the key items required to live successfully in the home. A property let without, for example, a bed or a cooker or a table or a refrigerator or chairs would, in each case, be likely to be treated as an unfurnished property. *The result could be that the tenant could acquire the right to stay on at the end of the tenancy.*

A holiday let is, officially, a letting that takes place during the recognised holiday season. That season is obviously different in a ski resort from in Bodrum. It generally covers at least the period from June to September.

The Letting Agreement

A suitably drafted tenancy agreement will protect you if you have a dispute with your tenant and, in particular, in the event that the tenant wishes to stay on at the end of the tenancy. This is especially important for non-holiday lets.

If your property forms part of a *site,* your tenants should agree to abide by the rules of the community; you must supply them with a copy of the rules or at least the part of the rules that governs their conduct.

In the rental contract, stipulate what things are going to be covered by your insurance and what are not. Typically the tenants' personal possessions would not be covered under your policy.

Taxation of Rental Income

If you are thinking about letting out your property it is *vital* that you get legal advice from a lawyer who understands the Turkish and English law and tax systems. All letting will have far-reaching tax consequences in both countries.

See **Financial Implications**, pp.158–62.

References

09

Major Resources in Britain and Ireland

Turkish Embassies in Britain and Ireland

Turkish Embassy in Ireland

11 Clyde Road, Ballsbridge, Dublin 4
t 0668 52 40
f 0668 50 14
turkemb@iol.ie

Turkish Embassy in Britain

43 Belgrave Square, London SWIX 8PA
t (020) 7393 0202
f (020) 7393 0066
info@turkishembassy-london.com
http://turkishembassylondon.org

For enquiries on aspects of living or owning property in Turkey:
Office of Economic Counsellor
43 Belgrave Square, London SWIX 8PA
t (020) 7235 2743
f (020) 7235 1020
london@turkisheconomy.org.uk

Turkish Consulate

Rutland Lodge, Rutland Gardens, Knightsbridge, London SW7 1BW
t (020) 7591 6900
f (020) 7591 6911
www.turkishconsulate.org.uk
For visas.

Specialist Estate Agents Dealing in Turkey

The *Homes Overseas* exhibition (**t** (020) 7939 9888, **www.homesoverseas.co.uk**) is held at a range of locations in the UK (including London, Manchester, Birmingham, Glasgow, Belfast, Leeds, Brighton, Exeter and Edinburgh) throughout the year and features agents for Turkey.

Specific email addresses and sites for estate agents include **property@dalyan.co.uk** in Dalyan; and **www.aeagency.co.uk** for properties near Fethiye.

To get you started, here are some of the UK-based estate agents that deal with Turkish properties. This is not a recommended list nor an exhaustive one, and the authors and publishers cannot vouch for them.

All Turkey Real Estate

3 Campbell Avenue, Leek, Staffordshire ST13 5RP
t (01538) 398254
f (01538) 398254
mike@turkeyrealestate.co.uk
www.turkeyrealestate.co.uk
Specialises in a wide range of coastal locations.

Black Lion

t 0090 (0)242 844 1345
www.2blacklions.com
Anglo-Turkish agency based in Kalkan.

Buzz Estates

99 Moor End Road, Mellor, Stockport, Cheshire SK6 5PT
t (0161) 449 5228
f (0161) 449 5227
realestate@buzzytravel.com
www.buzzytravel.com/buzzestate.htm
Specialises in the Ölüdeniz area.

EMP – Eastern Mediterranean Properties Ltd

219 Northfield Avenue, Ealing, London W13 9QU
t (020) 8579 7711
f (020) 8579 8945
info@emproperties.co.uk
www.emproperties.co.uk
Covers a wide range of coastal locations.

Headlands International

Waterside House, Station Road, Nene Park, Irthlingborough, Northants NN9 5QF
t (01933) 654000
f (01933) 654099
info@headlands.co.uk
www.headlands.co.uk
Specialises in new property only, sold off-plan.

Letsgototurkey

www.lgtt.com.tr
Developers based in Antalya.

My Turkish Home

t 0845 021 7717
www.myturkishhome.com
Anglo-Turkish agency based in Kalkan.

Prime Property Solutions

www.ppsturkey.com
Specialises in properties in Bodrum.

Samuel James, Property in Turkey Office

10–11 Harris Arcade, Friar Street, Reading, Berks RG1 1DN
t (0118) 956 9595
f (0118) 956 9993
turkey@samueljamesproperties.co.uk
www.samueljamesproperties.co.uk
Specialises in the Fethiye area.

Side Property Ltd

www.sideproperty.com
Specialises in properties in Side.

Tepe Villas by Carson International

t 01869 244774
www.carsoninternational.co.uk
Villa development based in Kalkan on the Turquoise Coast.

Turkey Expert

www.turkeyexpert.co.uk
Aegean properties and advice.

Turkish Holiday Homes Ltd

16 Foresters Drive, London E17 3PG
t (020) 8509 3691
f 08707 064849
info@turkishholidayhomes.com
www.turkishholidayhomes.com
Covers Kuşadası, Alanya, Bodrum and Altınkum.

Other Useful Addresses

Turkish Tourist Office

4th Floor, 29–30 St James's Street, London SW1A 1HB
t (020) 7839 7778
f (020) 7925 1388
info@gototurkey.co.uk
www.gototurkey.co.uk

Acacia International

100 New Kings Road, London SW6 4LX
t (020) 7610 3333
f (020) 7610 3358
info@acacia-int.com
www.acacia-int.com
Specialises in Turkish law, with offices in the UK and Turkey: Turkish property, tax, inheritance and investment matters.

John Howell & Co

English Solicitors and International Lawyers
The Vaults, Holborn Hall, 193–7 High Holborn, London WC1V 7BD
t (020) 7061 6700
f (020) 7061 6701
info@lawoverseas.com
www.lawoverseas.com
Lawyers specialising in Turkish property law.

DHB Bank (The Turkey Mortgage)

t 00 31 (0)10 440 6633
www.mortgageforturkey.co.uk
Dutch bank offering UK mortgages for properties in Turkey.

Major Resources in Turkey

British Embassy and Consulates

British Embassy

Şehit Ersan Caddesi 46/A, Çankaya 06680, **Ankara**
t 0312 455 33 44
f 0312 455 33 56
www.britishembassy.org.tr

British Consulate-General

Mesrutiyet Caddesi 34, Tepebaşi Beyoğlu 34435, **İstanbul**
t 0212 334 6400
f 0212 334 6401

Other Useful Addresses

British Council

www.britishcouncil.org/turkey

Posta Kutusu 34, Çankaya, **Ankara**
t 0312 455 36 00
f 0312 455 36 36
libinfo.ankara@britishcouncil.org.tr

Posta Kutusu 16, Besiktas, **İstanbul**
t 0212 355 56 57
f 0212 355 56 58
libinfo.Istanbul@britishcouncil.org.tr

PTT Pasaport Posta Md, Posta Kutusu 274, **İzmir**
t 0232 295 0053
f 0232 295 0027
libinfo.Izmir@britishcouncil.org.tr

Removal Companies

See generally: **www.international-movers.com**; **www.oneentry.com**. Check **www.google.co.uk**, and search 'pages from the UK' for removals + Turkey.

British Association of Removers

Tangent House, 62 Exchange Road, Watford, Hertfordshire WD18 0TG
t (01923) 699 480

f (01923) 699 481
info@bar.co.uk
www.removers.org.uk
Reliable companies should be members of this association.

Anglo Pacific

www.anglopacific.co.uk

5–9 Willen Field Road, Park Royal, London NW10 7BQ
t (020) 8965 1234
f (020) 8965 4954
info@anglopacific.co.uk

Unit 1, Townley Park, Hanson Street, Middleton, Manchester M24 2UF
t (0161) 653 4455
f (0161) 653 4466
north@anglopacific.co.uk

26 Eastmuir Street, Annick Industrial Estate, Shettleston, Glasgow G32 0HS
t (0141) 764 1010
f (0141) 764 1013
scotland@anglopacific.co.uk

Atlantis Overseas Removals

enquiries@atlantisltd.co.uk
www.atlantisltd.co.uk

Atlantis House, Bennett Road, Leeds, West Yorkshire LS6 3HN
t (0113) 278 9191
f (0113) 278 9197

1607 Pershore Road, Stirchley, Birmingham B30 2JF
t (0121) 451 1588
f (0121) 433 4034

Bishop's Move

branches nationwide
www.bishopsmove.net

PSS

Depots in London, Colchester, York and Glasgow
t (020) 8686 7733
f (020) 8686 7799
sales@p-s-s.co.uk
www.pssremovals.com

Useful Websites

Thousands of libraries and other community buildings offer free access to the Internet, if you don't have access at home. You may have to book a computer, and usage may be restricted to an hour or so at any one time.

There are many websites that may be of use to you, some of which are listed below.

www.avatar-turkey.com: Various aspects of the country.

www.bpe.com/food/ethnic_cusine/turkey.htm: Turkish cuisine guide (note the wrong spelling of 'cusine' in the web address).

www.calis-beach.co.uk/forum: Expatriate forum for residents of Çalış, near Fethiye.

www.fco.gov.uk/travel: Foreign and Commonwealth Office, in UK, with general travel advice on visas, health and safety.

www.findaproperty.co.uk/regi0099.html: Properties on the Mediterranean and the Aegean, as well as in Cappadocia.

www.gumruk.gov.tr: Turkish Customs Administration.

www.healthfinder.com: US Department of Health site; links to health organisations.

www.internationaleducationmedia.com/turkey: Directory of schools, colleges and universities.

www.internationalrealestatedirectory.com/country/turkey.htm: Directory of estate agents dealing with properties in Turkey.

www.mfa.gov.tr: Visa information for Turkey.

www.mymerhaba.com: Expatriate information for those living in Turkey.

www.pwc.com/tr/eng/ins-sol/publ/anexpatriateguide.pdf: Read 'Foreign nationals working in Turkey', a guide produced by PricewaterhouseCoopers in August 2003.

www.stanfords.co.uk: Online travel bookshop, with a huge range of guide books, general travel books and maps.

www.tefl.com: Guide to teaching English abroad.

www.travel-guide.com

www.travelleronline.com

www.travelturkeymag.com: Good general site on Turkey, with helpful Travel Guide.

www.tripprep.com: Travel health online.

www.turkeycentral.com: Wide range of info and advice on Turkey, including travel, business, food and language.

www.thy.com: Turkish Airlines.

www.ukpa.gov.uk: UK Passport Agency.

www.unesco.org: The definitive UNESCO list of World Heritage Sites.

www.virtualtourist.com: Click on Middle East for Turkey; useful forum for major resorts such as Bodrum and Marmaris.

www.worldclimate.com: World climate data.

National Holidays and Opening Hours

National Holidays

Banks and offices close on national holidays (*see* below). The movable festivals of Şeker Bayramı (the Sugar Festival, held over three to four days at the end of Ramadan) and Kurban Bayramı (commemorating Abraham's sacrifice and lasting four to five days, about a month after Ramadan) are also national holidays, and banks, post offices and government offices close, public transport gets totally booked up and resorts are completely packed.

Banks and offices stay open on 1 July (Navy Day public holiday).

There are local holidays in Istanbul on 29 May and in İzmir on 9 September.

During Ramadan (*Ramazan*), non-Muslim people in Turkey are little affected (and don't need to fast), and in resorts and major cities life carries on pretty much as normal.

1 January	New Year's Day
23 April	National Independence and Children's Day
19 May	Atatürk Commemoration and Youth and Sports Day
30 August	Victory Day (celebrating victory over the Greeks in 1922)
29 October	National Day (Anniversary of the declaration of the Turkish Republic)

Opening Hours

Government offices, tourist offices and museums: usually open Mon–Fri 8.30–12.30 and 1.30–5.30 (but often longer lunch breaks). Some museums close for a day between Monday and Friday.

Banks: open Mon–Fri, 8.30–12 and 1.30–5.

Shops: open Mon–Sat, 8.30 or 9.30–7 or later; some open on Sun.

Shopping malls: open daily 10–10.

Offices: in the Aegean and Mediterranean regions, many offices (including government offices) close in the afternoon in the summer months.

Further Reading

Eat Smart in Turkey, Joan Peterson, David Peterson, S.V. Medaris (Ginkgo Press). All about Turkish cuisine, including a dictionary of menu and market foods.

Crescent and Star: Turkey Between Two Worlds, Stephen Kinzer (Farrar, Straus and Giroux). A concise introduction to modern Turkey.

Atatürk: The Biography of the Founder of Modern Turkey, Andrew Mango (Overlook Press). A biography of the great Turkish leader and the way he transformed society.

The Ottoman Empire, 1700–1922, Donald Quataert, William Beik, T.C.W. Blanning (eds) (Cambridge University Press/New Approaches to European History). Scholarly but accessible account of the Ottoman Empire.

The Western Shores of Turkey: Discovering the Aegean and Mediterranean Coast, John Freely (I. B. Tauris). Accounts of journeys taken over two decades along the Mediterranean and Aegean coasts, delving into ancient sites such as Troy and Ephesus, and exploring Lycia.

Turkey Unveiled, Nicole Pope and Hugh Pope (Overlook Press). Good survey of Turkish current affairs and politics.

The Lycian Way: Turkey's First Long Distance Walk, Kate Clow and Terry Richardson (Up Country). Definitive guide aimed at walkers of all levels of ability.

The Lycian Shore, Freya Stark (John Murray Travel Classics). Epic account of a journey by boat along the coast of Turkey by one of the great travel writers of the 20th century.

A Fez of the Heart: Travels through Turkey in Search of a Hat, Jeremy Seal (Picador). An investigation of the country's cultural and spiritual facets and paradoxes.

On Horseback Through Asia Minor, Frederick Burnaby (Oxford Paperbacks). Burnaby's horseback exploits, accompanied by his servant Radford, during winter 1876 in the months running up to war between Turkey and Russia.

Portrait of a Turkish Family, Ifran Orga (Eland Books). Insightful work, first published in 1950, about the author and his family through the years when modern Turkey emerged.

Birds Without Wings, Louis de Bernières (Secker & Warburg). Complex novel from the author of *Captain Corelli's Mandolin*, about the inhabitants of a small coastal town in southwest Anatolia in the last days of the Ottoman Empire.

Turkish Vocabulary

For a pronunciation guide and introduction to the language, *see* pp.218–21.

Basic Phrases

yes	***evet***
no	***hayır***
please	***lütfen***
thank you	***teşekkür ederim/teşekkürler/teşekkür/mersi***
hello	***merhaba/selam***
goodbye	***hoşçakal/hoşçakalın*** (polite form) or ***allahaısmarladık*** (if you are the person leaving); ***güle güle*** (if you are the person seeing someone off)
good morning	***günaydın***
good evening	***iyi akşamlar***
goodnight	***iyi geceler***
How are you?	***Nasılsınız?/Ne haber?***
I am well	***İyiyim***
I don't understand	***Anlamıyorum***
Where is...?	***Nerede...?***
left	***sol***
right	***sağ***
here	***burada***
there	***şurada***
There is	***Var***
There is none	***Yok*** (generally used much more than ***hayır*** to denote 'no')
Excuse me	***Affedersin***, ***affedersiniz*** (polite form) or ***pardon***, ***özür dilerim***
Wait a minute	***Bir dakika lütfen***
cheap	***ucuz***
expensive	***pahalı***
airport	***havaalanı/havalimanı***
bus station	***otogar/terminal***
train station	***tren ştasyonu/tren garı/gar***
filling station	***benzin istasyonu/benzinci***
bank	***banka***
restaurant	***lokanta/restaurant/restoran***

Numbers

one	*nir*
two	*iki*
three	*üç*
four	*dört*
five	*beş*
six	*altı*
seven	*yedi*
eight	*sekiz*
nine	*dokuz*
ten	*on*
eleven	*onbir*
twelve	*oniki*
thirteen	*onüç*
fourteen	*ondört*
fifteen	*onbeş*
sixteen	*onaltı*
seventeen	*onyedi*
eighteen	*onsekiz*
nineteen	*ondokuz*
twenty	*yirmi*
thirty	*otuz*
forty	*kırk*
fifty	*elli*
sixty	*ıtmış*
seventy	*yetmiş*
eighty	*seksen*
ninety	*doksan*
one hundred	*yüz*
two hundred	*ikiyüz*
one thousand	*bin*
one hundred thousand	*yüzbin*
one million	*bir milyon*
one billion	*bir milyar*

Time

When?	*Ne zaman?*
yesterday	*dün*
today	*bugün*
tomorrow	*yarın*

later	***sonra***
in the morning	***sabahleyin, öğleden önce***
at noon	***öğleyin, öğlen, öğle***
in the afternoon	***öğleden sonra***
in the evening	***akşamleyin***

Days

Sunday	***Pazar***
Monday	***Pazartesi***
Tuesday	***Salı***
Wednesday	***Çarşamba***
Thursday	***Perşembe***
Friday	***Cuma***
Saturday	***Cumartesi***

Months

January	***Ocak***
February	***Şubat***
March	***Mart***
April	***Nisan***
May	***Mayıs***
June	***Haziran***
July	***Temmuz***
August	***Ağustos***
September	***Eylül***
October	***Ekim***
November	***Kasım***
December	***Aralık***

Signs

Stop	***Dur***
No entry	***Girilmez***
No smoking	***Sigara içilmez***
city centre	***şehir merkezi***
entrance	***giriş***
exit	***çıkış***
WC	***WC/Tuvalet***
Gentlemen	***Bay***
Ladies	***Bayan***

Dictionary of Useful and Technical Words

ağaç	tree
aidat	monthly payment for communal services
akşam	evening
akşam yemek	dinner
alıcı	purchaser or receiver
alış	purchase
alış bedeli	purchase price
ampul	light bulb
anasokak	main street
antika	antique, very old
apartman	apartment block
ara sokak	side street
araba	vehicle or car
arsa	plot of land
asansör	lift
at	horse
avukat	lawyer
bahçe	garden
bahçivan	gardener
bakiye	balance (money)
bakkal	corner shop, grocer
balkon	balcony, terrace
bank	bank
bank havalesi	bank transfer
bank hesabı	bank account
banliyö	suburbs
banyo	bathroom
bayram	religious holiday
bekçi	watchman
belediye	local municipality
berber	barber's shop (men only)
beton	concrete
beyaz	white
beyaz şarap	white wine
bilet	ticket
bira	beer
birahane	pub
bodrum	basement or cellar
borç	debt

borsa	stock exchange
boya	paint
boyacı	painter, decorator
bozuk para	change (money)
buzdolabı	refrigerator
büyük	big, large
cadde	avenue
cin	gin
çalışma izni	work permit
çarşaf	bedsheet
çatı	roof
çatı kat	loft
çay	tea
çek	cheque
çeşme	fountain or spring
çevre vergisi	annual environment tax (really a refuse charge)
çiftlik	farm
çiftlikevi	farmhouse
çimento	cement
çıkış	exit
dağ	mountain
daire	apartment, flat
değer	value
deniz	sea
deniz manzarası	sea view
deniz manzaralı	with a sea view
depozit	deposit (money)
dergi	magazine
dubleks	duplex
duş	shower
duvar	wall
duvar kağıdı	wallpaper
eczane	chemist
ehliyet	licence (normally driving licence)
ekmek	bread
elektrik	electricity
elektrik sayacı	electricity meter
elektrikçi	electrician

emlakçı	estate agent
emlak vergisi	annual property tax
emniyet müdürlüğü	central police station
eski	old
ev	house
faiz	interest (financial)
fatura	bill, invoice
feribot	ferry boat
fırın	oven
fiyat	price
gayrimenkul	real estate property, land
gazette	newspaper
giriş	entrance
giriş kat	ground floor
göl	lake
gümrük	customs
halı	carpet
harita	map
hastane	hospital
hava	weather
havaalanı	airport
havuz	swimming pool
hesap	bill
hol (koridor)	hallway
ikametgah	place of residence
il	province
ilçe	sub-province
inşaat	construction
iskonto or ***indirim***	discount
kahvaltı	breakfast
kale	castle
kalorifer	radiator
kaloriferli	centrally heated
kapı	door
karakol	police station
kasaba	town
kat	floor, storey

kat kaloriferi	central heating
kefalet	bail or financial security
kilit	lock
kıra	rent
kiracı	tenant
kıra bedeli	rent (amount)
kıralık	for rent
kırmızı	red
kırmızı şarap	red wine
kısa	short
kısa vade	short term
klima	air-conditioning
konut	housing
köprü	bridge
köy	village
kuaför	hairdresser
kuyu	well
küçük	small
lavabo	washbasin
mahalle	neighbourhood
marangoz	carpenter
merdiven	stairs
meşgul	occupied
meydan	town square
mimar	architect
mobilya	furniture
mobilyalı	furnished
musluk	tap
mutfak	kitchen
mühim	important
nalburiye	hardware store
noter	notary public
oda	room
okul	school
orman	forest
ortak	partner
ortaklık	partnership
otel	hotel
otobüs	bus

otobüs bileti	bus ticket
oturma izni	residence permit
öğle/öğlen	noon
öğlen yemeği	lunch
ödeme	payment
önemli	important
önemsiz	unimportant
özel	private or special
özel plaj	private beach
para	money
pasaport	passport
pasta	cake
pencere	window
peynir	cheese
plaj	beach
plan	plan
prim	premium
pul	stamp
rakı	Turkish strong national drink, similar to Greek ouzo
renk	colour
ruhsat	permission
salon	lounge
satıcı	vendor, seller
satılık	for rent
satış	sale
satış bedeli	sale price
satış sözleşmi	contract of sale
sayaç	meter
senet	promissory note
serbest	free, unoccupied
sermaye	capital (financial)
sigorta	insurance
sigorta policesi	insurance policy
site	condominium or site
sıcak	hot
sıcak su	hot water
soğuk	cold
soğuk su	cold water
sözleşme	contract

sokak	street
su	water
su borusu	water pipe
su sayaci	water meter
şarap	wine
şarküteri	delicatessen
şehir	city
şirket	company
şofben	water heater
tapu	title deed
tapu müdürlüğü	land registry office
tapu sicil	land registry
tatil	holiday
tazminat	compensation
tebligat	official communication
tepe	mountain peak or hill
ticaret odası	chamber of commerce
tren	train
tren bileti	train ticket
tripleks	triplex
tüketim	consumption
tuvalet	toilet
uçak	plane
uçak bileti	plane ticket
uzun	long
uzun vade	long term
üretim	production
valör	value date (for payments)
vatandaşlık	citizenship
vergi	tax
vergi dairesi	tax office
vergi numarası	tax number
yapı	structure
yapı ruhsat	permission for planning or construction
yastik	pillow
yatak	bed
yatak odası	bedroom
yemek	food

yemek odası	dining room
yeni	new
yorgan	bed quilt
zam	price increase

Internet Vocabulary

alt çiz gi	underscore/underline (_)
ana sayfa	home page
ara	search for
arama motoru	search engine
bağlan	link (n.)
büyük ve küçük harf duyarlı	case sensitive
çıkmak	exit (v.)
çizgi	hyphen (-)
dizin	directory
ek	attachment
e-posta adres	e-mail address
e-posta	e-mail
et	at (@)
geri	previous
geri dön	back (v.)
gir tuşu	enter key
girmek	enter (v.)
göz atmak	browse
hepsi küçük harf	all lower case
işaretle	bookmark
iki nokta üstüste	colon (:)
ileri	next
kapat	close (v.)
kullanıcı adı	user name
nokta	dot (.)
onaylamak	confirm (v.)
onaylamak/kabul etmek	accept
oturum açmak	log in
oturum açmak	log in/on (v.)
oturum kapamak	log out/off (n.)
parola/şifre	password
sil	delete
tıkla	click (on) (v.)

taksim	forward slash (/)
tamam	OK
tamam uygula	OK, done
tek kelime halinde	all one word
web sayfası	web page
web sitesi	website
www	www (pronounced the same as English: 'double-you double-you double-you')
yükle	download
yüklemek	download (v.)

Climate Charts

A Rough Comparison of British, Turkish and Other European Climates: Average Monthly Temperatures and Rainfall

	Jan	Feb	Mar	Apr	May	Jun	Jul	Aug	Sep	Oct	Nov	Dec
London												
Max. temp. (°C)	7	7	11	13	17	20	22	22	19	14	11	8
Min. temp. (°C)	2	2	3	5	8	11	13	13	11	8	4	3
Rainfall (mm)	61	36	51	43	46	46	46	43	43	74	46	58
Birmingham												
Max. temp. (°C)	6	6	9	12	16	18	21	21	17	13	9	7
Min. temp. (°C)	1	1	2	3	6	9	12	11	9	6	3	2
Rainfall (mm)	58	48	53	46	56	56	51	71	56	53	64	66
Manchester												
Max. temp. (°C)	7	7	9	11	15	18	19	19	17	13	9	7
Min. temp. (°C)	2	2	3	4	7	11	12	12	10	7	4	3
Rainfall (mm)	71	58	58	51	64	71	86	94	81	94	84	86
Edinburgh												
Max. temp. (°C)	6	7	8	11	14	17	19	18	16	12	9	7
Min. temp. (°C)	1	1	2	3	6	9	11	11	8	6	3	2
Rainfall (mm)	56	41	48	38	51	51	64	69	64	61	64	61
Cardiff												
Max. temp. (°C)	7	7	9	12	15	18	20	20	17	13	10	8
Min. temp. (°C)	3	2	3	4	7	10	12	12	11	8	5	4
Rainfall (mm)	91	64	74	53	64	64	69	76	84	91	99	94
Belfast												
Max. temp. (°C)	7	7	9	11	14	16	17	17	15	11	8	7
Min. temp. (°C)	4	5	6	7	9	12	13	13	11	8	6	5
Rainfall (wet days)	23	21	26	20	18	19	21	23	21	22	21	22
Dublin												
Max. temp. (°C)	8	8	9	11	14	17	19	18	16	13	10	8
Min. temp. (°C)	3	3	4	5	7	10	12	12	10	8	5	4
Rainfall (mm)	64	51	51	48	56	56	66	76	64	74	69	69
Nice (France)												
Max. temp. (°C)	13	12	14	16	20	23	27	27	24	20	16	13
Min. temp. (°C)	4	4	7	9	13	17	19	19	16	13	8	6
Rainfall (wet days)	7	8	7	9	8	6	3	3	6	9	7	7

	Jan	Feb	Mar	Apr	May	Jun	Jul	Aug	Sep	Oct	Nov	Dec
Malaga (Spain)												
Max. temp. (°C)	17	15	18	20	24	27	30	30	28	23	20	17
Min. temp. (°C)	11	7	12	11	14	17	20	20	18	16	13	10
Rainfall (wet days)	8	8	7	9	6	3	1	1	3	8	9	9
Antalya												
Max. temp. (°C)	15	15	17	20	25	30	34	35	28	21	16	15
Min. temp. (°C)	5	5	7	10	13	20	22	23	20	15	10	8
Rainfall (wet days)	12	11	9	7	6	3	2	2	3	11	13	12
Bodrum												
Max. temp. (°C)	10	10	14	19	25	30	33	34	30	25	16	11
Min. temp. (°C)	2	2	3	5	10	15	19	20	15	10	6	4
Rainfall (wet days)	16	14	11	8	7	3	2	2	3	11	13	12
Marmaris												
Max. temp. (°C)	10	10	14	19	25	30	33	34	30	25	16	11
Min. temp. (°C)	2	2	3	5	10	15	19	20	15	10	6	4
Rainfall (wet days)	16	14	11	8	7	3	2	2	3	11	13	12
İzmir												
Max. temp. (°C)	12	13	15	20	25	30	33	33	28	25	20	15
Min. temp. (°C)	5	5	6	10	15	20	22	23	20	15	10	8
Rainfall (wet days)	13	11	9	8	6	3	2	2	3	6	8	13

Source: USA Today/US Met Office

Appendix

10

Checklist: Do-it-yourself Inspection of Property

Task ✓

Title – check that the property corresponds with its description in the title:

Number of rooms

Plot size

Plot

Identify the physical boundaries of the plot

Is there any dispute with anyone over these boundaries?

Are there any obvious foreign elements on your plot such as pipes, cables, drainage ditches, water tanks, etc.?

Are there any signs of anyone else having rights over the property – footpaths, access ways, cartridges from hunting, etc.?

Are any parts of what you are buying physically separated from the rest of the property – e.g. a storage area or parking area in a basement several floors below an apartment or a garage on a plot on the other side of the road from the house which it serves?

Garden/Terrace

Are any plants, ornaments, etc. on site not being sold with the property?

Pool – is there a pool? If so:

What size is it?

Is it clean and algae-free?

Do the pumps work?

How old is the machinery?

Who maintains it?

What is the annual cost of maintenance?

Does it appear to be in good condition?

Walls – stand back from property and inspect from outside:

Any signs of subsidence?

Walls vertical?

Any obvious cracks in the walls?

Are the walls well pointed?

Any obvious damp patches?

Any new repairs to walls or signs of re-pointing?

Roof – inspect from outside property:

Does the roof sag?

Are there any missing/slipped tiles?

Do all faces of the roof join squarely?

If there is lead flashing, is the lead present and in good order?

Task ✓

Guttering and Downpipes – inspect from outside property:

All present?
Do they seem to be in good order?
Securely attached?
Fall of the guttering constant?
Any obvious leaks?
Any signs of recent repairs?

Enter Property

Does it smell of damp?
Does it smell 'musty'?
Does it smell of dry rot?
Any other strange smells?

Doors

Any signs of rot?
Close properly – without catching?
Provide a proper seal?
All locks work?

Windows

Any signs of rot?
Open and close properly – without catching?
Provide a proper seal?
Window catches work?
Any security locks? Do they work?
Any sign of excessive condensation?

Floor

Can you see it all?
If you can't see it all, will a surveyor be able to get access to the invisible parts easily?
Does it appear in good condition?
Is there any sign of cracked or rotten boards, tiles or concrete?

Under Floor

Can you get access under the floor?
If so, is it ventilated?
Any sign of rot?
What are the joists made of?
What is the size (section) of the joists?
How close are the joists?
Are joist ends in good condition where they go into walls?
What is maximum unsupported length of joist run?
Any sign of damp or standing water?

Task ✓

Roof Void

- Is it accessible?
- Is there sign of water entry?
- Can you see daylight through the roof?
- Is there an underlining between the tiles and the void?
- Any sign of rot in timbers?
- Horizontal distance between roof timbers?
- Size of roof timbers (section)?
- Maximum unsupported length of roof timbers?
- Is roof insulated – if so, what is the depth and type of insulation?

General Woodwork

- Any signs of rot?
- Any signs of wood-boring insects?
- Is it dry?

Interior Walls

- Any significant cracks?
- Any obvious damp problems?
- Any signs of recent repair/redecoration?

Electricity

- Is the property connected to mains electricity?
- If not, how far away is the nearest mains electricity?
- Check electricity meter:
  - How old is it?
  - What is its rated capacity?
- Check all visible wiring:
  - What type is it?
  - Does it appear to be in good physical condition?
- Check all plugs:
  - Is there power to the plug?
  - Does a plug tester show good earth and show 'OK'?
  - Are there enough plugs?
- Lighting:
  - Do all lights work?
  - Which light fittings are included in sale?

Water

- Is the property connected to mains water?
- If not, what is the size of the storage tank?
- If not connected to the water supply, how near is the nearest mains water supply?
- Do all hot and cold taps work?

Task ✓

Water (*cont.*)

Is flow adequate?
Do taps drip?
Is there a security cut-off on all taps between the mains and tap?
Do they seem in good condition?
Are pipes insulated?

Hot Water

Is hot water 'on'? If so, does it work at all taps, showers, etc?
What type of hot water system is fitted?
Age?

Gas – is the property fitted with city (piped) gas? If so:

Age of meter?
Does installation appear in good order?
Is there any smell of gas?

If the property is not fitted with city gas, is it in an area covered by city gas?
If it is in an area covered by city gas, how far away is the nearest gas supply?
Is the property fitted with bottled gas? If so:

Who is the supplier?
If there is a safety certificate, when does it expire?
Where are bottles stored?
Is the storage area ventilated to outside of premises?

Central Heating – is the property fitted with central heating? If so:

Is it 'on'?
Will it turn on?
What type is it?
Is there heat at all radiators/outlets?
Do any thermostats appear to work?
Are there any signs of leaks?
How old is the system?
When was it last serviced?
If it is oil-fired, what capacity is the storage tank?

Fireplaces

Is property fitted with any solid fuel heaters? If so:

Is there any sign of blow-back from the chimneys?
Do the chimneys (outside) show stains from leakage?
Do the chimneys seem in good order?

Task ✓

Air-Conditioning

Which rooms are air-conditioned?
Are the units included in the sale?
Do the units work (deliver cold air)?
If the units are intended also to deliver heat, do they?
What type of air-conditioning is it?
How old is it?
When was it last serviced?

Phone

Is there a phone?
What type of line is it?
How many lines are there?
Is there an ADSL line?
Does it all work?
Number?

Satellite TV

Is there satellite TV?
If not, is the property within the footprint of satellite TV?
Who is the local supplier?
Does it work?
Is it included in the sale?

Drainage

What type of drainage does the property have?
If septic tank, how old is it?
Who maintains it?
When was it last maintained?
Is there any smell of drainage problems in bathrooms and toilets?
Does water drain away rapidly from all sinks, showers and toilets?
Is there any inspection access through which you can see drainage taking place?
Is there any sign of plant ingress to drains?
Do drains appear to be in good condition and well pointed?

Kitchen

Do all cupboards open/close properly?
Any sign of rot?
Tiling secure and in good order?
Enough plugs?
What appliances are included in sale?
Do they work?
Age of appliances included?

Task ✓

Bathroom

Security and condition of tiling?
Is there a bath?
Is there a shower?
Is there a bidet?
Age and condition of fittings?
Adequate ventilation?

Appliances

What appliances generally are included in sale?
What is not included in the sale?

Furniture

What furniture is included in sale?
What is not included in the sale?

Repairs/Improvements/Additions

What repairs have been carried out in the last two years?
What improvements have been carried out in last two/10 years?
What additions have been made to the property in last two/10 years?
Do they have builders' receipts/guarantees?
Do they have building consent/planning permission for any additions or alterations?
Are any repairs needed? If so, what, and at what projected cost?

Lifts

Are there any lifts forming part of your own property?
How old are they?
When were they last maintained?
Do they appear to be in good condition?

Common Areas

What are the common areas belonging jointly to you and other people on the complex?
Are any repairs needed to those areas?
Have any repairs already been approved by the community?
If so, what and at what cost?

Disputes and Defects

Is the seller aware of any disputes in relation to the property?
Is the seller aware of any defects in the property?

Index